The Literary Zodiac

How writers express cosmic patterns in their writing

Paul Wright

Parlando Press

First edition published in 1987 by Anodyne and 1988 by CRCS Publications, Sebastopol, USA
Second edition published in 2011 by Parlando Press, Edinburgh

ISBN: 978-0-9556514-3-4

Author's preface to second edition

The first edition of *The Literary Zodiac*, published simultaneously in Britain and the USA, appeared in 1987 and has been out of print for some time now. This new edition, some 24 years on, is the product of a thorough revision in the light of further study. Having said that, the conclusions I arrived at in the first edition have not radically altered but, rather, have been brought into sharper focus, while the text has been rewritten in such a way as to be more accessible to those who have no or little knowledge of astrology.

I have studied astrology for more than 30 years and a number of books have been published along the way. My education was in science and I hold degrees in chemistry and technological economics. My academic qualifications in literature amount to an O level. I have, on the other hand, read with an innocent eye a great deal of fiction and non-fiction. I have also written a number of novels, one of which, *Cacknacker's Fury*, has been published. It was favourably reviewed by the *Scottish Review of Books*, which observed among other things: 'An intelligent wit hums through the text like electricity through wire'.

I would like to state here my appreciation for the Urania Trust's generous financial support for the production of this new edition. Thanks also to Chris Perry for the cover art, to my wife, Beverley, for her assitance and encouragement and to Jane Struthers for her excellent work proof-reading the typescript.

Contents

INTRODUCTION

The Literary Zodiac brings together two disciplines, literature and astrology, and attempts to demonstrate the remarkable potential for cross fertilisation that exists between them. Literature provides a route to a deeper understanding of astrology, for creative writers make actual, often in vivid and compelling form, the same essences (for want of a better word) that as we will see in due course are at the heart of astrology. At the same time, writers can discover in astrology a penetrating system of knowledge that encompasses the breadth of human nature in a way no other can.

These claims might seem extravagant to those whose impressions of astrology are drawn from the sun-sign columns of newspapers and magazines. It is true astrology has a trivial side, but so do many things and we should judge by the best rather than the worst. After all, there is more to music than advertising jingles. Equally, a divide exists between the prognosticators and those who seek through astrology a deeper understanding of life. At its best it represents a potent system of knowledge, a descriptive metaphor of life and a model of human totality. Perhaps most significantly, it offers every individual a unique statement of his or her essential being.

Astrology has exercised some great minds over the centuries and not a few of these have belonged to writers. It is not surprising to find the works of Dante, Shakespeare, Spenser and Marlowe sprinkled with astrological allusion for astrology was integral to the worldview of the times in which they lived. Yet a few years into the 19th century, when science had supposedly banished such things, we find the great German man of letters, Goethe, beginning his autobiography thus:

> On the 28th of August 1749, at midday, as the clock struck twelve, I came into the world at Frankfurt-on-the-Main. My horoscope was propitious: the sun stood in the sign of the Virgin, and had culminated for the day; Jupiter and Venus looked on him with a friendly eye, and Mercury not adversely; while Saturn and Mars kept themselves indifferent.[1]

More than a century or so later another great German writer, Thomas Mann, presents us with an astrological analysis of the young hero of

Joseph and his Brothers in which the boy's father makes some pertinent observations about the nature of astrology.[2]

The poet W B Yeats had a fascination with the occult and in March 1890 joined the Order of the Golden Dawn, becoming a full member of the second order in 1893. He studied, among other things, alchemical symbolism, Cabbala and astrology, including the drawing up of horoscopes. Louis MacNeice was another poet drawn to astrology and was commissioned to write a book on the subject. In 1998 the literary world learned of Ted Hughes's fascination with astrology with the publication of *Birthday Letters*.[3] More recently, in 2008, Michael Ward published *Planet Narnia: the Seven Heavens in the Imagination of C S Lewis*. The work details Lewis's passion for medieval astrology and makes the audacious claim that planetary symbolism is at the core of the Narnia novels. William Blake, Herman Melville, Rudyard Kipling, Hermann Hesse, August Strindberg, Samuel Beckett, James Joyce, Saul Bellow and Henry Miller are some other literary worthies who have demonstrated an appreciation of astrology in one way or another.

The Literary Zodiac, then, is about the common ground that exists between astrology and literature. Its basic thesis is that the creative substance of writers matches the symbolism of the zodiac signs, and that there is a consistency of literary theme among writers born under the same sign. It is built upon a study of the work of thousands of writers, either directly through their creative output, or indirectly through criticism. It will prove a rewarding read not only for astrologers and writers, but also aspiring writers, literary critics and, I believe, the open-minded lay-person in general.

What is the zodiac?

The zodiac is a zone of fixed stars, approximately 16 degrees in width, that marks the apparent courses of most of the planets and particularly the Sun about the earth. The ancients projected patterns on to the sky and the band of stars marking the sun's apparent yearly passage through the heavens became differentiated into 12 distinct groupings or constellations. The word 'zodiac' derives from the Greek for 'wheel of life' (*zoe* = life, *diakos* = wheel), although others have suggested *hodos* (path), rather than *diakos*, as a derivation.[4]

Critics of astrology often fall over themselves to point out that the constellations gradually shift relative to the earth, creating a difference between astro*nomical* and astro*logical* positions of the heavenly bodies. So that, for example, an individual born on 1 August will be an astrological Leo, while the physical sun will appear against the background of the constellation Cancer. The discrepancy arises because signs and constellations are different things, and this is explained further in Appendix 2. Suffice to say, the difference would only be important if astrology was held to operate through a cause-and-effect mechanism, that is, through some kind of energy beaming down from a particular part of the sky. This is not a widely held view among contemporary astrologers, who regard the heavens as mirroring life in an acausal fashion, and for whom the zodiac is more a useful working model of reality than reality itself.

Sun symbolism in astrology

The Sun in astrology at a basic level relates to the urge in an individual to externalise, to push out beyond the self, a fundamental sense of being. A reflection of this self is not so much a collection of character traits as a total life, an underlying pattern of existence as it has been consciously lived. The Sun nature forms the root of immortality, something beyond time and space, so that true works of art invariably outlive their creators. The Sun in its operation is both conscious and unconscious. It is unconscious in the sense that it represents a compulsive form of expression, and drives rather than is driven. But the Sun also represents an active detachment from the momentum of the past and a life that is purposefully wrought. The Sun symbolises that pressure, felt by some but not by others, to make a meaning of their life, at the same time giving Life an awareness of itself. It is through our Sun nature that we give novel and unique meaning to the raw material of consciousness. (These ideas are discussed further in the chapter on Leo, the sign associated with the Sun.) It can be a lifetime's work to act out our sense of self in a conscious manner, but it is when we are expressing and living our solar selves that we 'shine' and people take notice. The Sun represents the divine part of human nature, the individual analogue of a far greater consciousness. The solar urge is the desire to express our own divinity as one aspect of this total, and the quality of this single aspect is described by the sign in which the Sun is placed at birth.

In the same way, creative work is an externalisation of inner meaning and can represent a profound statement about a person. The writer John Hersey speaks for many of his fellows when he notes:

> If he is honest and at all able the [novelist's] work speaks his deepest self ... The work interprets him better than he can interpret the work.[5]

Alberto Moravia is another who touches upon this link between creativity and an individual attempting to externalise something fundamental to himself:

> Good writers are monotonous ... they keep rewriting the same book. That is to say, they try to perfect their expression of the one problem they were born to understand.[6]

A qualitative art – or, there's no such thing as a writer's sign

Astrology deals in qualities and it is difficult to encapsulate quality with numbers. For this reason, if we apply to it those quantitative methods favoured by science we are almost always disappointed. The psychologist Michel Gauquelin established some statistically significant links between writers and the planets (see Appendix 3), but good writers can be found in every sign and even if we take into account the extra information provided by a birth chart it is still not possible to astrologically fingerprint a writer.

All this is maybe as it should be. We find it convenient to classify individuals according to vocation but it does not follow at all that the universe does. This is the basic theme of Dennis Elwell's excellent book, *Cosmic Loom.*[7] He suggests people and the cosmos do not always talk the same language. Astrology makes more sense, he argues, when you regard it as a system of principles that cut across many of the 'artificial', if useful, compartments we make of the world. I do not think a birth chart distinguishes between a saint and a psychopath. It does, on the other hand, point to things like extremity, selfishness and social ineptness, and it can describe the particular quality of an individual's saintliness. Someone once said that finding the right answer is about asking the right question. If we ask the question, 'Is this a writer's chart I have before me?' we do not get a very good answer. But if we ask instead for a *qualitative* statement regarding an individual's creative nature then we do get an informative reply. And this is what *The Literary Zodiac* does.

There is a collection of poems by Richard Brautigan titled 'Loading Mercury with a Pitchfork.' The mercury he refers to is the liquid element and not the planet. It is a striking image and one that suggests 'gross inappropriateness of method'. Likewise, if we are too rigid in our approach to human nature and seek to capture its paradoxical, multi-dimensional fluidity in equations and formulas then we will lose what it is we are trying to grasp. The arts, astrology and religion are much better than science at plumbing human totality, if for no other reason than science excludes a good amount of it from its world picture. When scientists stray beyond the bounds of their reality model they make the same mistake as those clergymen who in the past sought to answer strictly scientific questions – such as the physical age of the earth – using passages from the Bible.

The science that evolved in northern Europe in the 17th century has proved very successful in understanding and exploiting the material world and, allied with technology, has lightened the burden of survival for many of us. Here lies its great value, in my view. But science represents only one way of looking at the world. It is a model of reality, and like any model it has its suppositions and limitations beyond which it is ineffectual. It can analyse the pigments that make up a painting but can not say why the same painting is regarded by millions as beautiful. Astrology likewise has its limits as a model and if science can tell us little about meaning and human nature then astrology is not very useful when it comes to guaranteeing daily bread. Each has its place. There is truth of the mind and truth of the heart and a healthy culture affords a place to both.

This describes something of the approach to *The Literary Zodiac*. It is a qualitative study, but, at the same time, an empirical one which draws on a wide body of objective data. While avoiding the Procrustean Bed, I have used common-sense empiricism to provide, I believe, a roughly adequate picture of something very complex. This approach seems to have yielded fruitful results.

Uncertain astrology

Astrology is an approximate science, one that deals with possibilities and probabilities rather than certainties. It is about judgement rather than the application of formula and is not as precise and consistent as is sometimes suggested. Astrology may be built on the Hermetic axiom 'As above, so below', but something is lost in the translation. The planets in the heavens are perfectly orderly and predictable, but we know human affairs are not.

The principles symbolised by the signs and planets operate at a certain level, at what Chinese philosophy terms the World of Thought. When they are made manifest in human affairs – or the World of Senses – the one becomes many, which is why it is so difficult to say just how the potential shown in a horoscope will manifest in actuality. When we are operating in the world of creative thought we are in a special place where divine and human come together. It is more ordered than the world of affairs, but even so there is variation and uncertainty, and the patterns we detect are not always clear and hard-and-fast.

There are reasons other than the limitations of astrology itself why not all written work bears the clear stamp of the author's Sun sign. A fair amount of the fiction that fills our bookshops is not creative in the sense I have described. Books are dictated by fashion, or are written to formula, with fame or fortune the main incentive.

And it is uncommon for even good novelists to express their creative self in every book. Creativity can not be willed as such; we can only put ourselves in the way of it, invoking it in some deeper sense. Books are often more consciously wrought, sometimes for experiment, sometimes for indulgence and amusement, and often just for practical reasons such as paying the rent. Such works can have merit and generate income, but they are less likely to outlive their author or to win critical acclaim. Some writers live through momentous times – wars, the collapse of political systems, disasters – and naturally enough these form the subject matter of their books. So powerful is this content that it often stands on its own, swamping any creative infusion from the author.

Apparent variety is created by accidents of time and place. In other words, the twelve signs as universal principles are given myriad form by individual writers who can not help but be part of the time and place in which they were born. The dramatist Molière and the novelist J D Salinger, for example, are separated by about three centuries and three thousand miles and at one level the writing of the two men is quite different. This is only to be expected. Molière was writing in the 17th century in the court of Louis XIV; Salinger wrote in the USA in the mid-20th century and in his most acclaimed work, *The Catcher in the Rye*, utilises the idiom of an urban teenager. And yet at another level their work is the same. They are both Capricorn Suns, and they both write about hypocrisy, as Capricorns often do.

Novels are compounded of a general and a particular part; a timeless and a contemporary. There are themes, and the material with which themes are decked out, and both are important from a literary point of view. A good idea is only part of a novel; realising it is another. The merit of a work often depends on the craft of a writer to give a theme compelling form. But it is at the general or universal level that the Sun-sign meaning reflects, and it is at this level that we must look for the connection between astrology and literature. It does not reflect, to use the above example, in the peculiarities of 17th-century France, or latter-day New York. This is an important point to make and one sometimes missed by literary critics, who can make the mistake of focusing over much on incidentals.

Systems of knowledge congruous with astrology

There are systems of knowledge aside from astrology that help us understand the inner workings of man. They are self-consistent formulations of the same essential wisdom, and while it does not do to transpose at the particular level there is something to be gained by studying the underlying teaching that has come to be associated with these disciplines. What we gain is a change of perspective and very often it is just such a reorienting that can crystallise understanding. I make reference in *The Literary Zodiac* to two such systems: the Cabbala, with its Tree of Life, and the *I Ching* (or *Book of Changes*). Further explanation of these is included in Appendix 4. I also often refer in the text to the man who has elucidated most clearly the essential meaning of the zodiac signs: the philosopher and composer Dane Rudhyar. Like all philosophers, he is not always easy to comprehend, though as with all good philosophers, it is worthwhile making the effort. Once again, a short summary of his ideas is presented in the appendices.

The following brief section is intended primarily for those who have little or no knowledge of astrology.

A potted history of astrology

Astrology is a system of knowledge whereby human life can be understood in terms of the heavens. It relies equally upon precise measurement and a body of symbolism associated with the signs of the zodiac and the planets. It is rooted in an ancient perception of the universe which holds that that which patterns the heavens likewise orders humanity: as above, so below. Joseph Campbell dates the appearance of the Mesopotamian astronomer/priests to about 3000 BCE. Through long and meticulous observations of the heavens they perceived the orderly motion of the planets and from this there evolved

> ... the insane, playful, yet potentially terrible notion that the laws governing the movement of the seven heavenly spheres should in some mystical way be the same as those governing the life and thought of men on earth.[8]

The earliest known astrological text, the so-called Venus tablet of Ammisaduqa, dates from about 1600 BCE. However, many historians put the effective beginning of astrology at around 800 BCE in Babylon, catalysed by the advent of an exact system of chronology and the first properly constructed tables of planetary movement. The discipline received further impetus in Classical Greece; it flourished in the Hellenistic period, whence it was probably transported to India, and permeated all levels of Roman society. Following the fall of Rome it became moribund, but revived around the 7th century CE, both in the Arab world and in northern Europe. It was a revival that was sustained for the next 900 years. Through the 18th and 19th centuries in Europe astrology was pushed progressively to the cultural periphery, although at the demotic level almanacs continued to sell in great numbers. The second half of the 20th century witnessed another revival in the West, with increasing numbers of educated people treating it as a subject worthy of study.[9]

Astrology, then, has stood the test of time. It does not thrive in strongly secular ages like our own, and sits rather uneasily alongside monolithic religion. But it blossomed in Elizabethan England and Renaissance Italy where existed a happy blend of humanism and religion, and in ancient Greece, where a passion for reason was combined with an equal leaning toward mysticism. Coincidentally, or otherwise, these are periods regarded as among the high points in the history of civilisations.

Astrology as it is practised today in the West differs significantly from that of other times. A good deal of astrology today has a New Age cast, often being used as a map of the psyche, and thus an aid to realising an individual's potential or solving psychological problems. But in the 16th or 17th century, for example, it was altogether more mundane. People wanted straightforward answers to simple questions. Oliver Cromwell, as well as consulting his military staff, sought the advice of astrologer William Lilly on the likely outcome of a siege. The Elizabethan astrologer Simon Forman was consulted by women anxious for the welfare of their seafaring husbands, merchants contemplating an expedition, or by doctors, for the horoscope was regarded as a valuable diagnostic aid. This is so-called horary ('of the hour') astrology, or astrology as oracle, which, like any other oracular method, is rooted in the idea that the answer to the question lies in the moment of its asking. Traditionally there are many ways of reading the moment, including studying cloud formations or the flights of birds, the scattering of yarrow stalks, or examining the entrails of butchered animals. But the horoscope represents the most sophisticated method. Horary astrology is related to electional astrology, which is concerned with choosing (or 'electing') the most favourable time to begin something, be this a marriage, a business, or a long journey. Electional astrology is commonly used in India today, and has enjoyed a revival in the West.

More definitions

Traditionally a zodiacal sign is characterised by an element (Earth, Air, Fire or Water), a quality (Cardinal, Fixed or Mutable) and a ruling planet. There are five pairs of signs which share ruling planets: Aries/Scorpio (Mars); Taurus/Libra (Venus); Gemini/Virgo (Mercury); Sagittarius/Pisces (Jupiter); and Capricorn/Aquarius (Saturn). This leaves Cancer, ruled by the Moon, and Leo, ruled by the Sun. Those planets discovered in modern times – Uranus, Neptune and Pluto –

have also come to be allocated to certain signs. When we say a planet rules a sign, it means, in effect, that there is an equivalence between the two, a congruence of meaning. One way of looking at it is to consider the planet as a sort of agent, something in tune with and capable of focusing the energy of the signs that it rules. Naturally there are similarities between certain signs because of the common factors they share, and most obviously this is between signs that share the same ruling planet.

One thing that has been impressed upon me by this study is the importance of polarity when it comes to understanding the deeper meaning of the signs. There is nothing too surprising about this. Science in its investigation of matter has come upon polarity at every turn, while religious and philosophical accounts of the created world are often founded upon the same phenomenon. The essential meaning of a sign seems to be built about the interplay with its polar complement, the sign that stands 180 degrees from it on the zodiacal wheel (see Page 231, Figure 4). For an individual to fully live out the meaning of a Sun sign involves a conscious shift of focus to embrace the qualities associated with its polar complement. So that, for example, Virgo, a sign usually associated with routine, order and control, must make room for some disorder, or mystery, or the 'unknown'. These are qualities usually associated with the polar sign Pisces, which in turn has to find room for more order in the life. It is not as if the signs change their nature. Virgo remains Virgo, and is never quite at home with chaos, just as there can be something rather desperate about Pisces' attempts to instil order, or find a stable point of reference in the life. The idea of polar equivalence is one that is disconcerting in a western culture that prefers dilemma to paradox, but ignoring it makes it difficult to get to grips with the root meaning of the signs.

The birth chart

The Sun is just one factor used in astrological interpretation; the Moon and other planets also play a part. The birth chart is basically a two-dimensional representation of a moment in time and space, or a snapshot of the heavens from an earthly perspective. It has become a fundamental tenet of astrology that an individual born of a moment can, to a greater or lesser degree, express the quality of it as a living personality. The quality is ascertained by the disposition of the planets among the signs and the symbolism associated with them (see Appendices for an example of a birth chart). These ideas are alien to the contemporary world view, which nonetheless has no problem with the idea of wine taking on an imprint of space and time.

The ascendant, or rising sign, is the zodiac sign situated on the eastern horizon and the time of place and birth. Along with another point, the so-called culminating degree or midheaven, it forms a sort of template that is superimposed on the planetary pattern within the zodiac and gives emphasis to certain planets, which include the Sun and Moon. In astrology these are termed planets because they *appear* to circle the earth in the way the others do (astrology essentially puts the observer at the centre of the universe). The signs in which the Sun, Moon and ascendant are situated in a horoscope are three of the most important factors in characterising an individual. There is no way of predicting which will predominate: it could be any one or a mix of them all.

However, creative expression is most clearly expressed in the meaning of the Sun sign, although the signs of the Moon and ascendant are sometimes evident (to a lesser extent). For example, the flavour of Ibsen's Moon sign, Taurus, is evident in some of his otherwise strongly Piscean works. Two of the most acclaimed novels of the last century are Thomas Mann's *The Magic Mountain* and *The Plague* by Albert Camus. At one level both works centre about illness and it is interesting to discover that both men have Virgo rising, for the broad area of health is traditionally given to this sign. And yet the essence of neither work is illness. There is something more fundamental to them, as we will see in later chapters, and that something equates to the meaning of their Sun sign. Two writers with Capricorn Suns are L P Hartley and Jack London. Hartley's best known work is *The Go-Between*, about a boy who acts as a messenger between two lovers having an illicit affair. The role of go-between, at whatever level, is one that traditional astrology ascribes to Mercury, the ruler of Gemini, which is Hartley's Moon sign. London has Gemini rising in his birth chart and his character Martin Eden is a man who betters himself through, and lays great store by, education – again something characteristically Gemini. However, in both these works, which are discussed in a later chapter, there is something deeper – the obduracy of class/caste systems – and this relates to the meaning of Capricorn, the Sun sign.

Notes

1. *The Autobiography of Goethe*, translation of *Dichtung und Wahrheit*, Sidgwick and Jackson, 1971, p3

2. When he was composing his book about Goethe, *The Beloved Returns*, Mann gave his own time of birth as noon, like his subject's. However his father recorded the time of birth as 10.15 in the morning. The horoscope Mann details in *Joseph and his Brothers* bears a passing resemblance to his

own 'adopted' chart. See *Thomas Mann, Eros & Literature*, Anthony Heilbut, Macmillan, 1997, p3

3. Neil Spencer's *True as the Stars Above*, Victor Gollancz, 2000, p227, gives more detail of Hughes's interest in esoterica (and Yeats's too). This volume forms a very readable introduction to astrology.

4. Bill Darlison, author of *The Gospel and the Zodiac*, Duckworth Overlook, 2007, personal communication

5. *Contemporary Novelists*, ed James Vinson, St James Press, 1976, p634

6. Alberto Moravia, quoted in *European Writers*, Vol 12, Charles Scribner's Sons, 1990, p2274

7. Dennis Elwell, *Cosmic Loom*, Unwin Hyman, 1984

8. Joseph Campbell, *Primitive Mythology*, Souvenir Press, 2000, p146

9. For a brief and straightforward account of the subject see: Nicholas Campion, *An Introduction to the History of Astrology*, Institute for the Study of Cycles in World Affairs, 1982. Keith Thomas's *Religion and the Decline of Magic* also contains much valuable material on the subject

ARIES

Writers with the Sun in Aries include: Nelson Algren, Hans Christian Andersen, Maya Angelou, Kingsley Amis, Jeffrey Archer, Alan Ayckbourn, Russell Banks, A L Barker, Charles Baudelaire, Stephen Becker, Samuel Beckett, John Braine, James Branch Cabell, Joseph Campbell, Samuel Delany, Henry de Montherlant, Isak Dinesen, Sebastian Faulks, Dario Fo, John Fowles, Anatole France, Robert Frost, Jean Giono, Nikolai Gogol, Maxim Gorky, Peter Greenaway, Arthur Hailey, Helene Hanff, Wilson Harris, William Hazlitt, Seamus Heaney, A E Housman, Richard Hughes, Henry James, Erica Jong, Anna Kavan, Violette Leduc, Heinrich Mann, Roger Martin du Gard, Patrick McCabe, Nicholas Monsarrat, Sean O'Casey, Octavio Paz, Christoph Ransmayr, Judith Rossner, Edmond Rostand, Budd Schulberg, Paul Scott, Tom Sharpe, Algernon Swinburne, J M Synge, Paul Theroux, Hunter S Thompson, Paul Verlaine, Edgar Wallace, Eudora Welty, Thornton Wilder, Tennessee Williams, William Wordsworth, Emile Zola.

Summary Often Aries writers create central characters that accord well with traditional astrological portraits of Aries types, which include pushy go-getters, strong independent women and idealistic males who take on the role of champion to rescue some lady in distress. More fundamentally, Aries themes concern intense awareness of separation, the jarring impact of individuals coming into contact with 'otherness' and the challenge of turning being into doing.

Live all you can; it's a mistake not to. It doesn't so much matter what you do in particular so long as you have your life. If you haven't had that what have you had?

Henry James *The Ambassadors*

'I am what I do,' said Celia.

'No,' said Murphy. 'You do what you are, you do a fraction of what you are, you suffer a dreary ooze of your being into doing.'

Samuel Beckett *Murphy*

The essential Aries

Aries is the first sign of the zodiac and at a fundamental level symbolises beginnings. It represents an agent through which spirit, or life energy, becomes embodied in action. Rudhyar describes the function of Aries in terms of the release of power through individual acts in order to set cycles unfolding. Aries is the hero, in the sense that Joseph Campbell defines it, the individual who unlocks and releases the flow of life into the body of the world.[1] As well as representing the birth of life, Aries also stands for a sense of existential aloneness, an intense awareness of separation, of being an individual consciousness surrounded by an otherness[2], generally perceived as something inimical to the self, or simply as an emptiness. Against the black of this otherness the white of the self is bright indeed. So Aries is a sign of intense self-consciousness in the sense that there is a compulsion to render the self conscious, or alive, through acts of assertion over the indifference and emptiness of what is not the self. We might liken Aries to a shooting star, a momentary brightness generated by friction in the atmosphere.

It's energy seeking an outlet. It is the urge, as the quotes at the beginning of the chapter suggest, simply to have a life and live it intensely.[3] This is a common experience among Aries Sun writers, as the following quotes suggest:

Stephen Becker
[A major theme] An existential concept of the self, men struggling with themselves, with nature and with circumstances to become fully alive and functioning beings.[4]

Jean-Marie Le Clezio
Le Clezio has single-mindedly pursued one adventure: to express what it means to be alive.[5]

Eudora Welty
Miss Welty has a wide range of strategies. But these all serve a concern that is strict, narrow, and unwavering: how persons respond to their opportunity to live.[6]

Henry James
One of the central recurring themes of James' novels is the desire to live, to achieve a fullness of consciousness which permits the richest yet most exquisite response to the vibrations of life.[7]

Brendan Kennelly
As I try to write I know that I am involved in an activity which is a deliberate assertion of energy over indifference, of vitality over deadness.[8]

A L Barker
Concerned with the jarring impact caused by a collision between innocence and experience.[9]

Aries character

When Aries is strong in a birth chart we often find energy, vigour, incisiveness and strong ambition (with the emphasis on rapid attainment). Aries people can be quick-witted but also wilful, headstrong and impulsive. They make for sharp critics. There is often an insensitive nature, which is rooted in the individual's difficulty in gauging the impact he or she is having on others. The skin can be thick and one is often left concluding that the gene responsible for embarrassment is absent in Aries individuals. Those strong in Aries can have a bullying nature, although this more often than not emerges verbally rather than physically.[10] Impatience can be marked, and there is often a provocative nature, a tendency to stir things up. They slot easily into the role of *enfant terrible*. Aries favours confrontation over harmony, competition over co-operation; it enjoys a fight, especially when this is for a cause, and can positively thrive on challenge and crisis. Those strong in the sign perceive the world simply, in a black-and-white way, and often idealistically. Aries types are often autocratic, independent and self-reliant. There can be a refreshing candour and naivety, and often the need for self-assertion.

The psychologist Wilhelm Reich was an Aries Sun and his ideas clearly bear the imprint of this sign. At the beginning of his career he was a follower of Freud and set out to discover a biological foundation for the sex drive. He postulated the concept of orgone, a great sea of energy from which all natural life originates. He believed that psychological health was the product of release of built-up sexual energy through orgasm. If energy is not released but allowed to build up, then neurosis could be the result. In the same way, he believed, a society was sick that trammelled its citizens' vitality in dead and sterile laws and bureaucracy.

Reich's personality bore many Aries character traits. He had a violent temperament and his mind worked very quickly. Everyone who came into contact with him spoke of a great vitality. He was very difficult to work with, driving others as hard as he drove himself, expecting others to share his same single-minded purpose. Equally his energy and enthusiasm often inspired others.[11]

It is common to find characters in novels who are personifications of their author's Sun signs. Samuel Glick is one character who fits well the picture of Aries painted above. He is the central figure in Budd Schulberg's *What Makes Sammy Run?* The rat-race might have been invented for Sammy; he wants to get to the top and to get there as quickly as possible. The novel charts his climb from copy boy on a New York newspaper to leading producer of a Hollywood studio. Sammy has no creative talent and no social grace. What he does have is a lot of push and 'a violent passion for his own future'.[12] He has a genius for self-propulsion, a great deal of energy, and no scruples when it comes to trampling on other people. Life is a race for Glick, with death the finishing line.

Aggressiveness and self-centredness are qualities often emphasised in descriptions of Sammy. For example: 'He had a quick intelligence, which he was able to use exclusively for the good-and-welfare of Sammy Glick.'[13] At the end of the book the narrator concludes: 'You never had the first idea of give and take ... it had to be you all the way. You had to make individualism the most frightening ism of all.'[14]

On more than one occasion his competitiveness is described in military terms:

> I saw Sammy Glick on a battlefield where every soldier was his own cause, his own army, and his own flag, and I realised that I had singled him out not because he had been born into the world any more selfish, ruthless and cruel than anybody else, even though he had become all three, but because in the midst of a war that was selfish, ruthless and cruel Sammy was proving himself the fittest, the fiercest and the fastest.[15]

A similar character to Sammy Glick is Joe Lampton in John Braine's *Room at the Top.* His progress is not quite as meteoric, but there is the same rise from humble beginnings, the same impatient desire for success, and the same willingness to use other people. There is also the same experience of loneliness at the top. As Schulberg notes, you can not have your brothers and eat them too.[16]

Helene Hanff's central character, Helene, in *84 Charing Cross Road* is another good example of Aries character (stage productions bring this out better than the popular film version). It is the story of a New York writer who prefers to order her books from a shop in London, and of how a relationship develops over a number of years through written correspondence (although the main characters never meet in the flesh). Helene is strong and demanding, blunt and impatient, a person who knows what she wants and says what she thinks. She is rather bossy, yet at the same time is an attractive character because of her fresh, no-nonsense approach to life.

Another fictional character to embody Aries character traits is Allie Fox, the central figure in Paul Theroux's *The Mosquito Coast.* He is single-minded, wilful, selfish, forceful, direct, and something of a bully. He thrives on challenge, particularly when the odds are stacked against him, and is fond of setting challenges for his family. He does not like anyone telling him what to do, even when the advice is sensible, as when a friend tells him not to build his house too close to the river, because the level rises dramatically in the rainy season. Fox ignores the warning and he and his family suffer the consequences. It is safe to assume Fox's sense of aliveness comes from asserting his will over the world. He likes to do things because they can be done, not necessarily because there is any real purpose in doing them. He uproots his family from a contemporary America he finds objectionable and sets up a community in a Honduran jungle. Things go well for a time. Homes are built and crops are grown where none grew before. But a madcap scheme to build a giant ice-making plant goes terribly wrong and ultimately leads to his death. He dies a man who failed to harness his formidable energy in a productive way.

Mars and Aries

Mars is said to be the ruler of the signs Aries and Scorpio, which in lay terms means there is a commonality of meaning between the three. Aries can be considered as an extrovert (or Masculine) face of Mars, Scorpio the introvert (or Feminine) face. An understanding of the symbolism associated with Mars (which, in astrological terms, equates to something specific in human personality) tells us much about Aries (and also, as we will see later, about Scorpio).

Mars symbolises the ego in the sense that Descartes (himself an Aries Sun) describes it, the intuitive knowledge that one exists:

> I then considered attentively what I was; and I saw that while I could feign that I had no body, that there was no world, and no place existed for me to be in, I could not feign that I was not ... from this I recognised that I was a substance whose whole essence or nature is to be conscious and whose being requires no place and demands no material thing.[17]

Mars and its signs relate to the idea of focus, or intensification. Mars it is that concentrates physical resources and attention, allowing, for example, the surgeon to perform gruelling operations, or the sportsperson to excel. Mars can also concentrate physical strength in response to threat or danger enabling, for example, an eight-stone woman to lift the vehicle that is trapping her infant. The capacity to focus strength at a given place in a given instant is the principle behind a discipline like karate. The martial arts are exactly that. So too are cutting and thrusting weapons an embodiment of the Mars principle. Pressure is force per unit area, so a blade with a very fine edge is simply a device which focuses and renders more potent the strength of its wielder. And strategists have long recognised that battles are won by concentrating forces, by getting there 'fastest with the mostest', as one American general put it.

Mars focuses awareness as well as physical strength, and most have experienced the intense quality of Mars consciousness. In times of stress, shock, illness or danger the surrounding world can be perceived very differently. It takes on a great vividness, and the artists and poets of this sign can sometimes describe their creativity in these terms. Similarly, certain recreational drugs can produce a tremendous sense of aliveness, a state of mind which makes everyday consciousness seem as a slumber.

A man about to be hanged has his mind concentrated, Dr Johnson assures us, paraphrasing the advice of Eastern sages to live every moment as if it is the last. There is the Chinese fable that tells of a man who when out walking is confronted by a tiger. He flees, but arrives only at the edge of a steep ravine. He begins a descent, but halfway down becomes stranded on a narrow ledge. The friable rock begins to give way under his weight. With a tiger blocking escape above, and a hundred-foot drop below, his time has plainly come. Just as his foothold gives way his eye catches a small flower growing from the cliff and we are told it was the most beautiful flower he had ever seen – once more, the vividness of Martial perception.

This leads on to what is a fundamental characteristic of Mars and the signs it rules: they are the enemy of abstraction. This has a number of implications for Aries writing. It is a sign better at showing and recording than philosophising. Its writers can excel at detailed realism that often makes no allowance for sensibility. 'Stark naturalism' and 'naked realism' are phrases often used to describe Aries writing – Emile Zola is a good example.

To Aries novelists, action is more important than comment upon or understanding of it, a point well expressed by one of the sign's dramatists, Thornton Wilder:

> The theatre is supremely fitted to say: 'Behold! These things are.' Yet most dramatists employ it to say: 'This moral truth can be learned from beholding this action.'

And he goes on to say:

> The point I've been leading up to is that a dramatist is one who from his earliest years has found that sheer gazing at the shocks and counter-shocks among people is quite sufficiently engrossing without having to encase it in comment.[18]

This conclusion could apply to many Aries writers. William Wordsworth was an Aries poet who found his voice in opposing abstraction. He began writing at a time when English poetry had lost much of the vigour of the mid-18th century, and become vague, florid, and introspective. The young Wordsworth revitalised it, so that poetry once again became simple, fresh and direct.[19] Wordsworth's poetry was a passionate response to life. He notes in the introduction of *Lyrical Ballads* that poets are 'possessed of a more than usual organic sensibility'. Because of this, he goes on to say, the scenes and events of the real world are etched that much more strongly into the mind of the poet. Many of Baudelaire's poems attempt to recreate the spiritual shock he received in his encounters with life and nature. Joseph Campbell is expressing his own Aries Sun nature when he notes of creative artists:

> Their task, therefore, is to communicate directly from one inward world to another, in such a way that an actual shock of experience will have to be rendered: not a mere statement for the information or persuasion of a brain, but an effective communication across the void of space and time from one center of consciousness to another.[20]

Mars-sign writers often mirror Existential or Absurdist ideas in their writing, philosophies that advance the notion that man is alone in the universe and must face up to this aloneness. They propound the view that there is no God, or at least not one that can be known, so that man must seek truth in his own being and actions and not through some transcendent ideal. The challenges of life must not be evaded in the name of a distant salvation. These ideas are more concretely expressed in Scorpio but are evident in Aries as well.

An interesting variation is found in the writing of Baba Ram Dass (an Aries Sun). Ram Dass started life as Richard Alpert, who was a successful academic. Like Samuel Glick and Joe Lampton, he reached the top quickly and reaped the material rewards. However, a deep dissatisfaction with his life developed and psychedelic drugs precipitated a search for a deeper set of values. He became a Leary LSD acolyte, and then travelled to India, where he met his guru and undertook some years of instruction. He returned to America, reborn as Baba Ram Dass, to set up a teaching network and to write *Be Here Now*, part autobiography, part spiritual guidebook.

On page 90 of this work we note:

> Ask yourself: where am I? Answer Here. Ask yourself: what time is it? Answer Now ... begin to notice that wherever you go or whatever time it is by the clock ... it is always here now.

Be Here Now is the essence of Ram Dass' philosophy, although it is not a call for hedonism or irresponsibility. Rather, it is a reminder to focus consciousness in an eternal present, for thus do we link up with the creative source of the universe and be an agent for the release of its energy.

On the Tree of Life Mars corresponds to Geburah, and descriptions of this sphere centre on strength and power, particularly as they are directed towards combating evil or curbing excess. The associated image is of a warrior king in his chariot, 'whose strong right arm protects his people with the sword of righteousness and ensures that justice shall be done'.[21] On the Tree of Life Mars sits in tandem with Chesed (which corresponds to Jupiter) and the two must operate as a mutually supporting polarity. Mars must counter the evasiveness, excess or over-expansiveness of Jupiter. Mars acts as a celestial surgeon who will cut away that which threatens the health of the total organism.[22] Equally, the principles and broad-viewed judgement of Jupiter work to guide and direct the Martial power.

Although Mars and its signs are direct and one-pointed they are also, to some extent, romantic and idealistic. If Mars likes anything more than fighting it is fighting for a cause, against what is perceived as injustice, evil or oppression. The image of St George and the dragon is very apt for Aries. Aries men often display a chivalrous nature and Zola forms a good example. In his younger days he set out to rescue his damsel in distress, in this case a prostitute fallen on hard times. They lived together for a spell and through his lofty perceptions of love he hoped to save her from a life on the street. Needless to say his idealism was somewhat blunted by the reality. This phase of his life is chronicled in his first novel, *La Confession de Claude*. We note that Vincent Van Gogh (an Aries Sun) lived for a time with an alcoholic prostitute, while for Charles Baudelaire the mulatto prostitute Jeanne Duval helped generate the intense passion from which grew his best poetry.

In Aries there is a quite singular tendency to idealise partners, though most commonly it is the men of the sign who are given to romantic projections. Possibly the root of this trait is the sense of isolation in Aries, which induces a desperate need to overcome this by connecting with another. Relating is not natural to Aries, although it is to the polar complement Libra. In Aries relating is something that has to be learned, so there can be an awkward and naive quality to it.The trait is evident both in the lives and fiction of Aries writers. William Hazlitt, the 19th-century essayist, was overcome in his middle life by a passion for his landlady's 19-year-old daughter. One critic has noted of this episode: 'he invested this unremarkable and flirtatious girl with a romantic aura that reflected his own emotional needs and had little objective reality.'[23] Similarly, Zola in his later life took for a mistress a simple girl, who was to become the mother of his children. Hans Christian Andersen developed a romantic pining for Swedish soprano Jenny Lind. Henry James' interest in women took the form of a 'rather distant worship', and for Baudelaire (aside from Jeanne Duval) too it was largely a case of distant worship. The theme of romantic projection crops up regularly in Aries novels. We see it, for example, in Heinrich Mann's best-known work, *Professor Unrat*, where a tyrannical schoolmaster becomes enraptured of the femme fatale Lola Lola. (The work was later filmed as *The Blue Angel.*) Rostand's portrayal of Cyrano de Bergerac is of a man who loves idealistically and at a distance. We note it in John Fowles' first novel, *The Collector*, in his later work *The French Lieutenant's Woman*, and in Henry James' *The American* and *The Portrait of a Lady*.

We'll consider these latter three in a little more detail.

John Fowles, *The French Lieutenant's Woman*

This novel is both a romance and a chronicle of the Victorian era in which it is set. It centres upon Charles, a young man about to be married and take up a position in society, prospects which do not induce in him a sense of wellbeing. Discontent develops in direct proportion to his contact with Sarah, the 'woman' of the title, whose full epithet derives from an affair she had with a French seaman. The affair, pursued out of desperate loneliness, left her more isolated than ever, an outcast in the Dorset town where she lives.

Sarah sees in Charles someone who is capable of understanding her and ending her isolation. Charles, for his part, is fascinated by Sarah. The first time he sets eyes on her it is against a stirring backdrop of storm and tempestuous sea and we are left in no doubt that he views her in an idealised way: 'she was more like a living memorial to the drowned, a figure from myth, than any proper fragment of the petty provincial day.'[24]

And later, when the relationship has developed:

> He became increasingly unsure of the frontier between the real Sarah and the Sarah he had created in so many dreams: the one Eve personified, all mystery and love and profundity, and the other a half-scheming, half-crazed governess from an obscure seaside town.[25]

His romantic image persists to the end. They become separated and Charles, imagining all manner of dire things to have befallen Sarah, sets out to find her. He is ready to play St George, but to his dismay he finds that she has acquired some sort of peace in an artists' residence:

> He had come to raise her from penury, from some crabbed post in a crabbed house. In full armour, ready to slay the dragon – and now the damsel had broken all the rules. No chain, no sobs, no beseeching hands.[26]

The theme of abandoning the reality of a safe (if, perhaps, dull) partner is quite common in Aries. Invariably the result is disenchantment.

Henry James, *The American*

Christopher Newman, the central figure of this novel, sees life as a challenge. It is one successfully met in his case, for by the age of 35 he has made a fortune from his business activities. 'What he had been placed in the world for,' we are told, 'was, to his own perception, simply to wrest a fortune, the bigger the better from defiant opportunity.'[27] Newman is vigorous, impatient and enterprising. He is a doer, a man of action, someone who bends circumstances to his will – 'exertion and action were as natural to him as respiration.'[28]

And yet he has a refined nature, lacking the brashness and ruthless selfishness of Samuel Glick or Joe Lampton. Indeed, Newman is an attractive character, one imbued with the ingenuous charm associated with Aries. He is a more high-mined Aries, one who has turned to his polar horizon and embraced some Libran qualities. He attempts to take 'otherness' into account, although not particularly successfully – and indeed, it is this failing that lies at the heart of the story. Newman's attitude to women is again characteristic of the sign: he idealises them, treats them with an exaggerated (hence slightly comical) courtesy. Yet at the same time he sees women in terms of his own needs and as individuals who must measure up to his rather lofty standards.

The American is basically a story of New World energy and optimism coming up against Old World reaction. Having made his fortune Newman has to decide what to do with it and how to spend the rest of his life. He travels to Europe with the intention of imbibing some culture and, more immediately, finding himself a wife. In Paris he is introduced to a certain Madame de Cintre, a woman who matches all his high ideals. She is a young widow, the scion of an old and aristocratic French family, and a woman dominated by a scheming mother and a conniving brother. It was they who arranged her first marriage to an unattractive but well-pedigreed suitor. They hope to do the same again.

When Newman learns of this he girds his loins and becomes a knight on a white charger intent on rescuing her. He resolves to marry Madame de Cintre then take her to America, where she will be free of her dreary home and scheming family and he will provide her with anything his money can buy. He almost succeeds. They become engaged. There is even a party to celebrate. But eventually it is the family's and not Newman's will that prevails. The family pressure Madame de Cintre so that she breaks off the engagement and enters a nunnery. He plots revenge, although this is never carried out. Newman seems the only one surprised by the turn of events. He feels himself 'a goodfellow wronged'.

At the outset Newman was confident that his proposal would meet with success and so plunges in boldly, against all the advice. But his is the confidence of naivety. He sees no problems because he sees things simply. He fails to comprehend or take account of the nature of what it is he is challenging. However, it is one thing to overcome dumb circumstance and wrest a fortune from it, quite another to pick a way through the intricate mores of French high society. The energy, will and directness appropriate in the first case are hardly so in the second. Established form, etiquette, the 'right' behaviour are not Aries' forte.

Newman feels it very unjust that something over which he has no control – his background – should be held against him. The family's concern with the 'right' credentials and upbringing bewilder and appal him. He is rich, attractive and available, and that should be the end of it in his eyes. Newman also fails to perceive the complexities of another person. It does not occur to him that Madame de Cintre does not want to be rescued and unconsciously colludes with her family because in her make-up there is a need for suffering and self-denial. Or that there is part of her that can not cope with relationships among equals, or is frightened of not living up to Newman's high expectations. There are hints that she is not all he perceives her to be, but James does not really explore her psychology too deeply.

Henry James, *The Portrait of a Lady*

Isabel Archer, the heroine of this work, forms another good example of Aries character, and at the same time illustrates the paradox that Aries is called upon to resolve. She is frank, energetic, high-spirited, eager and strong-willed; she carries within herself 'a great fund of life', and more than anything cherishes her independence. Another character in the work, Henrietta Stackpole, also embodies this idea of the liberty-loving, independent Aries woman. At a time when it was unusual for a woman to engage in any profession, she operates as a roving foreign correspondent. Henrietta is blunt, tactless, thick-skinned, and 'proof that a woman might suffice to herself and be happy'.[29]

Isabel travels from America to Europe for a fresh start in life, but also as a response to the nagging question: 'What was she going to *do* with herself?' (my emphasis).[30] At the time James was writing this was an unusual question for a woman to be asking, because there was an obvious answer: get married, have children, and look after house and husband. 'Most women did with themselves nothing at all,' writes James:

> They waited in attitudes more or less gracefully passive, for a man to come that way and furnish them with a destiny. Isabel's originality was that she gave out an impression of having intentions of her own.[31]

The dilemma faced by Aries is one of finding the middle way between constraining the momentum of life and accepting the need to harness one's energy to *something.*[32] It is through containment, however, that the self acquires contours and is more readily defined. The challenge is (to use James' words) to extract from 'the base, ignoble world ... some recognition of one's superiority'.[33] In other words, to win victories over life. Isabel Archer seeks, eventually, to define herself through marriage but makes a bad judgement and is damned by the consequences of her decision. (A not uncommon failing of Aries people; it's a sign that sees things too black and white to be a good judge.) She commits herself to a partner, a selfish and egotistical man who uses her for his own ends. In marrying she quenches the Fire, the exultations, the enthusiasms, the intoxication of possibilities, that's her birthright and in its place gets 'a dark, narrow alley with a dead wall at the end of it'.[34]

Sebastian Faulks, *Birdsong*

The theme of this novel is that of men whose lives are reduced to 'a narrow inferno of existence,' in a time of war, a brutal and perverted existence that allows for no fine distinctions, just life or violent death. Everything is stripped away, save the will to exist. In this it is similar to another well-known Aries novel, *The Cruel Sea,* by Nicholas Monsarrat, whose subject is the Atlantic convoys of the Second World War and the ever-present danger to their crews. The sea was hostile rather than indifferent because it held predatory U-boats and life was about survival and nothing much more. Most of modern, civilised life is removed from such raw intensity. But it's never far away and we can be plunged into it through death, birth or violence.

There are two main strands to *Birdsong.* The major one recounts the life of Stephen Wraysford in the years 1910-18. The first section of the novel, when he is a civilian living in France before the First World War, centres upon a passionate affair he has with Isabelle, the wife of the businessman he is lodging with. Stephen's affair bears comparison with Charles' in *The French Lieutenant's Woman*, in that he perceives Isabelle as a damsel in distress. She is physically abused by her husband and, in Stephen's view, trapped in a life that is not her own. He resolves to rescue her, and indeed they do run off and live together for a time. Isabelle falls pregnant but leaves before she has the child.

Stephen is strongly Aries in many ways. We are told of his 'openness and quick temper,'[35] and of a strong will, which because of a cruel accident of history could only translate into a determination to survive, as opposed to a full and rich life. We are told that while not necessarily a good soldier he was a 'terrific fighter'. His response to his own actions is also typical of Aries. After the escape from Isabelle's family the couple sit together in a railway carriage. Stephen:

> felt the simple elation of victory, the fact that it was he who had won, who had persuaded Isabelle against the weight of convention and sound argument to do the difficult and dangerous thing.[36]

Contrasted to Stephen's story and the horrors of the Trenches is the life of his grand-daughter Elizabeth in England in the 1970s. She undertakes a research project to discover something of her grandfather, whom she never knew. A huge gulf divides their generations, not so much of years but of experience. Elizabeth's uninvolved life contrasts with that of a young soldier whose photo she comes across in a book:

> his terror and imminent death were as actual and irreversible to him as were to her ... the ... fripperies of peacetime life that made up her casual, unstressed existence.[37]

What most irritated her was, 'the continued sense of the easy, the unessential nature of what she did'.[38] However, in the last pages of the book she is plunged into the sort of primal level of existence that was the lot of men like her grandfather. Pregnant by her lover she gives birth, not in a sanitised maternity ward, but like an animal in a cottage in Dorset without anaesthesia or even a midwife.

Notes

1. Joseph Campbell, *The Hero with a Thousand Faces*, Fontana, 1993
2. We can note the following comment on Beckett's writing: 'A mote in the dark of absolute freedom ... a tiny plenum in the immensity of the void, something autonomous and separate from the void ... such is the self in

Beckett: something undefinable in space, something dimensionless, but something (we can call it consciousness) and something which, because it is dimensionless, exists outside the world of space and time and is by definition unattainable within that world.' (Ross Chambers, 'Beckett's Brinkmanship', *J of Australasian Language and Literature Association*, 1963. Reprinted in *Contemporary Literary Criticism*, Vol 9, Gale Research, 1978, p78).

We think of one of Pozzo's speeches towards the end of *Waiting for Godot*: 'They give birth astride of a grave, the light gleams an instant, then it is night once more.' Critics have described the essence of *Waiting for Godot* as two characters aware of the need to persist in time.

In *Birdsong*, Stephen Wraysford views life as 'a blink of light between two eternities of darkness.' (ibid p12)

3. The critic Tony Tanner noted of Henry James: 'One of the first great modern novelists of the world within, the first to dramatise the inward effort and strain of the unique – and lonely – perceiving consciousness as it seeks to understand new and problematic worlds.' (*Henry James: Modern Judgements*, ed Tony Tanner, Macmillan, 1968, p35)

4. *Contemporary Novelists*, second edition, ed James Vinson, St James Press, 1976, p113

5. *Columbia Dictionary of Modern European Literature*, ed J A Bédé and W B Edgerton, Columbia University Press, 1980, p467

6. *Great Writers of the English Language (Novelists & Prose Writers)*, ed. James Vinson, Macmillan, 1976, p1278

7. Arnold Kettle, 'Henry James: *The Portrait of a Lady*,' in *English Novel*, Vol 2, Hutchinson, 1953. Reprinted in *Twentieth Century Literary Criticism*, Vol 2, Gale Research, 1978, p264

8. *Contemporary Poets*, ed James Vinson, Macmillan, 1980, 831

9. *An Encyclopaedia of British Women Writers*, ed Paul & June Schlueter, Garland Press, 1988, p22

10. Good actors can make something of any role but are often at their best when playing a character that harmonises with their own astrological nature. For example, Peter Capaldi is an Aries Sun with Scorpio ascendant and in astrological parlance would be described as a strong 'Mars' character. He nowhere better expresses this than in the role of Malcolm Tucker, a spin doctor in the BBC series *The Thick of It*. His spectacular tirades of verbal abuse and need (and ability) to dominate those around him demonstrate the harsher side of the planet and its signs. In the same mould is Alec Baldwin's character in *Glengarry Glen Ross*, whose 'motivational' talk leaves the staff of salesmen shell-shocked. Baldwin is an Aries Sun. While the violence inherent in Aries often emerges verbally, its physically brutal nature is well demonstrated by Robert Carlyle's portrayal of Francis Begbie in *Trainspotting*. Carlyle, a Sun and Moon Aries, sometimes plays more sensitive roles, or that of a social misfit on the fringe of society, but many critics agree that he is at his most impressive in screen displays of extreme anger and hairspring-sensitive violence. The same might also be said of Gary Oldman (another Aries Sun).

11. One biographer writes: 'Talking to friends and foes of Reich, one thing stands out above all others: his great vitality. It was always mentioned first,

the outstanding quality of the man in whatever connection, his élan, his energy, his almost overpowering strength." (Ilse Ollendorff Reich, *Wilhelm Reich, a Personal Biography*, Elek Books, 1969, pxix

12. Budd Schulberg, *What Makes Sammy Run?*, Sphere, 1971, p80
13. ibid, p12
14. ibid, p251
15. ibid, p208
16. The same idea of a scramble to the top is at the heart of Alan Ayckbourn's perennial favourite, *A Chorus of Disapproval.* We might also compare the central character in *The Gadarene Club* by the German writer Martin Walser (born 24.3.1927). 'A poor young man from the hinterlands ... who, with ambition, pluck and a talent for timing and one-upmanship makes a great success of his job ... but his climb to the higher reaches of society is accompanied by a loss of his sense of identity and respect ... he has become a bully and egomaniac.' *Dictionary of Literary Biography*, Vol 75, Gale Research, 1988, p244-45
17. René Descartes, *Discourses*, Part 4
18. Thornton Wilder, *Writers at Work*, Vol 1, ed Malcolm Cowley, Penguin, 1981, pp109-110
19. Hans Christian Andersen played a similar role in revitalising the Danish literature of his day.
20. Joseph Campbell, *Creative Mythology*, Secker & Warburg, 1968, p92
21 Dion Fortune, *The Mystical Qabalah*, Ibis, 1979, p174
22. Hence the following lines from *Two Noble Kinsmen* (attributed to Shakespeare). Mars is being invoked: 'O great corrector of enormous times/ Shaker of o'er rank states.'
23. R L Brett in *British Writers*, Vol IV, Charles Scribner's Sons, 1981, p131
24. John Fowles, *The French Lieutenant's Woman*, Vintage, 1996, p11
25. ibid, p410
26. ibid, p426
27. Henry James, *The American*, Bantam Books, 1971, p20
28. ibid, p19
29. Henry James, *The Portrait of a Lady*, Vintage Books, 2008, p51
30. ibid, p63
31. ibid, p63
32. This accords with the advice of the I Ching hexagram associated with Aries, number 34, 'The Power of the Great'. Its meaning centres upon the contrast between power and violent force. It marks a time when 'inner worth mounts with great force and comes to power', (p133) although the text goes on to warn that 'the superior man does not tread upon paths that do not accord with established order' (p557). Again, this suggests that Aries is not just about expending energy, but rather harnessing it to something.
33. *The Portrait of a Lady*, p440
34 ibid, p434
35. Sebastian Faulks, *Birdsong*, Vintage, p12
36. ibid, p82
37. ibid, p163
38. ibid, p334

Taurus

Writers with the Sun in Taurus include: Richard Adams, R M Ballantyne, Honoré de Balzac, Maurice Baring, J M Barrie, H E Bates, Frank Baum, Alan Bennett, Earle Birney, Charlotte Brontë, Robert Browning, Peter Carey, Angela Carter, R V Cassill, Cecil Day-Lewis, Walter De La Mare, J P Donleavy, Daphne Du Maurier, Stanley Elkin, Henry Fielding, Max Frisch, Ellen Glasgow, William Goyen, Hugh Hood, Ruth Prawer Jhabvala, Thomas Kinsella, Edward Lear, Harper Lee, Bernard Malamud, Robin Maugham, Armistead Maupin, Andrew Miller, Alistair MacLean, Archibald MacLeish, Christopher Morley, John Mortimer, Edwin Muir, Vladimir Nabokov, Novalis, Katherine Porter, Dennis Potter, Terry Pratchett, Frederic Prokosch, Thomas Pynchon, Ian Rankin, Dorothy Richardson, Dante Gabriel Rossetti, William Shakespeare, Samuel Selvon, Anthony and Peter Shaffer, Carl Spitteler, Graham Swift, Rabindranath Tagore, Sigrid Undset, Robert Penn Warren, Roger Zelazny.

Summary Money can be a theme in this sign, as can sex, though in a specific sense, with the emphasis often on the destructive aspect of sex (or of passion or obsession), and the need for individuals to learn to distinguish between lust and love. Eden, the Fall, lost innocence (and the urge to recapture it) all relate to this sign. There is also a 'psychoanalytical' strand to Taurean writing, where something from the past continues to exert a destructive influence on an individual's life and needs to be exorcised.

Love comforteth like sunshine after rain,
But Lust's effect is tempest after sun;
Love's gentle spring doth always fresh remain:
Lust's winter comes ere summer half be done.
Love surfeits not: Lust like a glutton dies.
Love is all truth: Lust full of forged lies.

William Shakespeare *Venus and Adonis*

Some astrologers have pointed to a relationship between the zodiac signs and certain of the enduring myths of ancient times. There are a number that relate to Taurus. There is the story of Midas, whose desire for wealth eventually destroys the thing he loves most. In popular astrology Taurus traditionally relates to money, which often enough assumes major importance for those strong in the sign and appears as a theme in Taurean literature. Much of Balzac's writing, for example, is about the struggle of the age in which he lived to amass money. One of his best known works is *Eugénie Grandet*, which features the miser Old Grandet. In Grandet, Balzac wrote, 'I have created Avarice'. Grandet is obsessed with gold; the dynamic of his life is the love of money, and the work tells of the impact this has on those around him. One critic[1] has described him:

> Grandet ... is a miser to the exclusion of all else. His physical make-up seems to have been shaped by his vice; even his awkward pronunciation serves his greed; his every word, his every deed, is determined by his unique obsession ... He has no religious beliefs, no political convictions, no pity, no self-respect, and no ambition of any kind apart from money. He has no desire to appear rich; enough that he is so ... the love of gain devours his aged body like a cancer ... he is a beast reduced to *the mechanism of an elementary instinct.*

The emphasis is mine, for it's an observation that points to the deeper meaning of the sign.

The Greek myth of the Minotaur also illuminates the meaning of Taurus. It's a tale that hinges on a broken pact and the chain of destruction this sets in motion.[2] Minos, king of Crete, in exchange for supremacy of the sea pledges to its master, Poseidon, a magnificent white bull. But when the time for sacrifice comes Minos offers instead a lesser beast. To take his revenge, Poseidon, acting through Aphrodite/Venus, instils in Minos' wife a powerful lust for the white bull. She is mounted by the animal and from the union is spawned the Minotaur, a beast part-human, part-bull with an insatiable appetite for human flesh. A shameful emblem of his misdeed, Minos has the beast enclosed in a labyrinth and sacrifices to it the sons and daughters of vassal states. It is the hero Theseus who puts things to rights by slaying the beast at the heart of the labyrinth. The Minotaur is brought into existence by two acts: the broken pact of Minos, motivated by greed and thirst for power, and the lust that befalls his wife. It is only through heroic deeds that the 'original sin' is undone, the cycle of destruction terminated, the world put back into kilter. This myth relates particularly to the 'psychoanalytical' dimension of Taurus, which we'll return to later.

Taurus also relates to the myth of Eden and the Fall, not as an objective historical event, but as a subjective experience, a subliminal awareness of some ideal way of life that has been lost (particularly because of some kind of interference by man in the greater scheme of things) and that the everyday world is but a pale shadow of something more beautiful and perfect. It's a continuation of the Aries theme of man as a self-conscious individual aware he is different from the rest of creation and who is cursed with the knowledge of an indifferent and disharmonious universe.

This is sometimes expressed in Taurean literature in quest stories, where the objective of the quest is recovery, or discovery, of some pattern that hints at a greater meaning in a world that seems devoid of love, beauty, or harmony.[3] The same idea also manifests in those strong in Taurus in more mundane ways for the sign is one of the more backward-looking of the zodiac. The past seems rosier than the present for the Venus-ruled signs; utopia is not something in the future waiting to be brought into being, but a past waiting to be re-discovered and restored. The following observations of Taurean writers by critics bear out the connection of this sign with the Fall:

> **Robert Penn Warren**
> A paradigm of [his] lasting concerns is found in the poem 'Original Sin: A short story', a short poem telling ... of the inescapability of man's knowledge of his fallen state.[4]
>
> **Camilo José Cela**
> One of the frequently recurring themes in [his] fiction ... is that Man is cursed by an original sin ... Cela has, in numerous works over the years, sought to give expression to his depressing vision of Man's Fall.[5]
>
> **Jorge De Lima**
> (Of *Annunciation and Encounter of Mira-Celi*) A volume of prose poems depicting the Fall as the origin of human misery.[6]
>
> **Tudor Arghezi**
> His ... yearning to know and understand human destiny, the torment of a soul longing in a world that shelters 'snakes and evil' to find the key to a pure, absolute, untarnished existence.[7]
>
> **Robert Pack**
> Poems like *Descending* interpret the terror implicit in the universe as the real cost of exclusion from paradise.[8]
>
> **Edwin Muir**
> The idea of Eden, a Fall, and a search for reconstituted unity and harmony is central to Muir's poetry.[9]

One of Muir's volumes is titled *One Foot in Eden*, and most of the individual poems are concerned with the road from innocence to experience, with all its dangers and benefits, for if we lose something in the Fall, we are also opened up to the possibility of doing positive good. Muir reflected the Fall myth in his life as well as his poetry and in his autobiography writes of two formative periods in his childhood centring upon loss of innocence. The first occurred when he was aged seven. He writes how in the early years of life a child holds a certain vision of harmony within life. But then,

> there comes a moment (the moment at which childhood passes into boyhood or girlhood) and this image is broken and a contradiction enters life ... the sense of an unseen tragedy being played out around me.[10]

He goes on to describe the experience as 'the destruction of my first image of the world'. At the same time, these childhood impressions remained vivid throughout his life, and he realised later that many of his poetic images were drawn from them.

A second period of childhood crisis came when he was 14 years old and his family moved from Orkney, where Muir was born and raised, to Glasgow. 'We were plunged out of order into chaos,'[11] he writes. Orkney was for him an Eden where life flowed according to the swing of the seasons. It represented a harmonious and protective order, while Glasgow, by contrast, represented a world askew, a squalid monument to capitalist competition, as opposed to the Venusian co-operation that pervaded Orkney. The move to Glasgow marked the beginning of the worst period of the poet's life, with uncongenial work, illness and the death of family members. It was also marked by a more general ennui, brought on, as his biographer notes, by his being 'at a loss to find any meaning in the life he saw round him'.[12] This is a theme that regularly crops up in Taurean writing.

Taurus and Venus

Astrologers associate the planet Venus with Taurus and also Libra, which means there is common ground between the two signs, although in other ways they are quite different. Peace, accord and diplomacy are watchwords of the Venus signs, although the shadow side of these qualities – laziness, procrastination, inability to act, difficulty in being firm – are also often apparent. Venus and its signs correspond with the charming, attractive quality we call charisma. The origin of the word 'Venus' relates it to charm and seduction. It derives from the Latin *venerari, veneror*, 'I work a charm [upon such and such a divinity] in order to [obtain a result]'.[13] Charm applies to both religion – to win grace and favour from a god – and to the profane world, as a form of power to get what we want.

Taurus is an Earth sign, and often earthy in the general sense of the word. Sex is a common enough subject among Taurean writers. It is common, of course, in modern writing in general, but in Taurus the slant is generally very specific: the destructiveness of an untrammelled passion, and the need for a man or woman to distinguish between lust and love. Venus symbolises the spectrum of love, from carnal to divine, and sometimes the challenge of its two signs is perceived as the need to move toward the spiritual end of the spectrum. A number of words connected to sex and love stem from Venus: venereal = concerning sexual love; venery = the pursuit of sexual gratification; venerate = to hold in deep regard.

Venus and its associated signs stand for our sense of right or wrong, both that which we absorb from family or society and something deeper and more instinctive. It's a quality well described by the archaic word 'ruth' – a word more familiar through its opposite, ruthless. It is that within us that recoils from injuring others or, when we do, assails us with remorse. 'Ruth' also means regret, a feeling of guilt for something we have (or haven't) done in the past and wish we could put right.

On a broader canvas the astrological Venus can be understood as that power which creates a harmonious order. It transforms chaos to cosmos, noise to melody and, at the social level, maintains a well-ordered and peaceful society. It holds things in their 'proper' place, in other words, orders through relationship. This same power is what the ancient Egyptians termed *Ma'at*, a word that can be translated as 'truth', 'justice,' or 'rightness'. *Ma'at*, like Eden, symbolised the pristine state of the world when it first came into being, the product of divine creation. Priests and the pharaoh worked to strengthen *Ma'at* through ritual, while the ordinary person helped maintain it through correct social behaviour, for when *Ma'at* was destroyed life became unbearable and meaningless. Whatever ran counter to *Ma'at* was termed *Isfet*.[14]

The Elizabethans too held this view of some principle of goodness and right holding together society, reflecting in peace, prosperity and harmony. It appears as a motif in the work of the era's most distinguished dramatist, William Shakespeare.[15] In his tragedies *Isfet* abounds when the harmony is rent by some 'unnatural' act. Lust for power overcomes Macbeth's moral restraint and he murders the king, an act which sets off a chain of evil and creates a state of bloody anarchy in his country. For his part Macbeth is isolated by his evil, and tortured by conscience. Venus stands for that which is right for the individual, his sense of morality, and this fight between the forces of the id and moral restraint is often enough the theme of Taurean writing. In one of the Bard's lighter works, *A Midsummer*

Night's Dream, we again have the idea of discord in the world of mortal and fairy harmoniously resolved.

Venus has its equivalent in cabbalistic teaching where it is regarded as a formative influence, one that patterns matter in the way that a magnetic field is seen to shape a scattering of iron filings. It is the same patterning capability that creates cosmos out of chaos, or harmony out of disorder. It is described in terms of free-moving force 'bound only into exceedingly fluidic and ever-shifting shapes'.[16] Venus functions as a bridge between matter and spirit, between man and his gods; in an individual it relates to the capacity to form images representative of some spiritual or psychic state. It is the tantalising emblem of a more perfect order, and is well symbolised by the likes of the aurora and the rainbow – things of elusive and insubstantial beauty.

The darker side of Taurus

Taurus symbolises a powerful but primitive current of life energy. It connects with vitality in the sense of will and ability to survive, where the need is for emotional resource that is robust and uncomplicated rather than refined and subtle. It was a Taurean Sun, Herbert Spencer, who coined the phrase 'survival of the fittest'. Taurus has a relationship to strong primitive emotions such as envy, lust, jealousy and obsession and this partly explains why some of the world's most evil men and egregious criminals have Taurus strong in their birth charts, and why five of the Seven Deadly Sins relate to the sign.[17]

The I Ching hexagram related to Taurus, number 43, refers to traditional failings of the sign such as greed and obstinacy and warns against the destructiveness of passion, the bane of the tragic Shakespearean hero, as well as other Taurean characters. 'Even a single passion still lurking in the heart has the power to obscure reason', counsels the text.

It suggests too that the best way to fight evil, 'is to make energetic progress in the good'.[18] Hexagram 43 is titled Breakthrough, or Resoluteness, and the time it describes is one of release after a long accumulation of tension, suggestive of the need-driven desire at the heart of the sign. There is also allusion here to the Taurean season of spring when the pressure of a hitherto subterranean life-force has grown strong enough to burst through the soil, and, in a surge of growth, push upward to the sky.

As we saw with Wilhelm Reich in the previous chapter, psychologists often reflect their essential nature in their ideas just as much as writers of fiction and we get an insight into the more fundamental side of Taurus through the thought of Sigmund Freud, who was a Taurus Sun.

Central to Freud's psychology is the concept of libido, a powerful life force or psychic energy congruous, at least at a primitive level, with the sex drive. It has been termed by one commentator, 'a fluid and malleable force capable of excessive and disturbing power'. Libido is something that needs to be discharged, either in the attainment of pleasure, or the avoidance of pain. Tied up with libido are concepts such as desire, need, and value. Desire springs from need, which can be understood as a releasing of tension, or the resolution of an existing unsatisfactory situation. Desire must find an object, and we value someone or something in proportion to the amount of psychic energy that is invested in them or it. When we value something it has force over us and can direct, even drive, our behaviour.

The work of another Taurean psychologist, Henry Murray, focused upon needs, and he talked of the 'press' of an object, meaning the power it has to affect the wellbeing of a subject. If the libido is thwarted, as it must be in the normal process of growing up, it is displaced, stored within the individual as a repository of repressed desire. In his topography of the psyche Freud established a fundamental duality between libido and that which restrains or represses it. It was a contrast between what he termed the id, on one hand, and the ego/superego on the other. The id for Freud was a source of energy, primitive urges for sensual gratification unchecked by any sense of right or wrong. The ego is a function of the reality principle, which accepts there are limitations on desires, while the superego results from an internalisation, usually through the parents and other authority figures, of society's moral imperatives.

It can be said that the causes and consequences of repressed desires are at the heart of Freud's psychology. Repressed desire is reflected in dreams – a memory, he suggests, not so much of real events as unfulfilled wishes. And this dammed-up life energy can also reflect as neuroses and complexes. Freud's methods were aimed at isolating such complexes and then releasing the life energy bound up in them. It could be said that Freud's methods involve a journeying into the labyrinth of the unconscious to discover, confront and destroy an individual's 'minotaur', that is, the thing which blocks, frustrates or warps an individual.

Essentially it is a delving into the past, although it is not just the recall of events that is important so much as the ability to positively create the past through the imagination in order to disentangle psychic energy and the things or events it is attached to. This is perhaps Freud's real contribution to the world: he demonstrated that the past could be redeemed.[19]

More examples of Taurean writing

J P Donleavy, *The Ginger Man*

Sebastian Dangerfield is a poor student living in Dublin, although his life revolves more around survival than studying the law. He yearns for the simple things in life – good food, drink, sex, a comfortable home – but is not prepared to work in order to secure them. And what fuels this unwillingness is the expectation of a large inheritance. When Sebastian's Irish debts become too intolerable he travels to London, where he learns of his father's death, and also of a codicil stating the fortune is not to be his for another 20 years. In effect he is cut off from his father's benevolence, from the money that was to have sustained him in a life of indolent indulgence. He can not go on cheating the laws of economic reality for another 20 years. If he is to survive then he must turn to his own productive resources and use them to create the kind of life he desires.

Beyond a tale about money a more basic theme is exile and loss of innocence. Sebastian Dangerfield is a person who is reluctant to accept the responsibility of life. He much prefers the Edenic existence of a pampered son, but ends up expelled from the Garden. In one sense the Taurus phase of the zodiac is about learning to leave Eden, accept exile, and work resolutely in a world at best indifferent, at worst hostile, to first discover, then recreate or regain, something meaningful. In one sense he is a boy who refuses to grow up emotionally, which is a characteristic of Taurus, and sometimes expressed in literature, most famously in J M Barrie's *Peter Pan.* There can often be a childlike quality about Taureans, men and women, so that although physically and intellectually developed, there remains an emotional immaturity, rooted in a desire *to be as* children, to hold on to an innocent view of the world, one that doesn't know sin or evil and can countenance fantasy.[20]

Peter Shaffer, *Equus*

There is a strong feeling of Freud to this tale of a dominating and destructive passion. It's a powerful drama, the story of an adolescent boy, Alan Strang, who blinds a number of horses with an iron spike, and a psychiatrist's attempts to unravel the complex motive. We learn that Alan formed an obsession for horses following a childhood incident when he was given a ride by a stranger. It was an exhilarating experience for the boy but, significantly, it was cut short by his father, an unimaginative man whose reality is built upon economic necessity, and who deplores his wife's attempts to interest Alan in religion. As it is, Alan seems to commandeer religion to feed his obsession. The high-blown prose of the Old Testament, suitably adapted, works as well to exalt a horse as God, not a particular horse, but an idealised essence of one – Equus.

Alan takes a weekend job at a stables and secretly, at night, strips naked and rides the horses bareback in a field. He is befriended at work by a young woman, Jill. They go out together one Saturday night and end up back at the stables. They prepare for sex, but Alan, although willing, is unable to perform. It is then, after sending the girl away, that he blinds the horses. Following arrest and a trial he is sent to a psychiatrist, Dysart, for treatment.

The childhood horse ride on the beach with the stranger is an incident that seems to trap Alan's psychic energy, so that horses become his passion, his obsession (the dividing line is thin). As Dysart notes at one point in his analysis:

> A child is born into a world of phenomenon all equal in their power to enslave ... Suddenly one strikes. Why? Moments snap together like magnets, forging a chain of shackles. Why? I can trace them, I can even with time pull them apart again. But why at the start they were ever magnetised at all – just those particular moments of experience and no others – I don't know.[21]

To use another term we mentioned earlier, horses have a great press for Alan, to the extent there is little psychic energy left for anything else. He finds little meaning in the world of his father, where passion has become diluted by restraint, compromise and necessity. He appears to find physical sex sordid, something degraded compared to what he experienced on the beach and on his midnight rides. 'I couldn't feel her flesh at all! I wanted the foam off his neck. His sweaty hide. Not flesh.'[22] This is how he describes his unhappy experience with Jill. There is pain in obsession, constant torment and censure, and it can be said that Alan's savage act is a desperate attempt to assuage it.

Yet although Dysart appreciates his patient's suffering he is also aware of something that will be lost if his therapy is successful. The psychiatrist is in a sense a victim of the Fall; his life lacks a vital element. He has adjusted well to ordinary life, but yearns for the past, for the heroic world of ancient Greece, where existence had a greater meaning. Dysart realises that Alan can be cured of his obsession, yet the cost is normality and acceptance of a shadow existence.

Vladimir Nabokov, *Lolita,*

This is another work whose subject is obsession. One of Nabokov's earliest works is *Laughter in the Dark*, the story of a middle-aged man and his yearning for a much younger woman. She is only interested in his money, although the man discovers this too late, after he has abandoned his family. It is essentially a tale of what happens when passion rules and temptation is not resisted.

The same theme, expanded and elaborated, lies at the heart of Nabokov's most acclaimed work, *Lolita.* It is a novel that has been much maligned, alas by those, it seems, who can't or won't read. It is plainly a tale of morality rather than pornography, for there are no coarse words, few erotic descriptions. Basically, with remarkable skill and some courage Nabokov plunges into an area of cultural taboo and emerges with an entertaining, amusing and, finally, sad and enlightening story.

The novel concerns Humbert Humbert and his obsession for a 12-year-old girl, Dolores Haze, the Lolita of the title. The two are brought together when Humbert takes up lodgings with the widowed Mrs Haze, whom he then marries. It is a brief marriage, terminated by accidental death, which is fortuitous for Humbert as it makes him Lolita's guardian. The two embark on a motor tour of the United States, staying overnight in motels and hotels, where Humbert sates his desire for young flesh. Lolita is willing at first, but soon tires of her stepfather's attention and has to be kept in thrall by veiled blackmail and numerous gifts. Humbert grows insanely possessive, suspicious of every male they meet. But Lolita eventually manages to escape with Clare Quilty, a lecherous playwright she met through her school drama class.

It is some years before Humbert and Lolita meet again. She was soon abandoned by Quilty and has married another. Pregnant, poor, old for her 18 years, she writes to her stepfather for money. He answers her plea for in their separation he came to realise the terrible toll his desire exacted. His lust has been transformed into a genuine love for Lolita. He tries to win her back, though without success. It is apparent – and Humbert is shattered to realise it – that in all their time together she had never felt for him. He was not a friend, lover or father, but simply a dirty old man indulging his sterile and selfish vice. Humbert's final act is to slay Quilty (the tale is told in retrospect from a prison cell).

Early in his recollections Humbert establishes the root of his obsession. He tells us:

> In a certain magic and fateful way Lolita began with Annabel ... that little

> girl haunted me ... until at last, 24 years later, I broke her spell by incarnating her in another.[23]

He is referring to an adolescent love affair, and a moment when he and his partner were interrupted on the point of a yearned-for consummation. The moment was lost for ever; two months later Annabel died, which consolidated the frustration, making of it 'a permanent obstacle to any further romance throughout the cold years of my youth'.[24]

It is the psychological residue of this traumatic event that fuels Humbert's desire for nymphets, a specific type of young girl which he defines very precisely in terms of physical and emotional development. In physical terms a nymphet seems to be that which invokes Annabel and the tantalising moment they shared. It seems to be an ephemeral state of fading innocence between girl- and womanhood. He insists he is not so much interested in physical sex as in trying to fix 'the perilous magic' of nymphets, the point where the 'beastly and the beautiful' merge.[25]

In one sense Humbert is a man who attempts to overcome the pain of existence by the pursuit of a fleetingly glimpsed perfection. Nabokov was a writer who was aware of the fallen nature of man and in his autobiographical writings he suggests there are ways back to a greater harmony, through art and creative memory – through the bridges of Venus, basically. Like Alan Strang in *Equus*, Humbert has an inner vision of beauty and it torments him, drives him into forbidden acts. For both, a delightful experience comes to be associated with a specific object.

When it comes to the desire for wealth, sex or power, Taurus needs to learn the lesson of detachment. The May full moon, symbolically at least, marks the birth and moment of enlightenment of the Buddha, whose teachings regarding desire relate to this sign. One Buddhist aphorism warns not to mistake the moon for the finger pointing at it. Matter is but the reflection of some higher order, and we should not mistake the idol for the something it represents. There is a paradox associated with this sign. The desire to possess something merely holds us in its thrall, and to truly possess something the need is to let go. The tighter one grasps the real, the more elusive becomes the ideal. Where Humbert goes wrong is in confusing the experience and the object, the moon and the finger. Other critics have remarked on this failing. In the following passage Humbert is being compared to the central character of *Laughter in the Dark*:

> Both have received a true intuition that the route to the infinite is through

> attachment to an adorable image or eidolon, yet both blunder, perversely and fatally by haplessly confounding the image with its illusory reflection or echo in the flesh of a child woman.[26]

Humbert seeks his Eden through the flesh of a nymphet, but is really only a slave to his passion. He learns too late that you can never really possess a physical object, no matter how much energy you vest in it. The lesson comes too late, because in the process of discovery he breaks the life and spirit of Lolita.

At the end of the work Humbert brutally slays the abductor Quilty. It seems in a way gratuitous, for Humbert has rid himself of the 'petrified paroxysm' that drove him to lust and which warped Lolita's life. He is truly sorry for what he has done. Yet the slaying seems in some way necessary to complete the process, to burn off the guilt, to put things right.[27]

Dennis Potter, *Brimstone and Treacle*

This is a play in which the Devil appears as therapist. Martin, the Devil in disguise, insinuates himself into the suburban household of the Bates family, mother, father and daughter Patti, who exists in an infantile state after being knocked down by a hit-and-run driver. She can not speak or care for herself, but simply lies in the living room all day making baby-like sounds. Martin appears to be an angel. He claims he knew Patti before the accident, had asked her to marry him, but had been rejected. He persuades the Bates to let him lodge with them and to help look after their daughter. Father has reservations, but Mother, upon whom the burden of care falls, agrees.

When they are alone in the house Martin has sex with Patti. This has the effect of snapping her out of her vegetative state. It functions as a therapeutic act that connects her with the traumatic experience that precipitated her condition. She vividly recalls finding her father in bed with one of her friends. It was in the course of fleeing from this unpalatable discovery that she ran into the path of a moving car. It seems Patti's condition is more a result of the shock of discovering her father *in flagrante delicto* than the physical impact of the car, while her infantile state can be viewed as a retreat to a safe and innocent past. Once again, we have an act of lust and betrayal setting up a chain of destruction that cripples the lives of daughter and mother, who is a slave to her daughter's needs.

Mr Bates is also a man stuck in the past. He is a racist and a member of a far-right organisation. He has a nostalgic view of the past when everything was 'right' in Britain. He remembers the happy

England of his childhood and equates it with an absence of coloured immigrants. Martin appears to agree with Mr Bates, coaxing him along a chain of logic to the unpalatable conclusion that his dream means in reality the extermination or transportation of England's coloured population. Mr Bates recoils, remarking: 'I simply want the world to stop where it is, and go back a bit.'[28] Of course, he can not go back, and unless he wholeheartedly embraces genocide, he has to compromise his wishes and accept life as it is.[29]

Brimstone and Treacle is a story of the Devil as psychiatrist, turning up a dark secret and laying the ground for a cure in what was a sick household.

Daphne du Maurier, *Rebecca*

Central to this novel is Manderley, a grand house set in expansive grounds on the Cornish coast, the property of Max de Winter. It is here that he brings his young bride, the nameless narrator of the story, not long after the death, apparently by accidental drowning, of his first wife Rebecca.

There is something of Eden about Manderley, with its flora and lawns and 'Happy Valley', and yet from the outset we suspect all is not perfect. Just as the original Garden had its serpent, Manderley had its interminable drive that 'twisted and turned' through the dark and silent wood, and 'luscious and over-proud' rhododendrons, whose beauty was mixed with menace. Nor is life anything like paradise for the young bride who comes to Manderley, 'a raw schoolgirl, red-elbowed and lanky haired'.[30] She is gauche, shy, desperate to please – in short, immature and hugely insecure. Moreover, she is haunted by the ghost of Rebecca, who, it seems at first, was everything she was not (and perhaps wants to be) – charming, beautiful, tasteful, poised, and the perfect hostess. But worst of all is her husband, who is cold, remote and tortured by some inner turmoil.

Life grows increasingly unhappy at Manderley, until a crisis is precipitated by a ship running aground in the bay. In the course of refloating the vessel a diver is sent down. He discovers Rebecca's boat, the one she was sailing the night she drowned. But it is the discovery of the body that's the real revelation, because it was believed she was swept away by the current and washed ashore some miles away. The body had been identified but, as it turns out, wrongly. A coroner's inquest follows, and other investigations, and despite certain suspicions to the contrary, the death is put down to suicide. But more significantly Max is forced to confess his guilty and awesome secret.

Rebecca was not what the world took her for. Quite the opposite. In Max's words she was 'vicious, damnable, rotten through and through ... incapable of love, of tenderness, of decency'.[31] Like most others he was taken in at first by her charms, but the marriage proved a sham. They led separate lives with Rebecca philandering as she pleased. Max admits that far from still loving her he had grown quickly to hate her. In a rage he shot her, put her body on the boat, then sank it in the bay. Yet his deed and her memory continued to haunt him, and at the same time tainted his relationship with his new wife.

Max admits he married his second wife because she was completely unlike Rebecca. She was a symbol of innocence for him, something that could 'lead him from the past', restore to equilibrium a life that has gone rotten. The new wife may be plain, lacking in poise, but she is decent and good. To Max she is like a child and for much of the book he treats her more like a daughter than a wife. However, events mature her, thrust her into the adult world of evil, death, sex, sin and pain. As her husband remarks: 'It's gone forever, that funny, young, lost look that I loved.'[32]

Manderley is destroyed by fire and the couple are exiled from their flawed Eden. It becomes just a memory of something lost. It transpires that Rebecca had been terminally ill with cancer and would have died anyway. That she was shot saved her a lot of pain, so not only is Max innocent in the eyes of the law, but is also spared the burden of guilt. Together the couple find a kind of peace abroad, listening to the county cricket scores, for them a timeless ritual, a symbol of an unspoiled England.

Notes

1. Marcel Girard, introduction to 1968 Everyman edition

2. The tale of the Pied Piper of Hamelin – immortalised by Taurean Robert Browning – with its greed, broken promise and vanishing children reflects the meaning of Taurus in the same way. Balzac's story *The Wild Ass's Skin* is about the destructiveness of desire; the skin has the power to grant wishes, but for each wish the skin shrinks a fraction, as does the life of the person wishing

3. The following lines by Browning, from *Fra Lippo Lippi*, suggest this side of the sign:

> The beauty and the wonder and the power,
> The shapes of things, their colours, lights and shades, changes, surprises ...
> This world's no blot for us,
> Nor blank – it means intensely, and means good;
> To find its meaning is my meat and drink.

In Henry Fielding's *Tom Jones*, the hero is expelled from Paradise Hall for sexual indiscretions and wanders the land searching for his beloved Sophie, garnering through experience the self-knowledge that might recapture the state of happy innocence of his youth

4. *Contemporary Poets,* 3rd edition, Macmillan, 1980, p1613

5. *Contemporary Author Series,* vols 21-24, ed Christine Nasso, Gale Research

6. *World Authors 1950-70,* ed J Wakeman, H W Wilson, 1975, p872

7. *World Authors 1970-75,* ed J Wakeman, H W Wilson, 1980, p31

8. *Contemporary Poets,* 3rd edition, Macmillan, 1980, p1148

9. Edwin Morgan, 'Edwin Muir', in *The Modern Poet, Essays from The Review,* ed Ian Hamilton, Macdonald, 1968, p43

10. Edwin Muir, *An Autobiography,* Hogarth Press, 1980, p33

11. ibid, p63

12. ibid, p33

13. *Encyclopaedia of Religion,* ed Mircea Eliade, Vol 15, Macmillan, 1987, p249

14. See, for example, *Ancient Egyptian Religion,* Henri Frankfurt, Harper Row, 1961; and *Cosmos, Chaos and the World to Come,* Norman Cohn, Yale University Press, 1993

15. There is no record of Shakespeare's birth date, but it is very likely he was born with his Sun in Taurus. There is a record showing he was baptised on 26 April, which equates to 6 May in the new style Gregorian calendar. The universal practice at the time was to baptise infants as soon after birth as possible, and it is unlikely it would have been left the sixteen days or so that would be necessary to put the Sun out of Taurus and back into the previous sign.

16. Dion Fortune, *The Mystical Qabalah,* Ibis, 1979, p222

17. Lust, sloth, covetousness, envy and gluttony relate to Taurus; anger belongs to the Mars signs, and pride to Leo and Scorpio

18. *I Ching,* Routledge & Kegan Paul, 1975, p166

19. In *Astrology and the Modern Psyche* (CRCS, 1978) Dane Rudhyar examines the work of a number of distinguished psychologists – Freud, Jung, Adler, Mareno, Assagioli and Kinkel – in relation to their birth charts. The interested reader is referred to this volume. The summary of Freud's theories is taken from Martin Evan Jay, *Encyclopaedia Britannica,* vol 19, 15th edition, and Calvin Hall and Gardner Lindzey, *Theories of Personality,* John Wiley and Sons, 1978

20. James Matthew Barrie, with a Taurus Sun, was a good example of this side of the sign in both his life and literary creations. He had difficulty relating to women in an adult way. He married, but it seems the marriage was not consummated. For him women were less flesh and blood, more ideal figments. His image of women is embodied in characters such as Mary Rose, and Wendy in *Peter Pan* – naive, sexless innocents. Barrie did have a Taurean way with money. He earned a great deal from writing and when he died he left £173,000 in his will (around £3.5 million in today's prices)

21. Peter Shaffer, *Equus*, Penguin, 1982, p76

22. ibid, p103

23. Vladimir Nabokov, *Lolita*, Everyman's Library, 1992, p8, 10

24. ibid, p8

25. ibid, p136-37

26. Julian Moynahan, *University of Minnesota Pamphlets on American Writers, No 98, Vladimir Nabokov*, 1971, p26

27. Compare the eponymous heroine of Maurice Baring's *Daphne Adeane*, who likewise has the power to invoke memories of former passions in a string of partners

28. Dennis Potter, *Brimstone and Treacle*, Methuen, 1978, p34

29. The author discusses this scene in these broad terms in *Potter on Potter*, Faber, ed. Graham Fuller, 1993

30. Daphne du Maurier, *Rebecca*, Arrow, 1992, p20

31. ibid, p284

32. ibid, p313

GEMINI

Writers with the Sun in Gemini include: David Ballantyne, Djuna Barnes, John Barth, Saul Bellow, Arnold Bennett, Isaiah Berlin, Maeve Binchy, Elizabeth Bowen, Andre Brink, Brigid Brophy, Lord Bulwer-Lytton, Raymond Carver, John Cheever, G K Chesterton, Arthur Conan Doyle, Dante, Margaret Drabble, Ralph Waldo Emerson, Allen Ginsberg, Ivan Goncharov, Dashiell Hammett, Thomas Hardy, John Hersey, James Kelman, James Kennaway, Charles Kingsley, Jerzy Kosinski, Federico Lorca, Thomas Mann, Mary McCarthy, Larry McMurtry, Bill Naughton, St John Perse, Alexander Pope, Alexander Pushkin, Barbara Pym, Kathleen Raine, Terence Rattigan, Theodore Roethke, Salman Rushdie, Jean-Paul Sartre, Vikram Seth, Harriet Beecher Stowe, William Styron, William Trevor, Arnold Wesker, Patrick White, Walt Whitman, W B Yeats.

Summary Gemini writers are sometimes criticised for being superficial, or for writing works whose parts do not add up to anything, but equally are praised for their flow of ideas or depiction of the particulars of life. It is easy enough to find characters in Gemini writing that fit the traditional picture of the sign, and we also find characters endeavouring to come to terms with the complex multiplicity of the real world. More fundamentally, though, Gemini is a sign where spirit wants to 'know' itself in matter and being has to translate into becoming. So we have stories of individuals who have to become less detached and theoretical and commit to the mill of life.

> How shall my eyes separate the beauty of the blossoming buckwheat field from the stalks and heads of tangible matter? How shall I know what the life is, except as I see it in the flesh?
>
> **Walt Whitman** *Complete Writings*

It is interesting to compare the words above, written by a Gemini writer, to those of Sagittarian William Blake in a passage from *The Vision of Judgement*:

> 'What', it will be questioned. 'When the Sun rises do you not see a round disc of fire somewhat like a guinea?' Oh no, no, I see an innumerable company of the heavenly host crying 'Holy, Holy, Holy is the Lord God Almighty.'

Gemini and Sagittarius sit opposite one another in the zodiac circle as polar complements and this is well reflected in these contrasting quotes. Sagittarius, as we will discover later, tends to look beyond the surface to search for significance in an underlying, often spiritual, stratum of experience. Gemini, on the other hand, is a sign that tends to demystify. Meaning for Whitman lies not in some distant or speculative beyond, but in the real world of matter, in the tangible forms of nature.

Just as Gemini represents the real over the abstract it stands for other variations of the same polarity: the parts over the whole, the particular over the general, the secular over religion. Gemini is time, as opposed to space, the temporal over the eternal, is pragmatic rather than dogmatic, inductive rather than deductive. It also represents multiplicity (or diversity) over unity, and differentiation as opposed to integration.

The fact that Gemini is a sensate sign focusing on the real or the parts is often borne out in comments on its literature:

Allen Curnow
[His poems] have led [him] consistently to the same preoccupation, weighing objective against subjective, real against ideal. In the real – the present place and time – and in that alone our salvation, or more simply our satisfaction, lies. It is the pursuit of the ideal that will damn us.[1]

W B Yeats
Yeats pins his faith on the actuality of ordinary life. Thus the 'minute particulars' of human life ... prevent the predominance of abstractions or theories.[2]

Larry McMurtry
[He] founds his stories upon such details of foreground landscape, vascular spoken language, vital character description, and realistic conception as make fictional events memorable for their authenticity rather than mythic effect.[3]

St John Perse
Perse observes the world and spells it out ... He enumerates all parts of the familiar world surrounding man.[4]

Walt Whitman
The aspects of nature, the forms and habits of animals, the sights of

cities, the movement and talk of common people, were his instant delight ... with Whitman the surface is absolutely all and the underlying structure is without interest and almost without existence.[5]

Thomas Hardy
Hardy ... was in the main line of Victorian rationalism, and it was this rationalism that ... convinced him that knowledge was available to reason and logic, and that truth was that which was verifiable; it excluded the spiritual, the intuitive, the mystical.[6]

Arnold Bennett
His world was as bright and hard-surfaced as crockery ... What was not precise, factual and contemporary could not enter into his consciousness ... Bennett was taking the thing that is for what it was, with a naive and eager zest. He saw it brighter than it was; he did not see into it and he did not see beyond it.[7]

Anders Österling
He came to feel that ... abstract heroism ... led in time to poetic sterility, and he turned instead for his poetic materials to life itself in its immediate, palpable, everyday aspects.[8]

Pär Lagerkvist
For him man's search for truth is not in the last analysis an abstract leap beyond the circumscribed conditions of existence but rather an immediate grappling with the confused profusion of life.[9]

Max von der Grün
Von der Grün seizes the issue of the moment and abandons the universal for the sensational.[10]

Alexander Pope
If he has a limitation ... it is that he does not feel the charm of the vague, the distant, of what can not exactly be defined.[11]

Harriet Beecher Stowe
She displayed the realist's aversion to mystery, mysticism and the legendising of history.[12]

One variation of this focus on the surface of life is found in those Gemini writers who produce work that is fragmented, whose parts do not seem to add up to anything. This can result in books that are plain banal and superficial but, equally, fascinating work that is packed with incident, information and detail. The word 'mosaic' occurs with some regularity in descriptions of Gemini writers, suggesting something sparkling, bright, crystalline, two-dimensional and fragmented:

Arnold Bennett
The bright, clear mosaic of impressions was continually being added to and all the pieces stayed in their places. He did not feel the need for a philosophy or for a faith or for anything to hold them together.[13]

Brewster Ghiselin
[His] two early collections offered many poems whose parts were so polished that it was very difficult to grasp the whole. The effect was that of Byzantine mosaics seen close, an effect of brilliant yet disparate atomies rather than of anatomy.[14]

John Cheever
[His first two novels] are packed with incident and rich in splendid anecdotes and set pieces, but this material, some readers thought, never coheres into a novel.[15]

Joyce Carol Oates
(Of *Wonderland*) Increases the growing suspicion that Miss Oates, a writer of excellent short stories, has yet to write a truly unified novel ... a sombre collection of bits and no illuminating coherent whole.[16]

Mark Adlard
[His] *Tcity* trilogy, *Interface, Volteface* and *Multiface*, makes up a whole less than the sum of its parts but is nevertheless a highly interesting and readable work.[17]

Federico Lorca Garcia
There are times ... when the prodigality of image does seem to be indulged in for its own sake ... the multiplication of ideas carries one too far and on too wide a front: too many things are required to be embraced at once.[18]

The essence of Gemini

Clues to the deeper meaning of this sign can be found in the I Ching, the Cabbala, the thought of Plato and even parts of the Old Testament.

Gemini is linked to the process of creation, although less to the creative spark, more to the embodiment of this in form. What is unique about Gemini and its associated planet Mercury is the fact that they represent a self-contained creative unit embodying both receptive and generative functions – and we are reminded that traditionally Mercury is regarded as an androgynous god. So things are not only given form in Gemini (Feminine), but are also developed by means of a process of dynamic becoming over time (Masculine).

The I Ching hexagram associated with Gemini is number 1, 'The Creative'. It is made up entirely of yang lines, a term which has been translated as 'banners waving in the sun', an image suggesting brightness and display. The commentary tells us:

> The beginning of all things lies in the beyond in the form of ideas that have yet to become real. But the Creative furthermore has power to lend form to these archetypes of ideas.[19]

There is similarity here to Plato's concept of the Demiurge (literally, 'skilled workman'), which effects the transition from divine 'idea' to sensible world,[20] and to the Egyptian Thoth, the enunciator of the divine will, the one who puts the primal urge to manifest into concrete being. Gemini has also been equated with the pillars of Isis, the twin halves of the universe, the manifest (*physis*) and the unmanifest (*psyche*).[21]

The text of hexagram 1 in the I Ching also tells us:

> The mode of the Creative is not rest but continuous movement and development. Through this force, all things are gradually changed until they are completely transformed in their manifestations ... In this way each thing receives the nature appropriate to it, which, from the divine viewpoint, is called its appointed destiny.[22]

Thus we can see Gemini as a process, the transformation of being into becoming. In a sense the two are equivalent: becoming is being filtered through the lens of space and time. Gemini is a sign of change, be this a self-contained development from a given pattern, or genetic-type change whereby different and more complex forms are created through the interaction of an individual life form with its environment.

Alice Bailey in *Esoteric Astrology* describes Gemini as a sign which produces change in time and space in order to create 'adequate' fields of experience for the unfolding of the self.[23] We have here the root of Gemini's thirst for variety, its adaptability and versatility, and the often diverse nature of the sign's creative expression. Gemini is a restless sign because at root it is seeking those conditions that will further the unfolding development of some inner pattern (or destiny).

Mercury's connection with movement and change is an ancient one, and is referred to in the *Iliad*, where we find Hermes/Mercury spoken of as a god of the road, where road means something specific: a kind of middle domain, a world in its own right, a volatilised region where nothing is fixed, but possibilities remain open. Hermes was regarded as being constantly underway, constantly in motion, a quality captured in statues of the deity, so that even when rendered in a sitting posture we recognise in Hermes an impulse to move on.[24] Homer attributes many qualities to Hermes, but primarily he emerges as a god of transitions, and as a guide, one who leads to destinations.

On the Tree of Life Mercury, Gemini's ruler, relates to Hod, or the sphere of 'formulation of forms'. Hod, from the Hebrew, means 'splendour', which again yields the idea of manifest divine radiance, of God displaying through His creations. Hod also translates as 'reverberation', which gives the idea of a dynamic polarity. The motive power of Gemini is based on a sort of dialectic polarity, where thesis and antithesis evolve synthesis, which in turn invokes anti-synthesis, and so on.

The Genesis version of creation also tells of an idea seeking to realise itself through space and time, and we are told it does so in stages of division and multiplication. Again, we have this idea of duality as a critical phase between unity and multiplicity.

Rudhyar suggests the Gemini phase of the zodiac symbolises the first clear division between life and mind, the reasoning mind that wins victories over nature and eventually distances us from it. Along with Mercury it stands for the translation of nature into intelligence: 'To think means for man to struggle with the multifarious, ever-changing problems which his experience of nature presents to him at every moment.'[25] It is also, he notes, a sign of 'extension in terms of particulars, of concrete experience'.[26]

It is common to find Gemini protagonists in literature engaged in this process of extension, eager to learn and to sate their curiosity about the world they see about them. It is indeed curiosity and inquisitiveness that draws Gemini to the phenomenal world. If we are curious about something we are attracted to it, perhaps because it is odd or puzzling but more generally because of its novelty. Curiosity draws us to things by prompting the questions, how, where, why, what lies behind the appearance and what's the place of this new phenomenon in a larger context? The search for new experience has its limits, and boredom is the bane of both the Mercury signs. It can be said that Gemini lives for the sake of new experience, as opposed to Aries, which lives for the sake of living.

Mercury and its signs relate to ordering and reductionism. There is the tendency to break down that which is vast into something manageable. In the way, say, that man's map-making instinct puts the world into proportion, giving each place on the globe a particularity through latitude and longitude, and through the compass points, which establish a relationship between an individual and any other place in the world. Mercury and Gemini are traditionally related to speech and language, which is a way of taming the world, by naming the parts, but is once more a function of ordering, by the imposition of a pattern on something – sound – that's inherently meaningless.

Finally in this examination of the meaning of Mercury it is informative to trace a connection with fate or destiny. The Old English word *wyrd,* and its modern equivalent 'weird', stem from the German *verden,* to become, in the sense delineated earlier in the chapter, the transformation of potential into actual. 'Weird' has come to mean something strange, or redolent of the supernatural, but originally, and particularly in Scotland, it meant relating to fate, or the Fates. So that Shakespeare's Weird Sisters in *Macbeth* were mediators of fate, the equivalent of the Scandinavian Norns. *Wyrd*/weird also relates to the old High German *wirt* or *wirtel*, meaning spindle. Fate is allegorically connected to spinning and weaving, because it is a process whereby the disordered and unusable fibres of a material are drawn out into a thread. Just as an individual human life spins out an unformed potentiality into a linear and evolving sequence of events.[27] This facet of Mercury seems to emerge in the work of Gemini and Virgo writers, where we find characters buffeted by forces they are unable to control, who can be made or broken by their response to a fateful circumstance. Mercury has a role of synchronising phantom, or an agent of fate who nudges us towards particular circumstances that are instrumental in furthering our own life story, or personal destiny, although this aspect of Mercury more often manifests through Virgo (the other sign ruled by Mercury).

The polar sign to Gemini is Sagittarius, so while it might remain focused at the real/particular end of the spectrum the shift to its complement often involves a striving towards wholeness, towards the general or ideal, towards something that will unite the complexity, or fuse the conflicting strands, of the world. Whether this is achieved is another matter. The composer Richard Wagner, a Gemini Sun, is a good example to point. He was a very intellectual character who wrote about music almost as often as he composed it, producing in all some 12 volumes of ideas and theories. His was the concept of the great unified artwork, a synthesis of music, drama and poetry. He established three discrete functions in man and equated these to the art forms thus: intellect = speech = poetry; heart = tone = music; body = gesture = drama. Each of the dissevered arts, wrote Wagner, 'longed' for reunion with the others. His attempt at synthesis took the form of grand opera and the majority of these are built about legend and myth because these in themselves are an expression of wholeness, of a way of thinking that is not fragmented and logical. Another good example, once more a Gemini Sun, is the German socio-historian Oswald Spengler. In *The Decline of the West* he seeks to establish something underlying the profusion of detail that constitutes the history of humankind, something

> beyond all the casual elements of the separate events, something that is essentially independent of the outward forms – social, spiritual and political – which we see so clearly. Are not these actualities indeed secondary and derive from that something?[28]

Indeed, Spengler, like that great Gemini creation Sherlock Holmes, is a master of induction (rather than deduction).[29] He works from details, observed facts, and builds a picture from these. He established certain unitary principles, which he called prime symbols, characteristic of a particular culture. These symbols, or ideas, are given form through individuals and groups and are inherent in the myths, religions, laws, ethics, arts, sciences and forms of state of a particular culture. The prime symbol runs a course through time; it is born, grows, flowers, declines and decays. In *The Decline of the West* Spengler delineates the prime symbols of the world's major civilisations.

His work reminds us that the form that 'truth' takes changes to meet the demands of time and place. Gemini is a contemporary sign and sometimes its challenge is to reformulate in terms of the times. Alexander Pope is a good example with his much-lauded translation of Homer for a contemporary audience, which took up a good deal of his working life. It was an adaptation of something remote in space and time into a form that the readers of his day could relate to, and this is very much the talent of Gemini: to change the form of things while being true to their essence.[30]

It is interesting to compare Pope to his contemporary Jonathan Swift (whose work will be considered later, in the chapter on Sagittarius). Swift's writing is more widely read than Pope's today because it transcends particularity. A lot of Pope's creative energy was focused on the people and issues of his day. So was Swift's, up to a point, but he was more universal in his approach so we do not have to know a lot about the times in which he lived to enjoy his writing. This is true of other Sagittarian writers; as a sign it is less restricted by time and place than Gemini. This doesn't necessarily make Sagittarians better writers, for shelf life is only one criterion. It is just that Gemini is focused more on the here and now. It is a contemporary sign that adapts well to change and this in itself can be a strength.

Two Gemini characters

Ebenezer in John Barth's *The Sot-weed Factor* fits many of the conventional descriptions of Gemini. The book is set in the 17th century and concerns a voyage from Europe to the New World. Its central figure is naive, young, interested in everything and everyone. He's 'dizzy with the beauty of the possible ... dazzled by all that might be done.'[31] He is also, as it happens, cast as a twin. His tutor, who delights in intrigue and adopting various guises, is very much a man of the world, whose philosophy is to engage with the world, but not be shackled by it.

This is a philosophy shared by Bill Naughton's Alfie. He is a character who occupies the 'road' in the sense the classical Hermes did. He remains uncommitted. He has no fixed job, lives in rented accommodation, has a few mates but no real friends, and believes in having at least three women on the go at any one time. Variety is the *raison d'être* rather than the spice of his life. Again and again he espouses his philosophy of non-commitment. At one point he remarks to a friend: 'You never want to let yourself get attached to anybody or anything in this life ...'.[32] And on another occasion, after ditching one of his many partners he says: 'I felt free again. ... I don't care who the bird is or who the mate is, but somehow I always feel better when I unload them.'[33]

Alfie is an embodiment of fickleness, which is a sort of negative by-product of the pursuit of variety.

Thomas Hardy, *The Mayor of Casterbridge*

A number of Gemini themes run through Hardy's novels. One is that of education as a means of betterment, another is of the impact of fate upon the lives of characters. His work also illustrates an essential duality associated with the sign, symbolised by a sky twin and an earth twin: the divide between the mind and matter. What we have in *The Mayor of Casterbridge* is a contrast between two different modes of being: the more instinctive, natural man, who must remain prey to the forces of chance, and the reasoning intelligence of the man who has divorced from nature and adapts his environment to suit himself. These modes are embodied in this work in Michael Henchard (the mayor of the title) and Donald Farfrae.[34]

Henchard is perhaps the most strongly etched of Hardy's male characters. He is primarily a sensual and instinctive man, one who personifies nature in its gross and unpredictable mode. His main qualities are vitality and energy. Significantly he is described as a 'vehement gloomy being who had quitted the way of vulgar men without light to guide him on a better way'.[35] He had the lost the luxury of innocence, though had not acquired the power of mind to win victories over life.

Farfrae is plainly not a man of energy. Descriptions of him revolve about his somewhat delicate physique but good brain. He is a thinker, a technologist. As one of the town's inhabitants notes: 'They like him [Farfrae] because he's cleverer than Mr Henchard, and because he knows more'.[36] He demonstrates power over nature and it is this that endears him to the community. He demonstrates his worth on first arriving in Casterbridge by redeeming Henchard's spoiled wheat (and hence the town's bread) by some knowledgeable means. And at the outset of the relationship between the two men Henchard himself establishes their difference:

> In my business, 'tis true that strength and bustle build up a firm. But judgement and knowledge are what keep it established. Unluckily, I am bad at science, Farfrae; bad at figures – a rule of thumb sort of man. You are just the reverse. [37]

Throughout the novel it is the Scot who rides the unpredictable twists of fortune. Henchard seems to suffer at every turn, a life-form who can not adapt. Farfrae becomes unwilling usurper, inheriting Henchard's position, business, house, lover and step-daughter. Events overcome Henchard and he dies before his time.

Jean-Paul Sartre, *La Nausée*

A number of ideas at the heart of Sartre's thought are suggestive of Gemini. It is a thoroughly secular philosophy and, as one commentator put it, he has 'an almost obsessive interest in the concrete and the actual.'[38] According to Sartre, objects are what they are. They hide nothing. Consciousness isn't pre-existent, but is created by the relationship of an individual with others and his environment. Man's being is created by reaching out into the finite world and the Sartrean man is a creature of perpetual becoming.

Integral to Sartre's thought is freedom of choice. There is no life without choice, although he believes that while man must commit to the world in this way, he does not have the ability to fundamentally change it. Sartre's concept of freedom typifies the contemporary (Mercury) view of freedom, and is quite different, the opposite in fact, from the medieval or Eastern definition, which is not about individual choice, but about the individual giving up desire and surrendering to something greater than the self, usually some ideal or faith.[39]

Sartre exhibited the characteristic Gemini versatility and gave his philosophy creative expression through prose, plays and novels. In *La Nausée* the protagonist, the historian Roquentin, undergoes a revelation about the nature of existence. At one point he observes: 'Things are entirely what they appear to be and behind them ... there is nothing.'[40] At the moment of epiphany, when the world for him takes on a viscous quality in which objects lose their particularity, he notes:

> Existence had suddenly unveiled itself ... the diversity of things, their individuality, was only appearance, a veneer. This veneer had melted away, leaving soft monstrous masses.[41]

His feeling of physical illness also relates to a realisation of the contingency of the world, its lack of purpose and its meaningless proliferation of things, again the antithesis of the traditional Christian view that the physical world exists to proclaim the glory of God.

Thomas Mann, *Tonio Kröger, The Magic Mountain*
Mann's interest in astrology sometimes emerges in his writing, most notably in the monumental *Joseph and his Brothers*, an imaginative rendering of the story of the Old Testament character, the son of Jacob. At one point in the story the young Joseph talks of a teacher who prepared for him a horoscope. He was born, we learn, in Harran, Mesopotamia: 'Midday in the month of Tammuz, when Shamash [Sun] stood in midheaven in the sign of the Twins and in the east the sign of the Virgin was rising.'[42]

Joseph goes on to describe Virgo and Gemini as signs of Nabu (Mercury), 'a sign of Thoth, the writer of tablets, a light and versatile god, as which he speaketh between things for their good and promoteth intercourse'. There is further elucidation of a birth chart that bears a passing resemblance to Mann's own. This work is a powerful evocation of times and places of which we know little. However, at the end of the day it is fiction rather than fact. Astrology was not as developed as Mann implies at the time the story is supposed to be set, which appears to be around 1000 BCE.

A significant amount of Mann's writing revolves about the theme of 'allegiance to the real', or put another way, learning to commit to the world of experience. He is also concerned with man's dual mental-physical nature. In an early work, *Tonio Kröger*, the eponymous hero is conscious of a divided self: 'I stand between two worlds,' he states. 'I am at home in neither and suffer in consequence.' He is an individual who as he develops from youth to man comes to associate more and more with the power of mind. Until, finally:

> He surrendered utterly to the power that to him seemed the highest on earth, to whose service he felt called, which promised him elevation and honours: the power of the intellect, the power of the word that lauds it with a smile over the unconscious and inarticulate.[43]

However, in the course of the story he is led to reflect on the burden of his self-consciousness. He begins to come to terms with his divided nature, and to accept the fact that his destiny lies not with intellect as such but with applying mind to the problems of life.

The themes of duality and allegiance to the real are treated on a grander scale in *The Magic Mountain*. The novel begins with its hero Hans Castorp journeying to a sanatorium in the Alps to visit his sick cousin. He ends up staying seven years because of fears about his own health. The sojourn forms an interregnum in Castorp's life. He dwells in a kind of timeless limbo, his destiny on hold, divorced from the world, distanced from the 'flatlands' below, which we can interpret as a realm of time, destiny and mortal corruption. Time in the Alpine sanatorium seems to have a different quality to that in the world below. It does not bring change or development, or the opportunity of it.

The writer Joseph Campbell[44] has suggested that the name 'Castorp' is derived from Castor and Pollox, twins in Greek mythology and the chief stars in the constellation of Gemini. Significant in the story of Castor and Pollux is that the latter is immortal, of the sky, and the other mortal, of the earth, and that they remain ever connected.

A coruscating dialectic between two of the town's inhabitants, Herr Naphta and Herr Settembrini, forms the creative thrust of the novel. Castorp stands between them, an eager young pupil intent, perhaps, on a synthesis and his own enlightenment. Naphta and Settembrini stand for opposing poles of a fundamental duality, what Mann termed Asiatic and European. The equivalents in astrology are Jupiter and Mercury, and in more mainstream sociological terminology, ideational and sensate.[45]

Over the past 1200 years or so the West has swung from an Asiatic to a European pole. When the former was dominant Christianity was at its apogee and the zeitgeist was marked by dogma, obscurantism and a yearning for spiritual salvation. The material world was of secondary importance. Great cathedrals dominated the landscape in the Asiatic period, their grandeur far outstripping anything secular, even the palaces of kings.

From about the 14th century onwards the power of the Church waned. There was a gradual movement towards a secular world, a motion highlighted by the Renaissance, the Reformation, the Scientific Revolution and the Industrial Revolution. In short, it was a progression characterised by the rise of humanism. Humanism favours natural religion, or none at all, and a practical morality. It stands against obfuscation and metaphysics, but favours empiricism, rationalism and common sense. It is egalitarian and dynamic, as opposed to the stasis of medievalism. For a time – the 17th and early 18th centuries – the two world views attained some sort of balance, with the spiritual and secular both afforded their place. Newton was theologian and occultist as much as scientist, and indeed most, if not all, of the leading lights of the Scientific Revolution had a place for God in the scheme of things. But the balance has been lost, and even more so in this new millennium than in Mann's day. We dwell in the West in a fragmented, over-secularised society. Mammon rather than religion dominates our skylines – factories and office blocks whose business is money and the material world.

These opposing spirits, then, are embodied in Naphta and Settembrini. The latter vaunts the body over the soul but, at the same time, the intellect over the body:

> I represent the world, the interest of this life against a sentimental withdrawal and negation, classicism against romanticism. But there is one power, one principle which commands my deepest assent, my highest and fullest allegiance and love; and this power, this principle, is the intellect ... the powers of reason and enlightenment will in the end set humanity wholly free and lead it in the path of progress and civilisation.[46]

Very apparent in Settembrini is a hatred of monolithic religion and the medieval world, which he regards as a dark and tortured epoch. He believes the only alternative to the reason he champions is chaos. Any deference to the Asiatic he perceives as a back-sliding to the Dark Ages. Settembrini's opinions are shared by many in the western world and this belief underlies opposition to such things as holistic medicine, astrology, religion, indeed anything that falls outside narrow, scientifically-defined boundaries.

Herr Naphta is not so naive as to advocate a return to nature or medievalism, but rather argues against an excess of secularism. Consistently in the debates he points to the inner emptiness of modern Western man, to his materialistic and pragmatic creeds, or what Mann terms the 'bourgeois' mentality. Naphta spares a good deal of his vitriol not for science as such, but for scient*ism*, or science as philosophy and pseudo-religion. He establishes it as a belief:

> ... only worse, stupider than any; the word science was the expression of the silliest realism, which did not blush to take at their face value the more than dubious reflections of objects in the human intellect; to pass them current, and to shape out of them the sorriest, most spiritless dogma ever imposed on humanity. Was not the idea of a material world existing for and by itself the most laughable of all contradictions.[47]

Mann's nomenclature for the opposing principles embodied by Settembrini and Naphta is rooted in the fact that Europe was the fount of humanism, while Asia, or more broadly the East, was for many centuries characterised by religion, dogma and collectivism. 'Asia' and 'Europe' must blend in the German Castorp, for Mann saw his own country as a crucible of ferment for these opposing principles. When we consider that the novel was first published in

1924, and how Germany was to become a divided nation, the interface of 'Europe' (capitalism) and 'Asia' (communism), it becomes apparent how perceptive a writer Mann was and how significant his subject.

Castorp has to acknowledge that it is Naphta who gets the better of the arguments although at the same time he feels more drawn to Settembrini as a person. The latter's greatest failing is one typical of Gemini: he is a theoretician. He likes the idea of a thing better than the thing itself and is afraid to commit himself to the real world. Yet it is just this commitment to the world – what Mann terms 'duty' – that is required of Gemini. The challenge is to accept that one is part of the flux of life. It is a sign, as was stated earlier, in which spirit must realise itself in form, which entails a willingness to accept life's vicissitudes and also to accept that corruption and death are part of the life cycle. Gemini is about learning that experience is superior to innocence. The sign in one sense exemplifies the difference between theory and practice. Theory tends to hitch on the sharp edges of reality, and the product of this interaction – as well as disillusion – we call 'problems', which have to be countered with a different type of thought, generally termed 'ingenuity'.

Two things jolt Castorp into an awareness of his 'duty'. The first is a near-death experience in which a vision of Eden gives way to one of three crones and the suggestion of earthly destiny. The second is the arrival at the sanatorium of the remarkable Mynheer Peeperkorn. He stands in marked contrast to the glib Castorp, and to Settembrini and Naphta, for unlike the garrulous duo, his talk is largely incoherent. Nevertheless, in his way he manages to communicate more powerfully than either, through gestures, looks, attitudes of hand that 'worked like a conductor to enjoin silence'. It is mind expressing as much through body as through words. He can speak clearly and precisely about things which are factual, but when it comes to larger questions his mind seems to scramble, as if opposites are merged within him. He speaks, Pieter Peeperkorn, as if to himself. He does not need answers, nor the polarity of an opponent.

Peeperkorn represents the difference between knowledge and experience. His poor health, his white hair, his deeply-etched forehead suggest he is a man who has suffered swings of fate and fortune. Indeed, his very name, at least in English, suggests an individual who has been through the mill of life. It has not generated in him an easy philosophy, one that can be translated into sparkling prose. It is only the 'chatterboxes' Settembrini and Naphta, and the young, naive Castorp, who has yet to experience life, who can do that.

Peeperkorn is a blend of Jove and Bacchus, with a huge presence, a huge appetite, a wrath like thunder, and a pagan love of the earth's bounty. He has travelled the world's surface and earned his fortune harvesting nature's bounty in Dutch colonies. But at the same time he has sacrificed his health. He dies in the sanatorium, although not before accepting Castorp as a 'brother'.

Castorp eventually ends his stay in the Alpine retreat to take up his duty in the flatlands below. The final pages of the novel see him firmly embroiled in the affairs of the world, as a soldier fighting in the Great War.

Notes

1. *Contemporary Poets*, ed James Vinson, Macmillan, 1980, p334

2. Raymond Cowell, *Perspectives in Literature: W B Yeats*, Evans Bros, p64

3. *Contemporary Novelists*, ed James Vinson, St James Press, 1976, p941

4. *Concise Encyclopaedia of Modern World Literature*, ed Geoffrey Grigson, Hutchinson, 1963, p282

5. George Santyana, 'The Poetry of Barbarism,' *Interpretations of Poetry in Religion*, (reprinted in *Penguin Critical Anthologies: Walt Whitman*, ed Francis Murphy, 1969, p162)

6. Samuel Hynes, *The Pattern of Hardy's Poetry*, University of North Carolina Press, 1961, p40

7. H G Wells, *Experiment in Autobiography*, Gollancz, 1934, p626

8. Alrik Gustafson, *A History of Swedish Literature*, University of Minnesota Press, 1961, p366

9. ibid, p407

10. *Dictionary of Literary Biography*, Vol 75, Contemporary German Fiction Writers, Gale Research, 1988, p236

11. George Fraser, *Alexander Pope*, Routledge & Kegan Paul, 1978, p27

12. *Great Women Writers*, ed Frank Magill, Robert Hale, 1994, p534

13. H G Wells, *Experiment in Autobiography*, Gollancz, 1934, p626

14. *Contemporary Poets*, ed James Vinson, Macmillan, 1980, p544

15. *World Authors 1950-1970*, ed J Wakeman, HW Wilson, 1975, p310

16. *Contemporary Novelists*, ed James Vinson, St James Press, 1976, p1049

17. *Science Fiction Writers*, St James Press, 1996, p5

18. Conrad Aiken, *Collected Criticism*, Oxford University Press, 1968, p277

19. *I Ching*, Routledge & Kegan Paul, 1975, p4

20. Desmond Lee, in the introduction to Plato, *Timaeus and Critias*, Penguin Classics, 1977, notes: 'One of the basic premises in Plato's philosophy is the distinction between two orders of reality, Being and Becoming.' (p9) Plato in *Timaeus* describes the Creator as: 'determined to make a moving image of eternity.' He also remarks: 'we must in my opinion begin by distinguishing between that which always is and never becomes from that which is always becoming but never is' (ibid pp 51, 40).

Ralph Waldo Emerson, a Gemini Sun, also reflects many of the ideas discussed here in his essentially dualistic philosophy. He wrote of a world of nature as an emanation of a world of spirit, and of the tendency of spirit, or Oversoul, as he generally called it, to express itself in form.

21. Robert Hand has suggested these associations – see, *Essays on Astrology*, Para Research, 1982.

22. *I Ching*, Routledge & Kegan Paul, 1975, p372

23. Alice Bailey, *Esoteric Astrology*, Lucis, 1976, p345

24. See *Hermes, Guide of Souls*, Karl Kerenyi, Spring Publications, 1986.

25. Dane Rudhyar, *An Astrological Triptych*, ASI, 1978, p121

26. Dane Rudhyar, *Astrological Signs, The Pulse of Life*, Shambhala, 1978, p46

27. See Jospeh Campbell, *Creative Mythology*, Secker & Warburg, 1968, p215. Also Nigel Pennick, *Runic Astrology*, The Aquarian Press, 1990, p31

28. Oswald Spengler, *The Decline of the West*, Allen & Unwin, 1922, p1

29. Holmes exemplifies the mental nature of Gemini when in *The Sign of the Four* he announces: 'Love is an emotional thing and whatever is emotional is opposed to that true, cold reason which I place above all things.'

30. The following comment on this work is also very suggestive of Gemini: 'We shall see what Pope is aiming at in his Homer if we ... think of [him] as aiming at a kind of harmony and contrast between an underlying principle of order and its bewildering and rich expression in life.' (George Fraser, *Alexander Pope*, Routledge & Kegan Paul, 1978, p54)

31. John Barth, *The Sot-weed Factor*, Secker & Warburg, p20, 23

32. Bill Naughton, *Alfie*, Allison & Busby, 1993, p93

33. ibid, p53

34. The same contrast is evident in Patrick White's *The Solid Mandala*, a novel centred upon twins Arthur and Waldo Brown. In one instinct is much to the fore, the other is an arid pseudo-intellectual

35. Thomas Hardy, *The Mayor of Casterbridge*, Macmillan, 1985, p114

36. ibid p103

37 ibid p63

38. Mary Warnock, introduction to Sartre's *Being and Nothingness*, Routledge, 1996, pxv

39. This concept of freedom, the freedom of an individual to make choices to create his or her life, crops up regularly in Gemini novels. Joseph, the central character in Saul Bellow's *Dangling Man*, for example, is in the grip of an existential crisis, stuck in a limbo awaiting war-time military service. Life is basically passing him by. He has freedom to do as he wishes, yet does not know what to do with it. His existence is a constant battle against boredom and futility, and a search for diversion to help the time pass. He finally commits himself to a course of action and enters the army. With this resolve comes a great sense of relief: 'I am no longer to be held accountable for myself; I am grateful for that. I am in other hands, relieved of self-determination, freedom cancelled.' (*Dangling Man*, Alison Press/Secker & Warburg, p191.)

A critic makes the following observation about the writing of Joyce Carol

Oates: 'In her first novel ... Oates introduces a theme that would pervade almost all the rest of her fiction works: the awful responsibility of freedom. Her characters struggle to divest themselves of their little lives in order to achieve personal freedom, but they are unable to cope with the consequences of their release from their former lives. (*Great Women Writers*, ed Frank Magill, Robert Hale, 1994, p371)

40. Jean-Paul Sartre, *Nausea*, Penguin, 1965, p140

41. ibid, p183

42. Thomas Mann, *Joseph and his Brothers*, Vintage, 1967, p67

43. Thomas Mann, *Tonio Kröger*, Penguin Modern Classics, 1982, p146

44. Joseph Campbell, *Creative Mythology*, Secker & Warburg, 1968, p636

45. The four-volumed *Social and Cultural Dynamics* (American Book Co, 1937) by 20th-century sociologist PA Sorokin describes the great cyclic sweeps of history in dualistic terms, with oscillating poles he terms 'sensate' and 'ideational'. His work gives an account of the manifestation of these twin principles (and others related to them) in the art, science, thought, religion and social forms of different civilisations. These principles seem to exist as a self-generating polarity, not unlike the yin and yang of Chinese philosophy, so that when one of the principles reaches a certain point of development, of necessity it begins to change into its opposite. Sorokin defines the sensate (Yang/Mercury/Gemini) mentality as one 'tuned to the ever changing aspect of the world and its parts and objects. It is the mentality of becoming ... its reality is incessantly changing, oscillating, vibrating, flowing.' On the other hand, the ideational (Yin/Jupiter/Sagittarius) mentality 'seeks in the universe and its parts their unchangeable ultimate reality, their being. This unchangeable being is thought of as the essence of the reality of a given object or of the whole universe. It lies behind and beyond the appearances perceived by the eye and the other organs of sense.' (Vol 1, p248)

46. Thomas Mann, *The Magic Mountain*, Minerva, 1996, p249

47. ibid, p691

CANCER

Writers with the Sun in Cancer include: Eric Ambler, Jean Anouilh, Richard Bach, Stan Barstow, Thomas Berger, Ingmar Bergman, Ambrose Bierce, Caroline Blackwood, Edward Bond, Pearl Buck, John Clare, A J Cronin, Anita Desai, William Eastlake, Louise Erdich, Winston Graham, Rider Haggard, Nathaniel Hawthorne, Robert Heinlein, Ernest Hemingway, Hermann Hesse, Elizabeth Jennings, Franz Kafka, Gottfried Keller, Laurie Lee, Candia McWilliam, Iris Murdoch, George Orwell, Mervyn Peake, Robert Pinget, Luigi Pirandello, Marcel Proust, Ann Radcliffe, Erich Maria Remarque, Jean-Jacques Rousseau, Antoine de Saint-Exupéry, Georges Sand, Nathalie Sarraute, Neil Simon, Jean Stafford, Christina Stead, Tom Stoppard, David Storey, William Makepeace Thackeray, Henry Thoreau, Vernon Watkins, Colin Wilson, John Wyndham.

Summary Again and again it is remarked how subjective are the writers of this sign, how dedicated to their own view of the world. But essentially Cancer has to learn how to come to terms with the public world, so we find characters who struggle with this challenge, who vaunt the autonomy of the individual and fear the intrusion of outside forces into their own, private, sphere of existence. Cancer is concerned with the past in the sense that it finds the familial home too small and feels the urge to break out into a larger sphere. However, it is a challenge not always successfully met and the characters that do uproot often simply flounder around in a sort of limbo. Cancer writers are usually strong on character and value content over form.

> This border region between loneliness and community I have crossed extremely rarely, I have even settled it more than in loneliness itself.
> **Franz Kafka**

The nature of Cancer

Cancer types have a strong sense of their own uniqueness and can appear to be odd, or idiosyncratic, because they are so much themselves, with little regard for what others think. Or, more accurately, they struggle to see beyond their own view of themselves. On the more negative side, those strong in Cancer can be like children, somewhat moody, self-centred, selfish, and aware only of their own needs and problems. The sense of being different from everyone and everything else can result in loneliness and isolation, and this is often a theme for the writers of this sign.

Cancer is probably the most subjective of all the signs, and the tendency to universalise from personal experience can result in a distorted or limited perspective. Equally, the sign's novelists make a merit of subjectivity by writing about their own experience to great effect. The most common observation made about Cancer writers by critics relates to subjectivity:

George Orwell
Orwell's concentration on himself leads him to see the outside world as an enlarged projection of his own personal problems. His preoccupation with himself and his own experiences prevented his enlarging that experience.[1]

Hermann Hesse
Hesse believed that his own moral and spiritual dilemmas were representative of those of modern man.[2]

Ernest Hemingway
He writes of what he knows from his own experience to be true.[3]

William Eastlake
An artist of uncommon personal stability and unusual dedication to his own view of the world.[4]

Martin Andersen Nexø
[He] is a fairly limited writer who reached excellence only when he depicted those fates or milieus that he knew from experience.[5]

Franz Kafka
[In *The Great Wall of China* Kafka] seems to argue that man can never know the secrets of his own existence in the world; we are so obsessed with our own experience that we can not form a synthesis of the collective experience of mankind. Those building the great wall see only the stretch on which they work.[6]

Frank O'Hara
His poetry is totally subjective, a playful disorder of undigested autobiographical notes.[7]

Juan Carlos Onetti
Some critics have objected that Onetti's reading of reality is a very partial one, limited by the author's own bitterly resigned view of mankind.[8]

Eino Leino
[His poems] are in essence profoundly personal philosophical visions that ... reveal his own inner world.[9]

> **George Borrow**
> His literary work is to an unusual extent a direct projection of his own personality, a re-creation of his particular quiddity.[10]
>
> **Jean Stafford**
> Her stories ... are not so much the result of observation and intellectual response as they are expressions of [her] personal view of life.[11]

Cancer is noted for its sensitivity and one manifestation of this is that those strong in this sign take things very personally. They are easily pricked by slight or insult – particularly by rejection – and will react aggressively or defensively, by retreating into a shell and sulking. It's a sign that forgives but rarely forgets, sometimes harbouring resentments for years. But Cancer is also sensitive in more positive ways. It can be sympathetic and caring, and readily absorbs impressions from its surroundings, which provides fuel for what can be a great imagination. Not only can the memory be astonishing, but these assimilated impressions, reproduced with any fidelity, can result in a rich, sometimes convoluted prose. Content tends to be more important than structure to Cancer writers, and plot subservient to character.

Cancerian sensitivity can often be hidden behind a tough or dour exterior (particularly in men). For the human qualities to emerge there has to be familiar and congenial surrounds and a trust in the company. If not there can be shyness and reticence, indeed a tendency to withdraw into a shell if an individual does not feel at ease in his or her environment.[12] In traditional astrology Cancer is portrayed as a home lover, because a house acts as a protective shell that separates us from the outside world. It is somewhere we feel we belong, where we can relax, where we can 'be our self'. Cancer (and the Moon) is the sphere of the private self, the one unmodified by external restraints. It's the sign that can least tolerate the intrusion of external forces into its own sphere of existence and can react aggressively, or at least petulantly, to such violation. Cancer is a sign that vaunts the autonomy of the individual. It hallows the freedom to do as it pleases rather than freedom as some ideal or abstract entity. A common Cancerian theme in literature is the negative impact the forces of society or the strictures of organisations can have on individual sensibility.

Cancer relates to the past, and to an individual's relationship to his or her past, although is perhaps more usefully related to time, for things like the past, memory, tradition, history and decay are all products of time, and Cancer writers are concerned with all these. Their focus is most commonly on a break with the past, rather than its glorification. Cancer often finds the circumstances of its upbringing too restricting, or otherwise unsuitable, and prefers to build its own, 'home' according to its own design. It is not an easy transition, however. Roots can be pulled up, the security of one's background abandoned, but then there is the challenge of a limbo. A sense of exclusion and isolation must be endured until a new source of security is discovered, often a spiritual home, or a sense of belonging in some community. Often in the sign's writing this is not attained and Cancer remains a wanderer.

Just like the other signs, Cancer turns upon a polarity, so it is not, in essence, a sign of unbridled individuality, but a sign that represents the first distant call of the collective upon the individual. Just as Cancer represents a turning point in the astronomical year,[13] so the sign marks the culmination of a particular type of individual growth. Rudhyar is once more the author who puts it most succinctly:

> The Cancer person is the most consciously individualised, yet most fearful subconsciously of the unavoidable pressure of the demands which life, society, humanity as a whole ... must and will make.[14]

Cancer looks out from a familiar, secure, inner world and wonders where it will find a place in the larger scheme of things. Capricorn, on the other hand, the polar sign, is essentially an outward sign that faces the challenge of re-connecting with an inner world. The essence of Cancer is an interplay between private and public worlds. As Rudhyar puts it:

> What the individual needs essentially at this Cancer stage of human development is to feel through and through that he belongs, and to realise that he has a definite place and a definite function, clearly his own, in the economy of society and in the life of whatever group is claiming him.[15]

This idea of characters needing roles is sometimes the theme of the sign's writing. Luigi Pirandello and Tom Stoppard, both Cancer Suns, are two dramatists often compared for the similarity of their view of human nature. Stoppard, particularly in his early plays, is concerned with individuals who fail to comprehend and are trapped by the world around them. In *Rosencrantz and Guildenstern are Dead* the playwright takes two of Shakespeare's most marginal characters and puts them at the centre of their own play, where they exhibit a profound lack of knowledge of what is going on around them and the parts they really play in that greater drama. Pirandello, like Stoppard, is concerned with the search for roles, most famously in *Six Characters in Search of an Author* and *Henry IV*. Both plays focus on the conflict between self and roles and on characters frozen in time but who seek to become part of a bigger picture. Both writers illustrate the subjective nature of the sign with characters that have only a partial view of life.

The I Ching remains distinctly inscrutable with regard to the meaning of Cancer. The Tree of Life, however, is more forthcoming. The Moon, which rules Cancer and shares something of its nature, relates on the Tree to the sphere of Yesod, whose function is connected to the formation of a self-image. One writer describes it as:

> The mind pivot of the world of materiality and action ... its English name 'Foundation' indicates its importance in perceiving the universe about us ... Yesod in man relates to that strange part of him wherein he forms images ... it gathers in all the information from the physical and psychological realms and focuses it into readable images.[16]

Mind is an encompassing term that equates to a number of astrological factors. The everyday survival-oriented mode largely relates to Mercury and the Moon. Mercury is more to do with observing, recording, making connections and building logical constructs. But the Moon creates images, weaving essentially flat and meaningless sense data into a rich and complex tapestry, unique for and characteristic of each individual. Everyday life as we experience it is a product of the interaction of our inner and outer worlds. One account of Proust's peculiar talent seems to capture this side of Cancer very well. His vision, the critic notes:

> transforms the cold facts of a closely-observed social world into the elements that compose the organic world of a single human experience. The individual consciousness records, registers, compares, contrasts and analyses the features it encounters, using its resources of sensibility and intellect. But it also does far more: it creates. It composes out of the fragments of perceived reality, a rich and interrelated world, imposing harmony and order where life seemed to offer mere confusion, and imposing identity on a self apparently doomed to discontinuity and fragmentation.[17]

The Moon forms a major part of what we call personality, that essential quality that distinguishes one individual from the next, and its sign is often as significant a factor as the Sun's when it comes to interpreting a birth chart. Rudhyar sums it up well when he describes the lunar nature as 'the feeling of being a person facing a complex environment and reacting to this environment in a characteristic, spontaneous and organic manner'.[18] This lunar nature is multifaceted and fluid, changing from time to time and situation to situation; we change as we get older, and we can be a different person at work and at home. And yet there is something that is constant and exists beyond these multiple personalities; the hero of Hesse's *Steppenwolf* searches for this still point, and Proust establishes it with his *moi-permanent.*

More Cancer writing

A fictional character who gives a good flavour of the Cancer type is David Brent in BBC Television's *The Office* series. Brent was created and played by Ricky Gervais, who is a Cancer Sun. Not everything about Brent is described by Cancer but astrologers will recognise something of the sign in this larger-than-life figure. He is obsessed with himself, is unable to see himself as others see him, he is rather sensitive and prickly, and is determined to play *pater familias* to his staff. He is insecure with a need to be liked and admired. And, what is ultimately his downfall, he is unable to fit into the organisational structure of even a small company. He is like a child who has not developed a persona that allows him to function comfortably in the public sphere, something that has filtered out the quirkiness of character, corrected the distortions of the subjective eye, and tempered the neediness.

David Storey, *Flight into Camden*

This novel is the story of a northern couple who attempt to escape the past and their clinging families. The man, Howarth, feels trapped in a marriage, the woman, Margaret, feels oppressed by her parents and brother. The moody Howarth expresses both their feelings when he observes:

> Families to me are just like vicious animals, radiant with solicitude and affection until you touch them. Then they rear up like crazed beasts ... in my experience they've destroyed far more than they ever created.[19]

They journey to London with the intention of starting a new life. Although they both find work and set up a flat together, a new life fails to germinate. They don't, in effect, find a safe anchorage and they drift back to their past and old securities up North – he to his clingy wife, who refuses to consent to a divorce, and she, bullied by emotional blackmail, to the home of her childhood and parents who refuse to let go.

Mervyn Peake, *Titus Groan, Gormenghast, Titus Alone*

The themes of time, change and escape from the weight of the past are strong in this trilogy, which can be summarised as follows: Gormenghast is a vast, decaying castle. It is an enclosed, isolated, self-sufficient world, in some ways no different from our own – the people are flesh and blood, the laws of physics hold. However, life in Gormenghast is dominated by the immutable Groan Law, founded in antiquity, perhaps in wisdom, but which over the years has lost its significance and degenerated into empty and absurd ritual. So it remains, a static world, until simultaneous events sow the seeds of change (and it is here that *Titus Groan* begins). Titus, the 77th Earl, is born heir to the throne and Steerpike, a castle menial, undergoes symbolic rebirth, the start of a quest to rule Gormenghast. The first two works of the trilogy chart the impressionable development of young Titus and his increasing restlessness and dissatisfaction with life in his ancestral home. The rise of Steerpike the usurper counterpoints this and the two are drawn together in a memorable and vividly wrought climax.

Rebellious Titus eventually leaves the world of his upbringing and the third work, *Titus Alone*, is the story of a restless wanderer unable to adjust to life away from Gormenghast. A number of characteristically Cancerian qualities and themes are to be found in this work. There is the creation of a circumscribed world with its own rules, history, people and geography, where the author is free to ordinate and create as he chooses. Content takes precedent over narrative so that detailed description produces an at times very dense prose, and in the first novel particularly there is little development. Other themes include the urge to escape the past, the conflict between individual sensibility and a rigid social structure, and loneliness and rootlessness (in *Titus Alone*).

Life in Gormenghast is simply a past which repeats itself.[20] The ritual which dictates life is plainly redundant but is adhered to simply because it has always been the case to do so. No one, save Titus, thinks to question it, and he does not want to change it so much as escape its jurisdiction. The idea of cyclic repetition, of time which does not bring improvement, relates more to Cancer, and its associated planet, the Moon, than to any other astrological factor. Rodney Colin, writing of the symbolism of the Moon, brings the Gormenghast ritual to mind with the following observation:

> The Moon rules that which has no conscious purpose in man, that which happens, mechanicalness ... For a very large part of involuntary and pointless movement takes the form of habit, that is, of some motion, action or reaction, originally performed for a reason, good or bad, but which goes on repeating itself ad infinitum, long after the original reason has been forgotten and the circumstances have changed.[21]

Cancer and the Moon in astrology relate to instinct and the security that is to be obtained from attachment to familiar behavioural patterns. But if life does not renew itself, it stagnates, just as Gormenghast does. It is, symbolically, in Leo, the sign that follows Cancer, that consciousness and purpose take the place of habit and instinct. In Leo the circle of Cancer becomes a spiral of evolution and victory is won over death and decay.

The character Steerpike is the antithesis of Titus and the tension and hatred between them is developed through the first two novels, finally to be resolved in a psychologically charged scene. Steerpike's murderous past catches up with him and he is hunted like an animal. A cataclysmic deluge comes upon Gormenghast and as the flood waters rise they swallow up hiding places until the quarry is eventually trapped. Titus engages Steerpike in mortal combat, a labyrinth of dense, convoluted ivy forming an arena for their battle. A Jungian would no doubt see in Titus's triumph the beginning of the process of individuation, overcoming his shadow in the underworld before embarking upon the road of conscious selfhood. And a Freudian might see in Titus's mother, Gertrude, a symbol of the All-Mother, someone nurturing and protective of natural life, full of instinctual wisdom, but also a dominating figure who embodies the stifling spirit of Gormenghast.[22]

Equally, we can regard the Titus-Steerpike struggle in terms of zodiacal polarity. Cancer always remains Cancer, an idiosyncratic, subjective, feeling, home-loving sign, but it must still look outward and come to terms with organisations, structures and the larger social unit. In short, those things symbolised by the opposite sign to Cancer, Capricorn. Steerpike, as he is described in the novels, embodies many of the more negative features of Capricorn. He is ambitious, calculating, callous, and has the ability to utilise people and circumstances to further his own ends. These are just the qualities that are needed, to some degree at least, if an individual is to establish himself in the world outside the home. They were qualities that Peake as a person lacked, for despite an abundant talent, both at writing and painting, he had difficulty making a living. To find a niche in the world at large is the challenge for Cancer. It was the challenge facing Titus in the last book of the trilogy, but as is often the case in Cancer novels, it was one unsuccessfully, or imperfectly, met.

Franz Kafka, *Metamorphosis, America, The Castle, The Trial*

Kafka's work is widely studied and a number of critics have alighted on the fact that his writings are studies in loneliness and isolation and explorations of attempts to break out of the citadel of the self. *Metamorphosis*, perhaps his best known story, tells of a young man who wakes up one day to find he has turned into an insect. He is loathed and rejected by his family and the story stands as a parable of human alienation, an inner feeling objectified by transformation into something completely unlovable that can not be integrated into human society, and so must remain painfully isolated.

Kafka's novels are often focused upon outsiders, and one such is Karl Rossmann, the central character of *America*. He is a typical Cancer hero, a wanderer cut off from his roots seeking the security of a new 'home'. Karl emigrates to the United States after he is rejected by his parents in Europe following indiscretions with the family maid. The greater part of his novel deals with his search for a suitable job. His life falls into a pattern of adoption and rejection by various people and organisations until eventually he finds a place and some security in the curious 'Nature Theatre of Oklahoma'. The precise nature of this body remains obscure, and like Gormenghast Castle it appears it could not have a wholly objective existence. But it seems to be a very maternal body in its willingness to cater for the assortment of misfits who come looking for work. Beyond a source of work it represented to Karl both a sense of acceptance and an opportunity to be assimilated in a strange country:

> Our Theatre can find employment for everyone, a place for everyone!... Everyone, that meant Karl too. All that he had done till now was ignored; it was not going to be made a reproach to him.[23]

America, like other of Kafka's novels, remains unfinished, but the author enlarged upon the ending and upon the Nature Theatre in a conversation with his friend and literary executor Max Brod. We learn that Kafka took particular delight in the Nature Theatre and intended it to provide a conciliatory note to the end of the novel. For in the limitless Theatre Karl was to find 'a profession, a stand-by, his freedom, even his old home and parents, as if by some celestial witchery'.[24] In one sense, then, the Nature Theatre can be seen as a kind of imaginative fulfilment of Kafka's own lifelong search for belonging.

The Castle recounts the efforts of a land surveyor, known simply as K, to become established in a village dominated by a mysterious castle. It is typical of a significant amount of Cancerian prose in that little happens; there is no plot as such, little sense of progression or time. K is an outsider who is trying to break *into* a world. He does not belong to the world of the Castle with its distant bureaucracy, nor can he find communion with the villagers, for he is not of their stock, and has no roots there. The novel was once again unfinished, but in the projected ending K would eventually be accepted by the community. As it stands, the theme is one of rejection and isolation, a tale of the land surveyor's fruitless attempts to reach the Castle and obtain confirmation of his appointment.

The Trial is the story of Joseph K, who is one day arrested in his flat and forced to defend himself against a charge never stated, within a legal system he can not comprehend and whose soul purpose seems to be the persecution of the individual. The system is complex, secretive and hierarchic so that just as he begins to come to terms with it at one level it becomes apparent that the real power to resolve the case is lodged with officials at a more remote level, officials we are told, who did not have 'right understanding' of human relations, since they were confined day and night to the working of the judiciary. Like *The Castle*, *The Trial* is very static, and one of the reasons Joseph K does not progress is because the people he talks to have only a partial knowledge – their own experience – of the system, which does not apply to his own case. He never does 'understand his situation clearly', and is in the end executed. What we might call Kafkaesque man, the individual who is ignorant of his role in a larger scheme of things, is common in Cancer writing.

In one sense *The Trial* is a tale of self-obsession and selfishness, for Joseph K is concerned only with his own problem. He is only interested in discussing those things which bear upon his case and which might help resolve it. *The Trial* is also the story of the impact of faceless bureaucracy on an individual sensibility, the futile struggle of a man against omnipotent authorities he can not understand, let alone defeat, but to which he is inextricably tied. In this regard it compares with one of the most acclaimed novels of the last century.

George Orwell, *Nineteen Eighty-Four*

Orwell was a writer who traced the malaise of the modern world to the decline in public life of what he called decency. What he meant by decency was an amalgam of things such as loyalty, honesty, sympathy, trust, qualities that thrive in an intimate atmosphere and which are commonly equated to Cancer. When these qualities were absent in public life inhumane systems and structures were the result. His dislike of hierarchy developed through his adult life but found compelling form in *Nineteen Eighty-Four*, the story of a totalitarian state that has the capacity to intrude upon and control every facet of individual life. He created a world where the concept of privacy had been eradicated, for no one was free of the all-seeing camera eye of Big Brother. This is the Cancerian nightmare.[25]

The core of the novel is Winston Smith's relationship with Julia, through which he seeks to keep alive his humanity. The couple appreciate that their illicit partnership will be eventually discovered and come to an end. But they believe they have with their love created something that the authorities can not take away:

> 'The one thing that matters is that we shouldn't betray one another, although even that can't make the slightest difference.'
>
> 'If you mean confessing,' she said, 'we shall do that right enough. Everybody always confesses. You can't help it. They torture you.'
>
> 'I don't mean confessing. Confession is not betrayal. What you say or do doesn't matter: only feelings matter. If they could make me stop loving you – that would be a real betrayal.'
>
> She thought it over. 'They can't do that,' she said finally. 'It's the one thing they can't do. They can make you say anything – anything – but they can't make you believe it. They can't get inside you.'[26]

But as Winston discovered to his horror, in Room 101, 'they' could get inside, the state could breach his personal citadel. It did have the power to destroy his last vestige of humanity, his feelings, and indeed considered it important to do so. Ironically the authorities accomplish this by tailoring their methods to individual sensibility. What lay in Room 101 was the death that each individual most feared – for one it might be impalation, for another drowning. For Winston it was having a rat burrow into his brain. Only in torment was their deference to the individual.

Hermann Hesse, *Steppenwolf, The Glass Bead Game*

Hesse was another writer who detested the kind of regimentation that crushes individuals, and these feelings found expression in an early novel, *The Prodigy*, the story of a youth sacrificed to a monolithic education system. More commonly, however, Hesse's heroes are loners and wanderers searching for some sort of spiritual home. *Demien*, for example, is the story of a young man caught between the desire for home and security on the one hand, and a life of wandering freedom on the other. For Demien we can read Hesse, for his life involved the same swings of motion and stasis.

Harry Haller, the central character of *Steppenwolf*, is also a restless loner caught in a limbo between a familiar world he has left behind and one not yet born. The novel's title translates as 'wolf of the Steppes' and the allusion is to the outsider who haunts the periphery of human society in the same way a lone wolf prowls the village boundary. There are many references in the early pages of the work to Haller's marginality:

> A wolf of the Steppes that had lost its way and strayed into the towns and the life of the herd, a more striking image could not be found for his shy loneliness, his savagery, his restlessness, his homesickness ... I came to see more and more that from the empty spaces of his lone-wolfishness he really admired and loved our little bourgeois world as something solid and secure, as the home and peace which must ever remain far and unattainable, with no road leading from them to him.[27]

This observation comes from the narrator whose account opens the work. Later Haller himself explains the attraction of the 'bourgeois world':

> I don't know how it comes about, but I, the homeless Steppenwolf, the solitary, the hater of life's petty conventions always take up my quarters in just such houses as this ... I live neither in palatial houses nor in those of the humble poor, but instead and deliberately in those respectable and wearisome and spotless middle-class homes, which smell of turpentine and soap ... the love of this atmosphere comes, no doubt from the days of my childhood, and a secret yearning I have for something homelike drives me, though with little hope, to follow the same old stupid road.[28]

Haller is similar to Kafka's characters in that he wants to belong somewhere. It comes to the point that he contemplates suicide to end his gnawing sense of loneliness. But he is drawn back into the flux of contemporary life by an assortment of pseudo-mythical characters. At the same time events are transfigured to a subjective level. Haller is subjected to the 'Magic Theatre', whose various sideshows teach him something of an eternal self that underlies a multi-faceted personality. It is the discovery of this focal point that constitutes an essential experience of this sign. It is this point that represents the thinker, rather than the thought, the perceiver rather than the perception, and that constitutes the home, or secure centre, that Haller seeks all along. As his companion states at one point: 'Ah, Harry, we have to stumble through so much dirt and humbug before we reach home. And we have no one to guide us. Our only guide is our homesickness.'[29]

The astrological symbolism of Cancer and the Moon also tells us something about the invention at the heart of Hesse's magnum opus. Twelve years in the writing, *The Glass Bead Game* is perhaps his most satisfying and substantial work, treating more confidently and successfully ideas he only really grapples with in *Steppenwolf.*

What Hesse has created in the game is an objective analogue of the lunar faculty. The name itself derives from the first form of the game in which a wire frame (representing a staff) strung with beads (note values) formed a device upon which musicians could exercise and develop their skill in theme manipulation. In essence the Glass Bead Game is a synthesising device, a method of integrating in an imaginative way the great thought and art of the ages. In the course of the game's development this thought and art came to be reduced to workable concepts, to ciphers and formulas that allowed one discipline to be expressed in terms of another. The first of these formulas, we are told, were derived equally from music and mathematics, and so, in effect, these two separate disciplines could be reduced to a common denominator and expressed in terms of one another. A sophisticated game language evolved that enabled parallels to be drawn between all manner of cultural symbols. In the hands of a skilled player it was possible to obtain a rich tapestry of association in much the same way the subjective mind creates an inner world from simple sensual input.

It is not explained precisely how the associative network of the game's structure was established, but we are given a clue through an incident in the life of the novel's central character, Joseph Knecht. He recalls an occasion when he was walking in the countryside and assailed by the distinctive odour from a broken elder twig. Later that day, he also recalls, he heard for the first time a particular Schubert song, and as the first notes hit his ear he experienced not only the sound but also the smell of elder. A sensual association had developed in his mind and from then onward he could not listen to that piece of music without experiencing the same aroma, or the joyful feeling of walking in the countryside in spring. There is something subtle linking the three, the product of the subjective mind. The difference between this individual's experience and the game's structure is that in the latter parallels are drawn through more universal associations. In *Steppenwolf* Hesse talked of the essential self that underlies the myriad personalities of the individual and exists as a kind of distillate of them. In *The Glass Bead Game* he suggests that the equivalent distillation of man's creations, the great art and thought of all ages, results in a more fundamental unity. The Game:

> represented an elite, symbolic form of seeking for perfection, a sublime alchemy, an approach to that Mind which beyond all images and multiplicities is one within itself – in other words to God.[30]

The novel's narrative returns us to familiar Cancerian themes: the need to break with the past, isolation, and the pressure of organisational structure on an individual. For the most part *The Glass Bead Game* is set in the fictional province of Castalia, a scholastic utopia set up to safeguard the country's cultural and intellectual values. Chief among the disciplines engaged in is the glass bead game. Outstanding students from throughout the country are creamed off for Castalia at an early age. One such is Knecht, and the novel centres upon his education and ascent within the province's hierarchy to the coveted position of Game Master.

He is an exemplary student and in many ways embodies the spirit of Castalia. Yet he is not satisfied with his life. His unhappiness is rooted in a sense of stagnation, the fact that the province has ceased to maintain a symbiosis with the outside world. Most of the Castalians are proud of their insularity, because they equate it with purity. But Knecht differs because at various stages of his life he has come into contact with worldly men, people with experience of the outside world who can put the Castalian vision of life into perspective. These encounters sow the seeds of doubt that take root within Knecht. What hastens his departure is the threat to his personal freedom from the burden of office. As he rises within the hierarchy he becomes less of an individual and more of a functionary. His friendships suffer; people talk to him as Glass Bead Game Master and not as Joseph Knecht. His own wishes become subservient to the demands of ritual and office.

We can note the similarities between this novel and Peake's *Gormenghast* trilogy. There is the same institution that will not change or grow. In both there is a central character who rebels against the weight of office. There are the same triggers of discontent – people who are the embodiment of a larger existence. Knecht, like Titus Groan, eventually cuts the umbilical cord to his alma mater. He renounces the Castalian order and pursues the simple life of a teacher. However, the uprooting seems to weaken him. His strength deserts him during an early morning swim in a mountain lake and he drowns.

The ending, in a broad way, typifies the novels of Cancer writers, who do not seem to know what to do with their heroes once they have uprooted them. Kafka is reluctant to finish his novels; Titus Groan wanders alone, as indeed do other of the sign's characters. In Cancer the emphasis is upon the need to break with the past and the struggle to find a new 'home', rather than public achievement. Symbolically this comes much later, in Cancer's polar opposite, Capricorn.

Notes

1. Tom Hopkinson, *Writers and their Work No 39 George Orwell*, British Council/Longmans, p6
2. *Columbia Dictionary of Modern European Literature*, ed JA Bédé and WB Edgerton, Columbia University Press, 1980, p362

3. Stewart Sanderson, *Writers & Critics:Hemingway*, Oliver & Boyd, 1961, p2

4. *Contemporary Novelists*, ed James Vinson, St James Press, 1976, p339

5. *Encyclopaedia of World Literature in the 20th Century*, Vol 3, ed Steven R Serafin, St James Press, 1999, p379

6. *Twentieth Century Writing*, ed Kenneth Richardson, Newnes Books, 1969, p340

7. *World Authors 1950-1970*, ed J Wakeman, HW Wilson Co, 1975, p1083

8. *World Authors 1970-1975*, ed J Wakeman, HW Wilson Co, 1980, p606

9. *Columbia Dictionary of Modern European Literature*, ed JA Bédé and WB Edgerton, Columbia University Press, 1980, p468

10. *Great Writers of the English Language: Novelists and Prose Writers*, ed James Vinson, Macmillan, 1979, p132

11. *Great Women Writers*, ed Frank Magill, Robert Hale, 1994, p521

12. We can note the following descriptions of two writers with Cancer Suns, Donald Windham and Nathalie Sarraute. Windham's stories show us 'human beings as displaced persons, pushing out their horns like timid snails in a world at once remote and familiar and then sharply withdrawing them again as the contact made proves harsh or unfriendly or startling.' (Cited in *World Authors 1950-70*, ed J Wakeman, HW Wilson Co, 1975, p1561)

Nathalie Sarraute's domain is 'the hidden emotional life of the depths in constant flux, with its subtle interchanges, its infinitesimal variations, which reveal, way beneath the rational social patterns of behaviour, the watchful, hunted, human hunter, peering like some small ferocious shell fish fearfully out of his shell.' (Germaine Brée, quoted in *World Authors 1950-70*, ed J Wakeman, HW Wilson Co, 1975, p1261).

13. The beginning of Cancer, around 22 June, corresponds (in the northern hemisphere) to the summer solstice, or midsummer's day. The sun has reached its point of maximum northerly declination at around 23 degrees north and from this time on, until mid-winter, the daily culminations move progressively south and the daylight hours become incrementally shorter. The winter solstice corresponds to the start of Capricorn, the polar sign to Cancer, and is once more a turning point in the astronomical year.

14. Dane Rudhyar, *An Astrological Triptych*, ASI, 1978, p28

15. ibid, p30

16. Z'ev ben Shimon Halevi, *Tree of Life*, Rider, 1972, p44

17. Valerie Minogue, *Studies in French Literature 23 Proust: du Côté de Chez Swann*, Edward Arnold, 1973, p46.

We find a similar comment regarding another Cancerian novelist, Anita Desai. The critic notes Desai was the first Indian-English novelist to be primarily concerned with the inner life of her characters, '... their fleeting moods, wisps of memory, subtle cerebrations. In her novels, Desai succeeds in capturing the evanescent moments of consciousness, preserving them from oblivion and investing them with the permanence of art ... Desai not only creates something of value for herself out of the endless flux of her own psyche but also provides for her reader an opportunity to share this rich inner life through her characters.' (*Great Women Writers*, ed Frank Magill, Robert Hale, 1994, p124)

18. Dane Rudhyar, *An Astrological Triptych*, ASI, 1978, p209

19. David Storey, *Flight into Camden*, Vintage, 2000, p68

20. Cancer is not the only sign that symbolises the past in astrology. Taurus, Libra and Leo also do, although in a different way to Cancer. The idea of ritual carried over from the past relates to Libra, and it is possibly significant that Peake had this as his rising sign. However, ritual is usually seen as a positive thing by writers with Libran Suns, something which imparts stability and harmony in a society, providing the rituals have not ossified and lost their meaning. The Venus-ruled signs Libra and Taurus both relate to this idea of a golden past, something wonderful that has been lost and which needs to be restored, or in some cases, as we saw in the chapter on Taurus, to be redeemed. Part of the meaning of Leo relates to a nation's, or a people's past, and the capacity of strong individuals to vivify this.

21. Rodney Collin, *The Theory of Celestial Influence*, Robinson & Watkins, 1973, pp112-113

22. *Gormenghast* seems to be an example of what Jung calls a 'visionary' novel, a work that is intuitive and spontaneous, as opposed to consciously wrought, and which reveals something of the author's inner world. Such a work is characterised by 'an exciting narrative that is apparently quite devoid of psychological intentions ... such a tale is constructed against a background of unspoken psychological assumption, and the more unconscious the author is of them, the more this background reveals itself in unalloyed purity to the discerning eye.' (C G Jung, *The Spirit in Art Man and Literature*, The Collected Works, Vol 15, Routledge & Kegan Paul, 1966, pp 88, 101)

23. Franz Kafka, *America*, Penguin Modern Classics, 1981, p246

24. ibid, postscript, p269

25. This idea was shared by Rousseau, who perceived a close connection between the moral condition of man and the structure of a society. Man was born good, believed Rousseau, and if he was unhappy or criminal it was because the environment was inimical to his nature. Like other Cancerians, Rousseau put the individual's welfare first, and he anticipated Schumacher in his belief that the size of community has a bearing upon individual wellbeing. The larger the community the less the individual was able to feel part of it and the more the few, through the growth of hierarchy, could control the many. One critic has described Rousseau as 'this outsider, this misfit, this vagabond, who felt that evil was thrust upon him by his position in a society where he could not feel spiritually at home.' (*Encyclopaedia Britannica*, vol 19, 1972, p662).

26. George Orwell, *Nineteen Eighty-Four,* Everyman's Library, 1992, p173

27. Hermann Hesse, *Steppenwolf*, Penguin Modern Classics, 2001, p22

28. ibid, p36

29. ibid, p180

30. Hermann Hesse, *The Glass Bead Game*, Penguin Modern Classics, 1976, p41

Leo

Writers with the Sun in Leo include: Conrad Aiken, Brian Aldiss, Isabel Allende, Fernando Arrabal, Piers Anthony, James Baldwin, Maurice Barrès, Hilaire Belloc, Enid Blyton, Ray Bradbury, Rupert Brooke, Emily Brontë, Charles Bukowski, Elias Canetti, Raymond Chandler, Walter Van Tilburg Clark, Paul Claudel, James Cozzens, Alfred Döblin, Alexandre Dumas (père), Paul Gallico, John Galsworthy, Dave Godfrey, Robert Graves, Alain Robbe-Grillet, Knut Hamsun, Gerard Manley Hopkins, Ted Hughes, Aldous Huxley, P D James, C G Jung, Philip Larkin, Malcolm Lowry, Guy de Maupassant, Hugh MacDiarmid, Rose Macaulay, Herman Melville, V S Naipaul, Dorothy Parker, Beatrix Potter, Thomas De Quincey, J K Rowling, Bernice Rubens, Walter Scott, George Bernard Shaw, P B Shelley, Robert Southey, Lord Tennyson, Frank Wedekind, Angus Wilson.

Summary Leo writers can be outstanding at writing for young people. They also excel at historical works and as exemplars of national values. At the deepest level Leo novels are built around the contrast between instinctive and purposeful existence. They express the idea of self-conscious individuals as the live end of some evolutionary spectrum, faced with the task of giving life an awareness of itself. For this, the individual must pit himself against *un*-consciousness – as in the raw stuff of consciousness – and in some way humanise, or spiritualise, this. A common lament of Leo writers is that people fail to capitalise on their birthright to grow into more conscious human beings, but instead dissipate their energies in amusements and pleasures.

Man's in the makin but henceforth maun mak himsel'.
Nature has led him sae faur, up frae the slime,
Gi'en him body and brain – and noo it's for him
To mak' or mar this maikless torso.

> Let him look to nature nae mair;
> For her will's to create ane wi' the poo'er
> To create himsel' – if he fails, she fails
> And the metal gangs back to the pot
> And the process
> Begins a'owre. If he wins he wins alane.
> It lies wi' himsel'
>
> **Hugh MacDiarmid** 'Man the Reality That Makes All Things Possible'

Many of the character traits traditionally ascribed to this sign revolve around the idea of self-centredness. It is common to find those strong in Leo described as attention-seeking, subjective, full of self-importance, with a tendency to self-dramatisation. It is a sign generally associated with pride, elitism, arrogance and autocracy. And yet while there is a high opinion of the self there is at the same time an acute sensitivity to the criticism or adulation of the crowd. None of this is very endearing, yet, like any other sign, Leo is a mixed bag with qualities often the obverse of its faults. Those strong in Leo will often succeed through strength of character, through what they are rather than what they do, or demonstrate by their work or vision the value of the individual in an increasingly depersonalised world. There can be a generous, high-minded, dignified side that embodies all that is best about the human condition, and which recoils at meanness, baseness and pettiness. The original 'warm and wonderful human being' was probably strong in Leo. Equally, Leo types seem to have the gift of perceiving and bringing out the best in others, and have a flair for connecting with young people. Fun-loving, romantic, gregarious, single-minded, a certain joie de vivre – these traits complete the popular portrait of this sign.

While this in its way is an accurate picture of the sign, these observable traits are but a reflection of something more fundamental. To state it briefly at this point, the deeper meaning of Leo centres upon inner quest and self-knowledge, and upon the idea of the individual as the live end of an evolutionary spiral.[1] It is to do with identity, the secret of the personality, and relates to what the celebrated psychologist Carl Jung terms individuation, the turning away from patterns of the past, individual and collective, to create a unique life based on a conscious awareness of one's true self.

Leo's traditional connection with acting has been overstated, although those strong in the sign can be dramatic (or melodramatic) in their everyday lives. Nevertheless the best Leo actors will often reflect the nature of the sign in their performances. Robert De Niro is a good example. There are three films I know of that illustrate well characteristics associated with his Leo Sun. Probably if we had to single out a scene most associated with him it is the one he improvised in *Taxi Driver* in front of a mirror. His 'are you talking to me?' monologue forms an excellent example of the foolish puffed-up pride and self-importance that is one of the more negative (though essentially harmless) faces of Leo. Travis Bickle, with his mission to purify New York, is also illustrative of another aspect of Leo: it can be an obsessive sign, although at its best this quality emerges as determination and a strong sense of purpose (and the one-pointed pursuit of this). One of De Niro's lesser known films is *This Boy's Life*, in which he plays the over-bearing, self-centred Dwight Hansen, an oppressive stepfather to Leonardo DiCaprio. Leos often slot into the role of father-teacher, but because Hansen is so self-centred his urge to nurture amounts to no more than vanity. He tries to mould his stepson in his own image (rather than bringing out the boy's individuality). Equally self-centred, but a much more likeable character, is Rupert Pupkin in *The King of Comedy* (written by Leo Sun[2] Paul D Zimmerman). Pupkin believes he is funny and wants nothing more than to front his own TV chat show. This is his obsession. He's vain and self-important, distinctly unfunny, but also determined, single-minded and self-confident. He never doubts that he's going to succeed. And because he also enjoys another common Leo trait – good luck – he does succeed.

Cancer, the sign preceding Leo, builds the foundation of selfhood from which we are able to operate in the social sphere. It is the *feeling* of being a unique individual. Cancer is a Water sign, and this element relates primarily to feeling. Leo, on the other hand, is a Fire sign, the element of emotion, which is the outward expression of some inner state of being. Leo is more to do with pushing the self outward – not in any spirit of co-operation (which does not come until the Libra phase of the zodiac) but simply to make an impression on the world. Rudhyar[3] describes the keynote of Leo as 'dramatic exteriorisation of personality in order to gain social recognition and increased self-assurance as a social unit.'

As with Cancer, the sense of being a unique individual is strong in Leo. 'Otherness' is still perceived, by and large, in a negative light. For one Leo writer, Elias Canetti, for example, it took the form of the crowd, a symbol of inhumanity capable of bestial acts, and a symbol too of equality and anonymity (the natural instinct in Leo is to stand out from the crowd).[4] The following observation of the poet Shelley, a Leo Sun, could apply to many Leo writers:

> To Shelley life was a straightforward problem: a struggle between the powers of good, which he believed to be reigning within himself, and a world quite external to the self.[5]

In Cancer the first seed of otherness, or what is *not* the self, is perceived as impersonal laws and organisations that seek to control the life of the individual. In Leo we find something less defined but in many ways more disturbing and powerful. The individual must come to terms with unconsciousness – in the sense of the raw stuff of consciousness. Or sometimes, this otherness is simply perceived as that which is not life and yet which works to negate it. In Leo the task is to spiritualise, or humanise, life in order to give it an awareness of itself, or (to put it another way) to redeem the holy which is bound up in the profane.[6]

The I Ching hexagram related to Leo is number 33, Retreat. The text is suggestive of the uneasy relationship between the light of the ego and the dark and danger that surrounds it. It also brings to mind the process of individuation whereby the individual must differentiate from the mass, and from an instinctive, unconscious, way of being. It counsels to show strength of purpose in one's quest for truth and notes: 'absolute firmness of decision is necessary if one is not to be led astray by irrelevant considerations'.[7] As we shall see presently, a single-minded sense of purpose in following one's own star is at the core of some of the more profound Leo writing.

Leo is ruled by the Sun in astrology, which has its equivalent in Tiphareth on the Tree of Life. Tiphareth sits central on the column of consciousness between earth and heaven, or in Christian terms, between humanity and God the Father. Tiphareth represents God the Son, divinity within the range of human consciousness. It is sometimes referred to as the sphere of the redeemer. From the perspective of earth Tiphareth is symbolised by the majestic god-king, but from those levels above it, it stands as a sacrificed god, divinity shackled by flesh. We have this same perspective in astronomy: the sun is the focus of all life on earth, but at the same time it is part of a larger system, a rather ordinary star in an incomprehensibly large galaxy.[8] Tiphareth is also related by cabbalists to the essential nature of man. As one writer puts it:

> Without Tiphareth [Sun] or a man's essential nature, the body ... would be a soulless automaton, a mere system of divine plumbing with no possibility of evolution.[9]

Leo has a connection with nationalism and racial consciousness, which we can attribute to the need an individual feels to bolster his identity with something larger than the self, something grand which he is proud to be a part of.[10] This abstract entity we call national character, an exulted summation of a country's land, culture and history, can sometimes be expressed in powerful form by an individual, and then we have the great patriot or national figurehead, of which a surprising number are Leo Suns. We can mention: Napoleon, Mussolini, T E Lawrence, Simón Bolivar, Bernardo O'Higgins, Fidel Castro, Habib Bourguiba (the 'father' of modern Tunisia), Daniel O'Connell, Marcus Garvey and Haile Selassie (the latter two being important figures to the emerging consciousness of the black races). We should also mention Sir Walter Scott, who for many came to embody the best of the Scottish character and helped forge an identity for the nation. The following observations about Leo writers also bear out this connection:

Cassiano Ricardo
[He] is remembered, above all else, as a leading proponent of literary nationalism in Brazil ... [his work] celebrates what the poet feels are the most salient and unique characteristics of the Brazilian people ... his foremost preoccupation as a poet: how to discover and bring to the attention of his fellow citizens all that was uniquely, truly, and unmistakably Brazilian in their land.[11]

Alois Jirásek
A spokesman for the Czech people in their efforts to gain national independence ... in his writings ... the Czech reader found a source of patriotic inspiration.[12]

Jorge Amado
My literature and my life have one characteristic trait in common: never to depart from the life and concerns of my Brazilian people.[13]

Antônio Gonçalves Dias
[His purpose in life] To use history to construct a distinctive national identity for Brazilians, and to create a literature capable of expressing that identity.[14]

Dave Godfrey
Some of his writing is an attempt to express our vital mythology in contemporary terms ... [he] gives shape to Canadian myth in the form of such men ... who represent the many races and cultures which make up the country.[15]

Vilhelm Moberg
[Of his nation] I wish to describe its deeds, explain its reticence, give it a voice and take part in its striving to discover itself. In my mind's eye I feel that this could be my true calling.[16]

Ferenc Juhász
For Juhász, to write about oneself is to write about one's past ... and that in turn is to write about the identity of one's nation ... as a poet ...

> his achievement is inseparable from his intuitive closeness to the traditions of the Hungarian people.[17]

More Leo writing

One of Leo's strengths is the ability to relate to young people and the writers of the sign, particularly the women, can be outstanding in the genre of children's fiction. This is more in a qualitative sense, rather than numbers, as measured by the impact the writer has had on the world of children's literature. We can mention: J K Rowling, Enid Blyton, Beatrix Potter, Hilaire Beloc, Pamela Travers (who created Mary Poppins), and Tove Jansson, whose Moomin series of books, like Harry Potter, grew into a global phenomenon. The sign's writers also have a flair for historical novels. In Walter Scott and Alexandre Dumas we have two of the most acclaimed exponents of the genre, while Robert Graves is another known for his capacity to vivify the past – the *Claudius* books, for example. In one sense Leo is a sign focused at the confluence of the past, present and future, a living now projecting the past into the future. But many of the weightier Leo writers focus in their work on the contrast between instinctive and purposeful existence, and upon the efforts of individuals to sustain their humanity in a profane world.

George Bernard Shaw, *Man and Superman*

Shaw is a good example of a creative evolutionist, which term he defines (when describing another, Jean Lamarck, also a Leo Sun) thus: 'you are alive, you want to be more alive. You want an extension of consciousness.'[18] *Back to Methuselah* and *Man and Superman* are his best known works which deal with the subject.

The latter is a play in four acts, three of which constitute a conventional drama about husband-hunting, while the other takes the form of a dream, much of it set in Hell, where more eternal, mythical figures discourse. The central female in the play, Ann, is not just a woman but Woman, the embodiment of fecund nature in its blind, procreative drive. John Tanner, a Don Juan figure and the object of Ann's pursuit, talks of women as having 'a purpose which is not their own purpose, but that of the whole universe, a man is nothing to them but an instrument of that purpose'.[19] Shaw is not being sexist here when he speaks of a woman's function as being the propagation of the species. Women, he owns, are quite capable of genius but in such instances a greater purpose simply over-rides the primal one. Nor do men rate particularly highly in the normal course of Shaw's scheme, merely serving as nature's instruments once removed. In both cases, hunter and hunted, instinct is at work, and the average man deserves his fate, suggests Shaw, if he is not prepared to forge a greater role for himself than that of husband and father. Those who were prepared to dissociate from the herd Shaw called supermen.

The superman he defined as that individual selected by Nature to carry on the work of building up the intellectual consciousness of her own instinctive purpose. Creative expression is one way in which this consciousness is built up and so for Shaw sex and creativity were mutually exclusive. Sex was a herd instinct, creativity its reflection on a higher arc, at the level of the superman. He notes in the play's introduction:

> What is true of the great man who incarnates the philosophic consciousness of Life and the woman who incarnates its fecundity, is true to some degree of all geniuses and all women. Hence it is that the world's books get written, its pictures painted, its statues modelled, its symphonies composed, by people who are free from the otherwise universal dominion of the tyranny of sex.[20]

The quandary of sex versus creativity is not an uncommon one amongst artists, but it does seem to come into some sort of focus in this sign. Often in Leo, at least among the individuated variety, there exists a certain repulsion of the bodily functions. Shaw was happily married, but it is said the marriage was not consummated.[21]

The Hell scene in *Man and Superman* takes the form of a dialogue on the question of purposeful as against conditioned existence. Tanner/Don Juan explains why he wishes to leave Hell to reside in Heaven, which places are not what we have been led to believe: Hell has no brimstone, Heaven no angelic choirs. Hell is characterised instead by hedonism; it is a place of eternal pleasure and amusement. It is a much easier place to abide than Heaven, just as the path of instinct, the line of least resistance, is easier to follow than the path of consciousness. Tanner/Don Juan is a superman. The life force flows strongly in him and he can not be content with the idle distractions of Hell:

> I tell you as long as I can conceive of something better than myself I can not be easy unless I am striving to bring it into existence or clearing the way for it. That is the law of my life. That is the working in me of Life's incessant aspiration to higher organisation, wider, deeper, intense self-consciousness, and clearer self-understanding.[22]

We have here the creed of the superman and the creative evolutionist. Don Juan goes on to rebuke the Devil:

> It is the absence of this instinct in you that makes you that strange

> monster called a Devil. It is the success with which you have diverted the attention of men from their real purpose ... that has earned you the name of the Tempter.[23]

Aldous Huxley, *Brave New World*

This work is similar to *Man and Superman* with its rejection of hedonism. Amusement and pleasure are held to be the highest good in Huxley's utopia, just as they are in Shaw's Hell. The population is conditioned to accept this by an almost foolproof system of eugenics – almost, because a few individuals begin to question the ideal of consensus happiness and demand the right to seek alternative ways. In the following passage we detect a clear parallel to Shaw's ideas. Controller Mustapha Mond muses upon a heretical treatise about individualism:

> Once you began admitting explanation in terms of purpose – well you didn't know what the result might be. It was the sort of idea that might easily decondition the more unsettled minds among the higher castes – make them lose their faith in happiness as the Sovereign Good and take to believing, instead, that the goal was somewhere beyond, somewhere outside the present human sphere; that the purpose of life was not the maintenance of wellbeing, but some intensification and refining of consciousness, some enlargement of knowledge. Which was, the Controller reflected, quite possibly true. But not in the present circumstances admissible.[24]

More than anything, however, it is the idea of babies in bottles that has come to be associated with *Brave New World*. Procreative sex, childbirth and motherhood are obsolete. We can note the same idea in the fifth of Shaw's *Far-Fetched Fables*, in which he describes a future world where sex has ceased to be a physical activity and geneticists perpetuate the race in the laboratory.

Hugh MacDiarmid

The poetry of Hugh MacDiarmid (Christopher Grieve) often focuses upon an evolution in consciousness. A good example is 'Man, the Reality That Makes All Things Possible', quoted at the beginning of the chapter. He establishes in this work that man's task is to become conscious of a greater purpose, but also laments the fact that the spiritual potential in most people remains untapped:

> The restless spirit of Man, the theme o' my sang,
> Or to the theme o't what Man's spirit and thocht
> Micht be if men were as muckle concerned
> Wi' them as they are wi' fitba' or wimmen.[25]

As with Shaw and Huxley, it is hedonism that diverts man from his real purpose. MacDiarmid was a great nationalist, and in some of his works self-consciousness is linked to race. A poem such as 'The Unconscious Goal of History,' for example, seems to suggest that self-aware individuals can activate some kind of primordial image that is capable of uniting a race. The protagonist of 'A Drunk Man Looks at the Thistle' symbolises the unenlightened mass and the poet is suggesting the Drunk Man can grow by remoulding himself in the archetypal image of his country.

Sri Aurobindo

The idea of spiritual evolution is at the core of the writing of the poet and philosopher, Sri Aurobindo. As a young man he was actively engaged in his country's struggle for independence and came close to being executed by the British authorities. His later years he devoted to poetry and writing at a retreat in Pondicherry in south-east India, where a spiritual community grew up around him and continues today.

According to his philosophy, life exists as a spectrum of consciousness and is built about a twinfold principle of involution, a process of densification of spirit, and evolution, its progressive liberation. Once again in Leo, it is the idea of spirit bound up in matter. The human challenge, says Aurobindo, is to awaken to greater levels of consciousness. So, life evolves from matter, mind from life, and spirit from mind. Each level is more conscious, more alive, more spiritual, than the one before. For the most part mankind has reached a full stop. In the West particularly we think that with the perfection of the rational mind we have reached the top. However, Aurobindo describes in some detail a number of higher stages in the chain of human potentiality, namely higher mind, illumined mind, intuitive mind and overmind. The illumined mind as he describes it is connected with the formation of archetypal images. To the intuitive mind belongs the power of truth-seeing, of inspiration, and the ability to immediately seize the significance of something. But the critical stage in his scheme is overmind, 'a vast horizontal expansion of the consciousness into some totality of the spirit'.[26] Overmind seems to function as a kind of booster phase, a transformer to make compatible the upward, essentially mortal current, with the downward, essentially divine. At the stage of overmind a universal individuality is attained with the ego becoming 'a point of relation for the action of a vast cosmic instrumentation'.[27] Overmind is only a midpoint on the scale, for above it are supermind and three other levels. The overmind acts as a mediator, in the same way Tiphareth operates on the Tree of Life. It is the task of individuals, and eventually mankind, to evolve to the level of overmind, for such an ascent triggers a descent from what he calls supermind consciousness. Such a descent is necessary, says Aurobindo, to reconcile finally the enigma of dark and light inherent in human existence.

Carl Jung

Jung's is a self-centred psychology, not concerned primarily with the relationships between individuals, or between individuals and the world, but with integration within the individual. It is to do with finding the self at the centre, the inner person. Jung himself has emphasised this:

> My life has been permeated and held together by one idea and one goal: namely to penetrate into the secret of the personality. Everything can be explained from this central point, and all my works relate to this one theme.[28]

Jung describes some of his insights into the nature of personality in his autobiography. He writes that from an early age he was aware of two distinct worlds, which he labels number one and number two. Number one was his everyday personality, while number two was 'God's world'. To this belonged 'everything superhuman – dazzling light, the darkness of the abyss, the cold impassivity of infinite space and time, and the uncanny grotesqueness of the irrational world of chance.'[29] In world number two were to be found meaning, a sense of continuity with the past, and the secret of the personality.

His first real clue as to the nature of the relationship between the two worlds came through a powerful dream. He saw himself in some unknown place making difficult headway against a storm. Mist and darkness surrounded him and all he had to guide his way was a small, flickering light. This, he later reasoned, represented his consciousness, and however dwarfed by the surrounding darkness it might be, it was all he had to use against it. His light was the number one world, the surrounding darkness, the unknown, the number two. He came to realise the border between them was not fixed and that it was part of the individual's duty to extend the borders of personality and embrace elements of the number two world. He was to speak of his life's work as hitting upon a 'stream of lava' and of attempting to incorporate 'this incandescent matter into the contemporary picture of the world'.[30]

Jung concluded from his dream that life must centre about the number one world, but at the same time, the demands of the number two could not be ignored. It was for the self-aware individual to assimilate some of the content of number two. Just as one element of biological life is the urge to perpetuate itself, so also there is a pressure in the life of the spirit, one not felt by all, to become more conscious, or more spiritualised. Jung saw himself as an unanswered question thrust out into the world of space and time. In discovering and living out the purpose of his own life he was at the same time, he believed, giving Life a greater understanding of itself.

Herman Melville, *Moby Dick*

The much-studied *Moby Dick* is one of the most extraordinary books ever written. It is open to a variety of interpretations but it is not difficult to find parallels with other Leo works.

On one level *Moby Dick* is an account of a whaling expedition and of the whaling industry in the nineteenth century. But on another level it is, as the author notes, 'a complete theory of the heavens and earth, a mystical treatise on the art of attaining truth'. Just as the solar hero in his search for significance and identity must leave the well-trodden paths of life to forge ahead in consciousness, so the whalers must forego the comforts and security of the land in their quest for the fruits of the sea. If the life of whalers was hazardous then so too, Jung assures us, is the path of individuation not to be followed lightly and only in response to deep inner compulsion.

In a number of passages Melville contrasts the land and the sea and the following reminds us of the distinction Jung makes between the ego self and the collective unconscious:

> Consider all this; and then turn to this green, gentle and most docile earth; consider them both, the sea and the land; and do you not find a strange analogy to something in yourself? For as this appalling ocean surrounds the verdant land, so in the soul of man there lies one insular Tahiti, full of peace and joy but encompassed by all the horrors of the *half-known life*. God keep thee! Push not off from that isle, thou canst never return.[31] (My emphasis)

The sea in this work represents unredeemed life, the raw stuff of consciousness that seeks expression and divinity through the individual. And despite the warning, whalers are drawn to the sea and confrontation with 'the horrors of the half-known life', from whence they return with oil to light up the lamps of the world.

The immediate focus of the book is Ahab's quest to kill the white whale. Monomania relates to Leo more than any other sign, sometimes reflecting as obsession, but more usually as less dramatic character traits such as loyalty, single-mindedness and determination. The symbolic meaning of the white whale has been discussed extensively over the years. An analysis by the distinguished American critic Lewis Mumford is very revealing, and is one which accords with the meaning of Leo. Mumford suggests the whale, and its element, the sea, stand for the inscrutable universe, with all its blind and threatening power, the same which can manifest as the outpouring of a volcano, as a tornado, or as the 'mere aimless dissipation of unused energy into a ... void'.[32] Ahab, he suggests, 'is the spirit of man, small and feeble, but purposeful, that pits its puniness against this might and its purpose against the black senselessness of power'.[33] Man must create a purpose to offset the 'inscrutability' of the world, give himself significance, even though he might be puny in comparison to the great task. Ahab does just that, although perishes in the process. He is deranged by his obsession; it is not possible to directly overcome such force as is embodied in the whale. There exists a balance between the conscious mind and the unredeemed life seeking expression through it. The individual acts as a transformer for a powerful current, or as a dam restricting a great head of water. And the nature of the raw flux itself is bizarre; it's all-life, the base and disgusting mixed with the holy and the wondrous, although this too can be disturbing, as Pip the cabin boy discovers when he falls overboard in the chase for the whale, and goes mad after his exposure to the 'number two world'.[34]

> The Sea had jeeringly kept [Pip's] finite body up, but drowned the infinite of his soul. Not drowned entirely, though. Rather carried down alive to wondrous depths, where strange shapes of the unwarped primal world glided to and fro before his passive eyes; and the miser-merman, Wisdom, revealed his hoarded heaps; and among the joyous, heartless, ever juvenile eternities, Pip saw the multitudinous, God-omnipresent coral insects, that out of the firmament of waters heaved the colossal orbs. He saw God's foot upon the treadle of the loom and spoke it; and therefore his shipmates called him mad.[35]

It is true that the material of man's quest are 'the horrors of the half-known life,' but the way to overcome them is not to be bound to them by hatred (as Ahab is to Moby Dick) but to transform them, as the alchemist must turn base matter into gold.

Elias Canetti, *Auto Da Fé*

This novel is split into three sections titled 'A head without a world', 'Headless world', and 'The world in the head'. It is a story about madness associated with individualism and the demands of the unconscious, or as Canetti calls it, the mass (or crowd) within. It is a book that in a sense mourns the divide between flesh and spirit.

The central character, Peter Kien, is a bibliophile and sinologist.

Thanks to his father's legacy he is able to live a narrow and rarefied life in his library of rare books, studying, collecting, and writing theses and commentaries. His reality is the wisdom of the East distilled into erudite texts. For Kien these represent Truth and the only thing in this life worthy of his consideration. The pursuit of happiness he regards as the 'contemptible life goal of illiterates'.[36]

Kien's goal is knowledge and truth, his ambition was to 'be true to himself'.[37] It seems strange to class the physically feeble scholar as a superman, but he does fit Shaw's definition of a man working to create consciousness. The vast majority of mankind – 'a bog of illiteracy' – Kien despises. He will not even enter into a conversation unless there is a compelling reason to do so. Neither does he have time for fellow academics, for he holds himself a world authority in his field, with nothing to learn from anyone else. Whatever else, Kien is a man tainted with the Leo sin of pride.[38]

'You draw closer to the truth by shutting out mankind',[39] believes Kien, but in a moment of delusional weakness he marries his housekeeper, Therese, an appalling woman, vain, grasping, foolish and unattractive. She gradually takes over the house, tries to steal his money, beats him, and eventually throws him out on to the street. Kien languishes for some time in the 'headless world', that is, the world unredeemed by consciousness, where he begins to suffer delusions. He is eventually rescued and restored to his library by his psychiatrist brother, George. But his experiences in the 'bog of illiteracy' derange him and he sets fire to his library.

Auto Da Fé reflects the meaning of Leo in a number of ways. The idea of essence or spirit trapped inside a bodily prison is characteristic of all the Fire signs. And one strand of the story reminds us of Shaw and his view of the Feminine, as something that deflects man from his true purpose. Kien perceives the relationship with his wife thus:

> this stainless spirit in a wretched body had struggled for twenty years to lift itself out of the mire of its surroundings. He was forced to impose enormous sacrifices on himself, never losing sight of his glorious goal – a free mind. Therese, no less determined, dragged him for ever back into the slime.[40]

Kien and his brother spend many pages detailing the frailty of Woman, citing in their support authorities (admittedly male) such as Buddha, Confucius, and Homer.

Auto Da Fé is also the story of an isolated consciousness who, willy-nilly, must heed the call of the unconscious, or the life-awaiting-consciousness. But Kien is not strong enough to meet the challenge. He is destroyed by the mass within, the 'world in his head'. Fire, as

Canetti notes in *Crowds and Power*, is a symbol of the mass, and in the last pages of the book it destroys the humanity bound up in his rare tomes.

It can be argued that Kien is involved in a sort of alchemy. As he notes at one point, he does not write for gold, but what he writes is worth its weight in gold. The content of his books represents humanity's highest endeavour, the seed of the divine extracted from the dross of brute reality. Yet redemption of this sort requires contact with the raw material. When he is in his library, in his 'head', this is hardly the case. In this mode he is supremely arrogant; his contempt for other people – even the brother who rescued him – is marked. The only sign of a bond with another human is when he is in the 'headless' world and meets up with a dwarf called Fischerle who has both a talent and a passion for chess. In Kien's view this passion gives the dwarf, whom most despise, a shred of human dignity. When he is playing chess he is treated like a human being, but abused when he is not. We are told: 'He [Fischerle] has clutched at one tiny corner of the world of the spirit and clings to it like a drowning man ... those wooden chessmen recover his human dignity.'[41]

Kien's brother George runs an asylum. He takes an unusual view of lunacy, believing his patients are simply individuals who have created their own reality and who believe fervidly in it. He also relates madness to the 'mass within', a concept which seems to have a parallel with Jung's collective unconscious. The mass soul, George tells us, 'foams, a huge, wild, full-blooded, warm animal in all of us, very deep, far deeper than the maternal ... its goal is the future. We know nothing of it.' And he adds, 'countless people go mad because the mass in them is particularly strongly developed and can get no satisfaction'.[42]

Leo, while an individual sign, marks a phase in the zodiac when the influence of the mass or collective is growing stronger, although it is not until the Scorpio stage that its pull becomes irresistible. To surrender to the mass has its rewards in Scorpio, but not in Leo, where it seems to be to court madness. It is in Aquarius, the polar sign to Leo, that we find another formulation of the collective in the concept of mankind. George Kien refers to mankind as the mass soul watered down into an idea. And yet, in its way, Aquarius represents some of the more positive aspects of Leo in a collective mode. Leo writers are often of the view that humanity resides in individuals rather than the mass; when individuals act together in a crowd this humanity can be dissipated, resulting, sometimes, in barbarous acts. Yet humanity can exist in a collective form, in the Welfare State for example, where qualities such as caring for others are crystallised into structures – once more the domain of polar Aquarius.

This latter sign is also to do with elevating consciousness, or attaining the truth that preoccupies Peter Kien, but specifically that of the mass. It is the sign of the true teacher or educator raising others up to his level. As is the case with all the signs, the light is beginning to dawn on the polar horizon, and Leos are often enough happily placed as teacher, seeking to awaken others to a fuller potential. We even see it in Peter Kien, for when he is plunged into the sea of humanity he resolves to educate the dwarf Fischerle. But Kien is too feeble and subjective to operate in the world of flesh and take on the challenge on the mass within. So he goes mad.

Notes

1. The lion symbolism of Leo may relate to the long-established ideas of life divided into levels of being. At each level of being it was held that there is one form more advanced than the rest. Amongst the fishes it was the dolphin or whale, amongst the birds the eagle. Of the flowers the rose was supreme, of the precious stones the diamond, and the metals gold. In the animal kingdom it was the lion. Equally the symbolism could have a more primitive correspondence, in that the male lion, with its shaggy golden mane, suggested the aureole of the sun

2. According the site www.filmreference.com he was born 3 August 1938. Some sources give 3 July 1938

3. Dane Rudhyar, *Astrological Signs, the Pulse of Life*, Shambhala, 1978, p65

4. Elias Canetti, *Crowds and Power*, Penguin, 1992

5. Andre Maurois, *Byron*, Constable, 1984, p268. The picture that emerges from Shelley in this (and other) works was of a man rather aloof and self-absorbed but one aware of his duty as a creative artist. His life was full of dramatic incident and he possessed a strong sense of purpose and a single-mindedness much admired by Byron. In all this there is Leo. His desire to better humanity, his atunement to the revolutionary spirit of the day, along with his own eccentricity and non-conformity are more suggestive of the close conjunction of the planet Uranus with his Leo Sun. The muddled, chaotic nature of a life spent in flux is more indicative of his Pisces Moon.

6. The critic Keith Sagar (*Writers and Their Work No 227,* British Council/ Longmans, 1972) has suggested that inherent in Ted Hughes' poetry is the idea that man is neither spirit nor matter, but that which must struggle to preserve itself at the expense of the other. Hughes' poem 'Crow Blacker Than Ever' suggests this very well:

> When God, disgusted with man,
> Turned towards Heaven,
> And man, disgusted with God,
> Turned towards Eve
> Things looked like falling apart

But Crow Crow
Crow nailed them together,
Nailing Heaven and earth together –

So man cried, but with God's voice
And God bled, but with man's blood.

Then Heaven and earth creaked at the joint
Which became gangrenous and stank –
A horror beyond redemption.

The agony did not diminish

Man could not be man nor God God

Collected Poems, Faber & Faber, 2003, p244

7. *I Ching*, Routledge and Kegan Paul, 1975, p129

8. Dane Rudhyar, *The Sun is also a Star*, Dutton, 1975

9. Z'ev ben Shimon Halevi, *Tree of Life*, Rider, 1972, p41

10. The French writer Maurice Barrès (a Leo Sun) wrote a trilogy in his early years titled *Le Culte du Moi* (*The Cult of the Ego*), and its subject is a young man who admits to but one reality, his own self. However, he is eventually forced to recognise the limitations of the ego and that fullness of life involves relating with the fellow men he professes to despise. Barrès later came to identify with his region and his country, and a second trilogy was titled *The Novel of National Energy*

11. *Encyclopedia of World Literature in the Twentieth Century*, Vol 3, St James Press, 1999, pp661-662

12. ibid, vol 2, p556

13. *World Authors, 1950-1970*, ed J Wakeman, HW Wilson Co, 1975, p42

14. *Encyclopedia of Latin American Literature*, Fitzroy Deerborn, 1997, p377

15. *Contemporary Novelists*, ed James Vinson, St James Press, 1976, p532

16. Author quoted in Alrik Gustafson, *A History of Swedish Literature*, University of Minnesota Press, 1961, p501

17. *Contemporary World Writers*, St James Press, 1993, pp280-281

18. George Bernard Shaw, *Back to Methuselah* (preface), Oxford University Press, 1945, pxxiii

19. George Bernard Shaw, *Man and Superman*, Penguin Classics, 2000, p61

20. ibid, p20-21 (Epistle dedicatory)

21. A number of Leo males have wrestled with the sex in the manner we describe here. We can mention T E Lawrence, Robert Graves, Malcolm Lowry and Aldous Huxley. One critic notes that the poet Philip Larkin grew up to 'regard sexual recreation as a socially remote thing ... and nothing happened to alter this view' (*World Authors 1950-1970*, ed J Wakeman, HW Wilson, 1975, p835). We are reminded too of Napoleon's legendary rebuttal: 'not tonight Josephine.' We don't know a lot about Melville's sex life, but critic Lewis Mumford was moved to remark: 'There was ... something in Herman Melville's life that caused him to dissociate women from his account of man's

deepest experience' (*Herman Melville, a Study of his Life and Times*, Secker & Warburg, 1963, p138). This trait is no doubt truer of those Leos who find a greater purpose in life than recreational or procreative sex.

22. George Bernard Shaw, *Man and Superman*, Longman's Green, 1956, p152

23. ibid, p152

24. Aldous Huxley, *Brave New World*, Chatto & Windus, 1970, p145

25. Hugh MacDiarmid, 'There is no Movement in the World Like Yours', *More Collected Poems*, McGibbon & Kee, 1970

26. Sri Aurobindo, *Life Divine 2.26*, reprinted in *The Future Evolution of Man*, Sri Aurobindo Ashram, 1974, p104

27. ibid, p105

28. C G Jung, *Memories, Dreams, Reflections*, Collins, 1971, p232

29. ibid, p91

30. ibid, p255

31. Herman Melville, *Moby Dick*, Everyman Library, 1991, p295

32. Lewis Mumford, *Herman Melville, a Study of his Life and Times*, Secker & Warburg, 1963, p125

33. ibid, p125

34. The dramatic, inflated prose characteristic of Melville in this work is very appropriate for the symbolic level at which it moves and characteristic too of the Romantic ethos. Romanticism, the concern with things wonderful, mysterious and remote from the everyday world, equates to astrological Fire, particularly the signs Leo and Sagittarius. The latter was his Moon sign and the author had the love of travel and adventure tradition links to Sagittarius.

35. *Moby Dick*, p434

36. Elias Canetti, *Auto Da Fé*, Picador, 1978, p194

37. The text of Leo's I Ching hexagram is relevant to *Auto Da Fé*. For example, the counsel to show 'perseverance in single acts of resistance' reminds us of Kien's ambition to 'persist stubbornly in the same manner of existence ... for the whole of his life he would be true to himself.' (*Auto Da Fé*, p13)

38. Frank Wedekind's most acclaimed play is *King Nicolo* and this is a work that has parallels with *Auto Da Fé*. It is about a king who abuses his authority, is deposed by one of his subjects, a butcher, and forced to wander among the common people. As other critics have pointed out, the theme of the play is human dignity and its vulnerability in a hostile environment.

39. Nagel, the central character in Knut Hamsun's *Mysteries*, is likewise a man who rejects the masses, who basically detests everything that isn't Nagel.

40. *Auto Da Fé*, p170

41. ibid, p170

42. ibid, p 377

VIRGO

Writers with the Sun in Virgo include: Dannie Abse, Martin Amis, Sherwood Anderson, Gillaume Apollinaire, Antonin Artaud, Malcolm Bradbury, Robert Benchley, Jorge Luis Borges, John Buchan, Michel Butor, John Creasey, Agatha Christie, James Fenimore Cooper, Julio Cortázar, Roald Dahl, Robertson Davies, Theodore Dreiser, Dorothy Dunnett, C S Forester, Frederick Forsyth, Janet Frame, Michael Frayn, Théophile Gautier, Wolfgang Goethe, William Golding, Julien Green, O Henry, James Hilton, Oliver Wendell Holmes, Christopher Isherwood, Alfred Jarry, Samuel Johnson, Ken Kesey, Stephen King, Arthur Koestler, D H Lawrence, Stanislaw Lem, Ira Levin, Maurice Maeterlinck, Louis MacNeice, Brian Moore, Michael Ondaatje, J B Priestley, Wilhelm Raabe, Mary Renault, Jean Rhys, Upton Sinclair, Mary Shelley, Edith Sitwell, Alexander McCall Smith, Stevie Smith, Leo Tolstoy, Edward Upward, Fay Weldon, H G Wells, Franz Werfel, Charles Williams, William Carlos Williams, Jeanette Winterson.

Summary: Virgo writing often focuses on the contrast between the primitive (or a natural existence) and the civilised, in the sense of modern man's desire for an ordered, predictable, sanitised world. We also find stories in which narrow lives are interrupted by the intrusion of some kind of otherworldliness, and characters whose lives are dominated by the vagaries of fate, or who, more generally, feel insignificant in the face of vast forces they can not control or understand.

> Having occasion to go to London, he marvelled as he returned, thinking of naked, lurking savages on an island, how these had built up and created the great mass of Oxford Street or Piccadilly. How had the helpless savages, running with their spears on the riverside, after fish, how had they come to rear up this great London, the ponderous, massive, ugly superstructure of a world of man upon a world of nature?
>
> **D H Lawrence**, *The Rainbow*

Virgo is the second sign of the zodiac associated with Mercury; Gemini represents its bright, 'day' face, Virgo the more introverted 'night' face. There is some common ground between the writing of the two signs – in the concern with fate and destiny, for example – but for most part the creative output of each is quite distinct.

Mercury can be understood as the principle of change and exchange, and this sometimes reflects in everyday language, where we find words like commerce and merchant (from Latin, *mercari*, to trade), and mercenary, from the Latin *merces*, wages, which originally meant anyone (not just a soldier) who worked for pay. Virgo traditionally relates to what we call our work or trade, a process through which we exchange our physical or mental energy and skills for the things we need both to survive and enjoy life. When it comes to producing books there is no substitute for sitting at a desk hour after hour, day after day, and writing, which is why this workaholic sign tends to be very productive when it comes to words. It is said, for example, that Upton Sinclair bequeathed eight tons of writing to the University of Minnesota, while John Creasey produced more than 500 books.

Mercury stands for that drive in humankind to differentiate itself from nature in order to gain control over circumstances, particularly to make life as predictable as possible. It is also the prime symbol of reductionism, standing for that part of human nature that seeks to reduce the sensible world beyond the boundaries of the self to mental correlates, which can then be manipulated by the intellect, or by a computer. Mercury and its signs seek security through knowledge, the reduction of complexity to simplicity,[1] the unfamiliar to the familiar. What it can't comprehend in terms of its own mental constructs[2] it tends to ignore – or deride.

The Mercury signs are associated with the urge to abolish mystery, regarding it simply as an unstable transitory state, an unknown waiting to be resolved into a solution. We should reiterate here that the sign's meaning simply *turns* upon this point. While there are some Virgo individuals who refuse to sanction anything that is unscientific, there are others, particularly among writers and artists, who recognise the limitations of orthodox science in explaining the full spectrum of reality.

In traditional astrology Mercury and Virgo are related to ritual magic, because this was the first way man attempted to alleviate his fear of the unknown and to influence the course of life. Sir James Frazer talks about this in *The Golden Bough*. Ritual magic, he notes, involved first the anthropomorphising of nature into particular spirits with characteristics of their own. This is essentially a process of reduction, breaking things down so they cease to overwhelm. A second aspect of the process involved the carrying out of a well-established ritual, for by acting out his wishes – perhaps successful hunting, or fertility – man hoped to induce the same outcome in nature. This is so-called homeopathic magic, and we perhaps also have the root here of the talent of the Mercury signs to impersonate and imitate. We also see a connection with Virgoan anxiety, the discomfort and sense of helplessness when faced with an unfamiliar situation, and the same feeling when things don't go according to plan, or machines break down or routines are disturbed. Such occurrences suggest the encroachment of disorder. Virgo's relationship with the future is an uneasy one. It is not tuned to future possibility in the way the Jupiter signs (Sagittarius and Pisces) are, but rather tries to pin it down and forestall calamity by being prepared for all eventualities (what we call anticipation). Another side of Virgo's anxious nature is worrying about things which may or may not happen.

Virgo has a traditional connection with virginity, although we should look beyond the common meaning of sexual purity to get an understanding of this relationship. In cultures throughout the world and across the ages the virgin is a figure who acts as a conduit through which the unmanifest is given form in order to participate in the life process. Through the virgin, spirit (or the supernatural) enters human affairs in the only way it can, so it is an expression of the union between divinity and the material world. By maintaining a place in human life that is physically 'pure' or, more broadly, not of the profane world, the flow between spirit and matter is facilitated. Children were once used in hunting because it was believed their innocence made them receptive to those animistic forces of the earth and forest that could guide a hunter to his prey. For much the same reason, their receptivity to the divine, they were also utilised in certain ceremonials. A carry-over of this is the use of bridesmaids and pages in modern weddings.

Virgo is connected with humility, which sometimes emerges in fiction that focuses on lack of free will or a feeling of insignificance in the face of forces perceived to be far greater than the individual. The following criticisms bear this out.

William Golding
Golding's revelation ... is of ultimate forces that no man can ever hope to understand.[3]

Theodore Dreiser
Dreiser feels keenly the plight of each individual human soul at the mercy of chance and of forces beyond his control.[4]

Jean Rhys
Relentlessly she develops her single vision of a world in which free will is a myth and the individual has no power to control his destiny.[5]

Giovanni Verga
Typical of Verga's fictional universe ... the overwhelming role of destiny and the inability of characters to change their circumstances.[6]

Hjalmar Bergman
Bergman's intensely personal world is ultimately one of puppets, of people animated by forces, internal or external, over which they have no control.[7]

Henry Livings
Very crumpled little people are the subject of his plays ... waging battles which only serve to underline their own insignificance.[8]

Ernst Weiss
[In his last work he] finds a term for the overwhelming omnipotence of an impersonal destiny – his main theme ... 'that which crushes' ... the picture he conveys of the unalterable nature of the decrees of fate.[9]

May Sinclair
Her books, especially those written after 1913, deal with the psychological tension between determinism and free will.[10]

The positive outcrop of this sense of smallness is a modest and unassuming nature, but equally it can result in a sense of inferiority. Virgo often needs to develop a trust in life, to wait patiently to be opened by it (and again there is something of the virgin symbolism here). Of all the signs Virgo seems least to be master of its own destiny. Rather, fate is the navigator, and the individual often ends up buffeted by winds and tides, at a place other than planned. Chance is often fate's agent, that which furthers, often dramatically, some inner pattern tense with potential. Often some trivial event, perhaps a meeting, can have profound consequences because there is a resonance with some inner state ripe for development.[11] In mythology Mercury is often viewed as a trickster, and this seems to be one aspect of it: a synchronising phantom who manipulates circumstances to bring about that inner unfoldment that leads us to become what we essentially are.

It is the Virgo sense of helplessness that sets up a compensatory urge to make the environment a more comfortable, predictable place, one where men's minds rule, and not capricious Fate or Nature. Virgo is one of the signs traditionally related to agriculture, which was a major step in the evolution of man, for it necessitated settlements, long-term planning, and the development of skills and tools. Moreover, it eliminated the hand-to-mouth existence of hunting and foraging and so reduced man's susceptibility to chance. By the application of practical intelligence (or technology) man wrested power from Nature in the same way, but more efficiently, than his magic did.

In recent centuries science has been at the forefront of the civilising process, and in many ways has made the world a better place. But this has come at a price. The interface that once existed between man and the natural world has been eroded. The reasoning mind has prised the two apart and in the West we no longer live close to the soil and by the swing of the seasons. Some degree of distancing is necessary if we are to evolve in a positive way, but man is, whatever else, an organic creature, rooted in a subtle way in the energies of the living earth. Virgo in one guise manifests as this process of abstraction taken to extremes so that man cocoons himself in an artificial environment and suffers accordingly from both vital and spiritual inanition. This contrast between the 'civilised' world, and a pagan vitality is a common theme in Virgo writing. For example:

Leo Tolstoy
The contrast between the natural man and the spoiled product of sophisticated society deeply interested Tolstoy.[12]

John Knowles
Throughout all his writing there is a theme which most attracts John Knowles - it could be called wildness in the midst of civilisation.[13]

Gerd Gaiser
He believes that nature ... is man's source and his salvation which he ignores at his peril. Gaiser's heroes are those inevitably lonely individuals who understand this, who have not lost contact with nature.[14]

D H Lawrence
The great achievement of *The Rainbow* is its demonstration that man's power over nature, attained at the cost of an immense effort of abstraction and detachment, means a radical alienation from the life of nature.[15]

Sherwood Anderson
[Being compared to Lawrence] Both men were rebels against industrial civilisation with all of its implications, including the suppression and crippling of the natural exercise of sexual and all other emotions.[16]

Bernard Wolfe
Each of his works is a strong indictment of the life-denying impulses of our age.[17]

Maurice Maeterlinck
He wrote essays that reflect his profound understanding of the mysteries of matter and the need of modern man for unfathomable domains in his overly scientific, mechanised and industrial society.[18]

Virgo's repolarisation involves (to some degree) embracing mystery, disorder or uncertainty. What can induce this shift is a powerful sense of ennui, dissatisfaction with mundane experience and the sense that life is lacking some vital dimension. This is the shadow side of having everything routine and predictable: life gets very dull. What seem to proffer a solution to the ennui are things like adventure, religion, drugs, or perhaps the glamorous worlds of music, film and theatre. These things appear to contain something of the vital element that is missing from life. They appear portals to a life that promises freedom, creativity, spontaneity, vitality. Something like adventure is just the opposite of routine for it entails relinquishing control and trusting to chance. So the truer representation of Virgo is of a sign of order periodically interrupted by phases of disorder (in the broadest sense). Virgo soon enough creates out of the changed circumstances new order and routines. Thus we observe the sign as a spiral-like pattern of growth seeking to create order out of disorder at ever inclusive levels. And once again we observe the dialectic nature of the Mercury signs (although it is more apparent in Gemini): order gives birth to its contradiction, and vice versa.

The idea of an order-disorder polarity is common in Virgo literature and appears in a number of guises. We get stories set on the border of the mundane and the fantastic, when a perfectly logical and ordinary situation can slip unobtrusively into fantasy before returning once more to normality, almost as if nothing had happened. Some of H G Wells' stories feature this interplay, as does some of the work of Borges. In J B Priestley's *The Good Companions* the central theme is escape from a dreary life, when chance draws three individuals together and presents the opportunity of a life on the road with an ailing concert party. In Goethe's *Faust* the hero laments his arid life and seeks to connect with something more vital. The wager in this story revolves around the notion that interest in the material world can not be sustained, and this same idea seems to be at the heart of Samuel Johnson's *Rasselas* and *The Vanity of Human Wishes.*

More Virgo writing

William Golding, *Lord of the Flies, Pincher Martin, The Inheritors*

Lord of the Flies, Golding's first book, was written in a six-week period when he was 41. It is one of those legendary books that inspire would-be writers, for it was rejected by a number of publishers, including, at first, its eventual publisher Faber, whose reader apparently dismissed it as absurd and uninteresting fantasy. Nevertheless, it was rescued from the slush pile by a more perceptive employee, has since sold millions of copies, been translated into 28 languages and made into two films.

It is the story of a party of schoolboys marooned on a desert island following a plane crash. Their world – post-nuclear – seems to have destroyed itself through a surfeit of knowledge. They do not behave in the manner of other fictional marooned characters but instead divide into a 'civilised' faction, the commonsense thinkers intent on organisation and rescue, and a primitive faction, who become as savages, painting their bodies and skewering pigs. They are only prevented from slaying the civilised group by the timely arrival of adult rescuers. Coincident with the atavism is a fear of the unknown, which is anthropomorphised into a beast which must be stalked to its lair.

What Golding seems to suggest in this novel is that humans are not so different from animals. Most animals can be tamed, and yet this domestication is just a veneer. It is well known that even cats and dogs can become feral if they are removed from human proximity. Similarly, domestic pigs, if returned to the wild, will begin to take on the attributes of the wild variety.[19] As with other Virgo writing, we are presented with the idea that civilisation is only a pattern we impose upon a natural, vital and frightening world, an artificial order created by our reasoning intelligence.[20]

This is a theme taken up in *Pincher Martin*. This book employs a non-linear time sequence and for the most part is set out of time in a spaced-out split second between life and death. Apparently the action takes place on a desolate rock in the middle of the Atlantic, but in fact we witness the hallucination of a drowning sailor and, it transpires, a symbolic re-enactment of his life. The drama on the isolated rock stresses the appalling insignificance of a single person in a universe of immense natural forces. Nevertheless, Pincher Martin is convinced he can survive by using his intelligence. At one point he proclaims:

> I am netting down this rock with names and taming it ... What is given a name is given a seal, a chain. If this rock tries to adapt me to its ways I will refuse and adapt it to mine. I will impose my routine on it ... I will use my brain as a delicate machine tool to produce the results I want.[21]

He plainly has great faith in the power of the rational mind. He faces the angry sea and says: 'I don't claim to be a hero. But I've got health and education and intelligence.'

And later:

> The solution lies in intelligence. That is what distinguishes us from the helpless animals that are caught in their patterns of behaviours, both mental and physical.[22]

To exploit nature is to escape its patterns; if we stand still – like the 'savage' group in *Lord of the Flies* – we succumb. In one sense, *Pincher Martin* is the story of a man who is frightened to surrender, to the unknown, to mystery, and desperately tries to create his own ordered, solid, existence.

The Inheritors centres upon two tribes who represent stages in the development of modern man. It is set at that time in pre-history when Neanderthal Man was being usurped by Cro-Magnon. The Neanderthals are portrayed as heavy, simian creatures living close to the natural world. They use their feet as much as their hands to grasp and manipulate objects. Their thought processes are just beginning to develop, but most of the time they live unreflectively through their senses. They experience the world vividly, though are unable to make any sense of it. This ultimately is their downfall, for they are unable to adapt to a change of circumstances. The second tribe contrasts both physically and mentally with the primitives. In appearance they are more like modern man with refined features and high foreheads (emphasising cranial capacity), and have developed language and other skills, and through these, tools and weapons.

Most of the book is recounted through the eyes of the Neanderthals. The reader is placed at their experiential level, sharing the same confusion, the same struggle to comprehend. Toward the end of the book, however, the focus is transferred to the level of the second tribe and we are immediately struck by a sense of familiarity, for we are viewing life through mind. The thought processes of the 'civilised' tribe are relatively sophisticated and akin to our own. The shift in perspective provides an omniscient view of a situation hitherto not really comprehended, because the reader has been restricted to the primary sensual level of the Neanderthals.

The novel is basically about the primitive-civilised contrast, but also about fear of the unknown and the need to adapt to change. The rational tribe have built canoes and explored beyond their own territory. They have paddled up-river to the forests and mountains, which happen to be the summer resting ground of the Neanderthals. In the ensuing encounter the explorers are frightened into retreat, although not before they have exterminated the Neanderthals. The book ends with the Cro-Magnons homeward bound, glad to be drawing nearer their own familiar world and to be putting distance between themselves and a wilderness peopled by primitives.

Michael Frayn, *A Very Private Life*

This tale is set far in the future when the world has become broadly divided between the insiders, those who do the 'thinking, arguing, persuading', and outsiders who do the physical work necessary to sustain life. The insiders lead a hermetic existence, for the most part sealed off from the natural world and from the presence of other people. For 'private' we can read 'detached', 'removed' or 'insulated'.

In this world, the intelligent elite live in homes that function as controlled environments. Food, water, energy and entertainment enter through tubes from the outside world and nothing can enter their homes that has not been screened and purified. Drugs act as chemical firewalls to keep out unwanted feelings, such as unhappiness or discontent, while sex has ceased to become a physical activity (babies arrive, on request, through the tubes). Instead, couples use pills to create orgasms that are less to do with sensation, more to do with projection into a world of soaring fantasy and the creation of imaginative correlates to the visceral experience. In short, it is a sanitised world in which the inhabitants are protected from anything that might harm or unsettle them. Life inside is calm and ordered.[23] The insiders form

> part of a happy and secure world which stretches all over the globe. Step outside it and you're in another world altogether – the old primeval world ... where anything can happen.[24]

The insiders do not have to suffer the 'corruption of indiscriminate human contact'. Individuals communicate not in the flesh, but through the projection of holographic images. Even within an individual house walls are built to separate family members from one another. There is communication and relationship, but very little in the way of physical or emotional contact.

Unhappy in this world is the book's heroine, Uncumber. She is curious about the outside world and her urge to experience its reality is quickened by a chance encounter with one of its inhabitants on the holovison. She discovers a secret door in her home and one day escapes and has an adventure in the outside world. She is transported thousands of miles to a remote region and lives for some time in a primitive community, experiencing pain, cold, hunger, disease and the general squalor and disorder associated with the real world and its people. She meets up – in the flesh – with the man she encountered on the holovision and finds herself strongly attracted to him, even although he has many physical imperfections ('a body shaped by long and close contact with the world').

They have sex, in the natural, visceral, tactile way. It seems to give her little pleasure, but does mark the turning point in her adventure. Having lost her purity and experienced the earthy outside world, she returns once more to the controlled, sterile environment of home. We are left with the impression that she is still not content with the inside world, even though her encounter with nature was not a happy one.[25]

Ken Kesey, *One Flew Over the Cuckoo's Nest*

This novel tells the story of Randle McMurphy, a petty criminal who gets himself transferred from prison to a mental hospital in the hope of an easier time. It is the story of the impact he has upon the institution, particularly upon the antiseptic ward of Nurse Ratched. McMurphy is a strong character, vital and instinctual, in contrast to many of the other ward inmates, who suffer not from lunacy in the traditional sense but from an assortment of the trivial neuroses that Western industrial culture seems to spawn. Indeed, most are voluntary admissions; that they do not leave is because their fear of the outside world is stronger than their hatred of the ward.

At one point McMurphy proposes a deep-sea fishing expedition. Although this stimulates the inmates, there is still a fearful reluctance to give up the stupefying routine of the ward, even for a day. Nurse Ratched does her best to bolster these fears, but the trip goes ahead, and the inmates get a taste of freedom, and contact with an elemental activity. The outing seems to sow the seeds of dissatisfaction, for eventually a number of the inmates find the courage to challenge the nurse and leave the ward, although only after the sacrificial death of McMurphy.

Many critics have seen this work as allegorical. The inmates have cut themselves off from life, swapping a vital, perhaps hazardous, existence for something safe, dull and routine. The raunchy McMurphy is the emblem of a more vital – essentially earthy – existence. The story is seen through the eyes of one of the inmates, Chief Bromden, an American Indian. As an aborigine, one whose race was the victim of genocide, he represents that part of human nature that has been suppressed in the name of scientific and material conquest of the natural world.

Antonin Artaud

The theories of this French actor, dramatist and writer, born in 1896, had a major influence on European theatre. He is another example of a Virgo writer whose creative note turns upon the instinct-reason duality.

He wanted the theatre to be 'a double', or equivalent, to a vital life force that lay buried under layers of domestication and reasonableness. Artaud sought to develop a theatre that would strip away the bloodless reason that insulates people from this mode of existence. He wanted a theatre that would galvanise, shock and touch the audience at a primal level. As one critic has put it, Artaud's theatre

> is an assembly of human beings striving to establish contact with the profound mainsprings of their own being, the dark forces of physical emotion which lie beyond the trivialities of everyday existence.

The same critic also concludes:

> ... the one strand of total consistency that runs through [Artaud's] oeuvre – that it was the spirit of rationalism, analytical and discursive thought, formal logic and linguistic pedantry, which has desiccated the fullness of man's emotional life and cut him off from the profound sources of his vital being.[26]

When life is filtered through mind it becomes safe and comfortable. But if we bypass these systems of 'analytic and discursive thought' we find existence is not only vitalising, but also dangerous, inhuman, and cruel. Hence he called his art The Theatre of Cruelty. It was one that emphasised physicality over abstractions and language; it made use of primitive ritual, and communication based on rhythmic sound rather than words, because words, he believed, had lost contact with the reality they represented.

D H Lawrence, *The Rainbow*

This work, centred on a family and its generations, is primarily a parable of the civilising process, a contrast between a life linked to nature and one symbolised by the advancing industrialism of early 20th century England. The contrast between instinct and reason is established early on in the work. Instinct is personified by the family men, the urge to transcend it by the women. There were

> full built men, masterful enough, but easy, native to the earth, lacking outwardness and range of motion ... the teeming life of creation ... poured unresolved into their veins.[27]

The women, on the other hand, 'wanted another form of life than this, something that was not blood intimacy'. The Brangwen women

> looked out from the heated blind intercourse of farm life to the spoken world beyond. They were aware of the lips and mind of the world ... [they] faced outwards to where men moved dominant and creative having turned their back on the pulsing heat of creation, and with this behind them, were set out to discover what was beyond, to enlarge their own scope and freedom.[28]

The original Brangwen wife, we are told

> craved to achieve this higher being, if not in her self then in her children. That which makes man strong even if he be little and frail in body ... it was not money or power not position ... She decided it was a question of knowledge.[29]

It is Ursula who gains access to the domain of knowledge. She attends college and then works as a teacher. Yet her life does not bring contentment. School soon becomes a 'stupid, factitious duty' and a 'barren nothing'. The college professors are not, as she had hoped, 'priests initiated into the deep mysteries of life and knowledge', but simply middlemen passing on sterile and antiquated facts. The point of her college was not education or enlightenment, but passing exams so she would have a higher commercial value later down the line. Like Faust, Ursula finds only emptiness in her studies and in the common activities that seem to satisfy others. Her ennui is only finally quelled by the discovery of a new inner life.

Virgo is in one sense a kind of outward marker buoy within the zodiac. The zodiac is sometimes divided into two hemicycles, one (the personal) bounded by Aries and Virgo, the other (the transpersonal) by Libra and Pisces. The first relates to a process of differentiation, the process of becoming whereby Life unfolds into myriad form. Lawrence himself has written about this process of differentiation:

> It seems as though one of the conditions of life is, that life shall continually and progressively differentiate itself, almost as though this differentiation were a Purpose. Life starts crude and unspecified, a great Mass. And it proceeds to evolve out of that mass ever more distinct and definite particular forms, an ever-multiplying number of separate species and orders, as if it were working always to the production of the infinite numbers of perfect individuals, the individual so thorough that he should have nothing in common with other individuals. It is as if all coagulation must be loosened, as if all elements must work themselves pure and free from the compound.[30]

Virgo is the culmination of this process, so it symbolises Life fully expressed in form, but at the same time, most buried within it. In Virgo, we are at the point at which the journey back to Life or spirit must begin. The second half of the zodiac, as we will see in the following chapters, is more one of integration, with atomies becoming aggregates and then once more a homogeneous mass. So we have something of the crisis that is at the heart of Virgo: the discovery of life as an exhausted vein of material and mundane satisfaction.

In another sense, Virgo seems to represent a journey between nature and the spirit, through the mind – this is how the ancients viewed Mercury, this sign's ruler, as a kind of link between heaven and earth. But mind, intellect, is only a means, a journey, not a destination. There is no meaning to be found in mind in isolation. There is life in an instinctual existence and life in the spirit. But between the two, there is only disequilibrium, a movement between the known and the unknown. Part of the discovery of this inner, virgin, birth is the realisation that the individual's will is not paramount in the universe. This realisation is not borne of fear but of a limitation consciously, perhaps joyfully, accepted. Instead of the primitive's malignant crushing forces the perception is of a sustaining spirit which seeks only inclusion in a greater harmony. This is the experience of humility. This is the pot of gold that comes to Ursula at the end of *The Rainbow*, and also to other Virgoans both in life and literature.[31]

H G Wells

In Wells' early works the theme of escape is strong. We note it in books such as *Kipps* and *The History of Mr Polly*, and in *The Sea Lady* and *The Wonderful Visit*, where mythical creatures – a mermaid and an angel – materialise in the midst of ordinary lives as emblems of a magical realm. The theme of escape is also present in *The Time Machine*, although more essentially this story is about the contrast between the primitive and the civilised.

It tells the tale of a scientist who constructs a machine to transport himself into the distant future. He discovers a world populated by two races: the Eloi, an enfeebled people, the degenerate product of some distant civilisation; and the Morlocks, simian creatures who dwell underground but venture to the surface periodically to feed on the flesh of the Eloi. The book is a straightforward tale of the traveller's explorations and his friendship with one of the simple Eloi.

He finds a world where the civilising process has triumphed:

> The work of ameliorating the conditions of life – the true civilising process that makes life more and more secure – had gone steadily on to a climax. One triumph of a united humanity over nature had followed another ... the ideal of preventive medicine was attained. Diseases had been stamped out ... I saw mankind housed in splendid shelters, gloriously clothed, and as yet I had found them engaged in no toil.[32]

This is the realisation of the Virgoan dream, to make life safe, comfortable and certain through the scientific manipulation of nature. However, for all the creature comforts, something is far amiss in Wells' future. Beneath the simple contentment of the refined Eloi there is the predatory relationship with the primitive Morlocks. As man detaches from instinct and nature in order to gain some control over his world, as he puts mind between himself and his immediate experience, so a duality is established, which eventually becomes so polarised that inversion takes place. Primal forces begin to infiltrate the veneer of civilisation as the Morlocks crawl from their underground lair to feed on the Eloi. The decadent people, drained of their vital earthy forces, are powerless to help themselves.

The Time Machine is a prophetic work, although perhaps not quite in the way Wells imagined. If a nemesis stalked the Eloi then equally it does Western man, who still seeks the security of a subjugate nature and who still, by and large, worships on the altar of reason. Already the fissures seem very evident in our life-denying culture, and a number of times in the last century our civilisation was plunged into chaos by the forces of unreason. Further eruptions and more social sickness seem inevitable unless reason and instinct can establish a more wholesome relationship.

For forty years or more Wells was dominated by a single idea – The New World Order. When we examine this idea we find it once more reflects the symbolism of Virgo, particularly as it emphasises control over the natural world and a distaste for unreason in any form. It was an expression of the common Virgo characteristic to instil order into that which is perceived as disordered and inefficient. But equally we find the signature of Aquarius, which is strongly accented in Wells' natal chart, with the Moon and ascendant placed there.[33] Aquarius, whether through Sun, Moon or ascendant, is commonly connected to the desire to better society and contribute to it in a unique and inspirational way.

As Wells perceived it, mankind had reached the threshold of a new age. Immense energies were being released through the advance of science and technology, energies that held the promise of human betterment through their power to ameliorate toil and pain. What disturbed him, however, was the possibility that this potential might not be realised. As things stood, contemporary structures – man's systems and the mould of his mind – could not accommodate this new energy effectively, and unless steps were taken to establish a compatibility then mankind would be lost. In his utopianism, then, he was basically concerned with establishing a new system that could channel the new type of energies available to 20th-century man. His New World Order was in one sense simply a form capable of accommodating a new evolutionary impulse. It was to be a rationalist's paradise, governed by an intellectual elite. Thanks to science and technology it would be free from material want. It would also be free of emotion, woolly-mindedness, muddled thinking, indeed any type of unreason. It would be international, for nationalism was rooted in unreason and men destroyed themselves in its name, as they did in the name of religion – another irrationality that had no place in Wells' vision. Men would be bound by their common humanity and not by root loyalties. Even relationships would be rationalised. Sex would be free of taboo and the need for commitment; liberated free love would replace the mires of jealousy and possessiveness.

In some ways Wells' ideas seem sound enough and yet despite many millions of words and 40-odd years of application his vision was not encapsulated in a single great, enduring work capable of lighting men's minds. It is interesting to consider why. He was correct in his conclusion that the human race had reached a critical phase in its evolution, and indeed may have been one of the first to grasp this. He was also right, but only half so, in believing unreason to be destructive. As we are discovering to our increasing discomfort, it is an unhappy amalgam, the undigested remnants of an atavistic past and the immense power that has been released by the rational mind. He was mistaken, however, in believing that unreason could be theorised away. He should have known from his own tumultuous sex life that unruly passions do not respond to reasoned argument, and from his own first novel that you can not just bury primitive instincts.

He was only half right in his views on unreason because he only seemed to see one side – the dark side – of it. He did not appear to realise that it also contains in its fertile flux the seeds of creativity. Vision capable of moving men and of enduring beyond space and time lies in the 'irrational', and not in the ordered intellect. To deny one's 'unreasonable' side is to deny creativity and thus we have the dry, lifeless prose that forms a good amount of Wells' later output. In a sense, he epitomises Western Man with his towering intellect but spiritual and emotional paraplegia, and his inability to realise that the problems of the 21st century can only ever be solved with reference to higher levels of being. Book titles such as *Men Like Gods* underline the fact that Wells could not conceive of anything greater than rational man. His utopia was an end in itself, an earthly end, and one can not help but compare it to one of those medieval paintings of Heaven where life seems to be one long cathedral service. A life of free love and being terribly reasonable would surely prove equally as tedious.

Wells did leave a message for our salvation, but it has little to do with the New World Order. It is wholeness we must strive for and not the schizoid sundering of instinct and the rational mind. This was the message of *The Time Machine*, his first book. The work of his later life obscures rather than enhances this message.

Notes

1. The Virgo capacity for creating order out of disorder can manifest in many guises. In Dr Johnson's case it involved the English language, as the following extract, from the introduction to his dictionary, suggests:

> When I took the first survey of my undertaking, I found our speech copious without order, and energetic without rules; wherever I turned my view, there was complexity to be disentangled and confusion to be regulated; choice was to be made out of boundless variety, without any established principle of selection.

2. Robert Hand, in a perceptive essay on the symbolism of Mercury, talks of the planet as a modulator, something which imposes a pattern on what would be otherwise random and meaningless: 'For example, a pattern imposed upon radio waves converts the waves from being mere noise, through use of a carefully designed instrument, the radio receiver, into music or speech. Music and speech are examples of superimposing order on to intrinsically meaningless sound waves in order to give them significance in human consciousness.' (Originally published in *Journal of Geocosmic Research*, Vol 1, 2)

3. Anthony Burgess, *The Novel Now*, Faber & Faber, 1967, p65

4. W A Swanberg, *Dreiser*, Charles Scribner's Sons, p175

5. E W Mellown, 'Character and themes in the novels of Jean Rhys', in *Contemporary Women Novelists*, ed Patricia Meyer Spacks, Prentice Hall, 1977, p135

6. *European Writers*, Charles Scribner's Sons, Vol 7, 1985, p1548

7. *World Authors 1950-1970*, ed J Wakeman, H W Wilson, 1975, p147

8. *Contemporary Dramatists*, ed James Vinson, St James Press, 1977, p488

9. *Handbook of Austrian Literature*, Ungar Publishing, 1973, p271

10. *Dictionary of British Women Writers*, ed Janet Todd, Routledge, 1989, p618

11. In Robertson Davies' *The Fifth Business* it is a misdirected snowball that sets in motion three interconnected destinies. The work of Theodore Dreiser also focuses on characters buffeted by chance.

12. *Encyclopaedia Britannica*, vol 22, 1973, p63

13. *Contemporary Novelists*, ed James Vinson, St James Press, 1976, p766

14. *World Authors 1950-1970*, ed J Wakeman, H W Wilson, 1975, p518

15. Jacques Berthoud, 'The Rainbow as Experimental Novel', in *D H Lawrence*, ed A H Gomme, Harvester Press, 1978

16. *Twentieth Century Authors*, ed. S Kunitz and H Haycraft, H W Wilson, 1942

17. *Contemporary Novelists*, ed James Vinson, St James Press, 1976, p1537

18. *Encyclopaedia of World Literature in the Twentieth Century*, Vol 3, St James, 1999, p154

19. Rupert Sheldrake in *The Rebirth of Nature* (Century, 1990) writes:

> Many feral animals revert not only in behaviour, but in bodily form as well. Feral pigs, for example, become more bristly and tend to redevelop their tusks, while the coloured stripes of young wild pigs reappear in their young. (p 112)

Sheldrake also cites Darwin's observation in *The Variation of Animals and Plants Under Domestication*: 'We can only say that any change in the habits of life apparently favours a tendency, inherent or latent in the species, to return to their primitive state.'

20. Similar in essence are tales based on the character Tarzan, the creation of Virgoan Edgar Rice Burroughs.

21. William Golding, *Pincher Martin*, Faber & Faber, 1972, pp90-91

22, ibid, p81 and p177

23. *Stepford Wives*, by Ira Levin (a Virgo Sun) is not great literature and yet its central idea has lodged firmly in the contemporary consciousness. A Stepford wife is a bland, sanitised abstraction of a woman, somebody domesticated and submissive, untroubled by feelings or inner conflict

24. Michael Frayn, *A Very Private Life*, Dell Publishing, 1969, p20

25. Franz Werfel's final novel, *Star of the Unborn*, is a future vision of a world over-burdened with technology that has lost contact with the wellspring of nature

26. Martin Esslin, *Artaud*, Fontana Modern Masters, pp 83 & 108

27. D H Lawrence, *The Rainbow*, Penguin, 1974, p8

28. ibid, p9

29. ibid, p10

30. D H Lawrence, *Lawrence on Hardy and Painting*, Heinemann, 1973, p 43

31 For example, Levin in *Anna Karenina*. It is widely held that there is much of the author in Levin, who forms a good embodiment of the male Virgo character

32. H G Wells, *The Time Machine*, Everyman, 1969, p35

33. Wells' most enduring works are his early scientific romances and it is these that most obviously reflect the core meaning of Virgo. This is in line with what was said in the introduction about more consciously-wrought work – in this case Wells' social ideas – often reflecting the other major factors in a birth chart, while more inspired work bears the mark of the Sun

Libra

Writers with the Sun in Libra include: Peter Ackroyd, Alain-Fournier, Monica Ali, Louis Aragon, Louis Auchincloss, Jurek Becker, William Beckford, Italo Calvino, Truman Capote, Michael Crichton, Miguel de Cervantes, James Clavell, S T Coleridge, T S Eliot, William Faulkner, F Scott Fitzgerald, Elizabeth Gaskell, Caroline Gordon, Simon Gray, Graham Greene, Günter Grass, Frank Herbert, A L Kennedy, R D Laing, Ursula Le Guin, Doris Lessing, Katherine Mansfield, François Mauriac, E Y Meyer, Arthur Miller, Eugenio Montale, R K Narayan, Friedrich Nietzsche, Eugene O'Neill, Harold Pinter, J C Powys, Mario Puzo, Arthur Rimbaud, Claude Simon, Wallace Stevens, C P Snow, Gore Vidal, Irvine Welsh, Nathanael West, Oscar Wilde, P G Wodehouse.

Summary Libran characters often have to learn to establish a balance between self and others, but in the opposite way to Aries. Libra has to learn to be less deferential, less dependent upon others and upon social norms and expectations. Libran novels sometimes revolve around the family, particularly in the sense that the family unit forms a society in microcosm in which the individual learns how his or her actions affect others. There is a concern with values that have lost their meaning and can no longer harmonise a society. The second of the Venus signs shares with Taurus the theme of lost perfection and the need to restore the equilibrium or harmony in some way. Libran writers seem to be of the view that in a fallen world we need hope, a vision of something better.

> Some sort of divorce there has been along the long path of this race of man between the 'I' and the 'We', some sort of terrible falling away.
> **Doris Lessing** *Briefing for a Descent into Hell*

Libra is the seventh sign and in terms of overall structure it marks the beginning of the so-called transpersonal hemicycle of the zodiac, the phase where, symbolically, socialising forces *begin* to hold the balance at the expense of individualising ones. Rudhyar says of this sign:

> The entire purpose [of Libra] is that of making ... more tangible ... the reality of living together within an organic, stable, permanent structure of communal behaviour.[1]

Other writers have referred to it as a sign where the 'aspiration for return to unity' first becomes felt.[2] Libra can be thought of as part of a sequence of four signs beginning with Leo and ending in Scorpio. In this scheme the zodiac is split into three groups each containing a Fire, Earth, Air and Water sign. Aries, Taurus, Gemini and Cancer then form a personal quaternary, and Sagittarius, Capricorn, Aquarius and Pisces a collective one. The intermediate grouping forms a transition from one to the other and stands for the gradual assimilation of the individual into the collective. The first point of Libra marks the halfway stage in this process and brings the relationship of the individual to his environment into some sort of climax. Personal and collective are balanced at the autumn equinox, the first point of Libra. Therefore both the sense of being an individual and the urge to be associated with some larger grouping are strong. Individuality is not subsumed at this phase of the zodiac. It is the work of Libra and Scorpio, as it were, to prepare the individual for participation in collective life and so in both signs we find a focus upon community and communion. In Libra we have the first intimation of a sacred web of inter-relatedness, and a poignant awareness that individual actions affect other people. In Libra there may be guilt for putting self above others, but it is not until the next sign, Scorpio, that the real work of purging away the boundaries of the ego takes place.

While those whose birth charts are strong in Libra tend towards deference and putting others' happiness first,[3] more essentially Libra is about establishing a balance between self and others, or between self and the dictates of some external morality – between what 'I want' and what 'I ought or should'. Just as the polar sign Aries has to learn to temper selfish tendencies with a greater regard for the needs of others, so Librans are often faced with the task of developing will and self-reliance.

Representing, symbolically, the first stage of collective life Libra acts as an induction phase whereby the individual can, as it were, acclimatise through some microcosm which embodies the essentials of the social world on a limited scale. The family is one such microcosm and indeed forms a subject for many Libran writers. One who discusses it in some detail is R D Laing. Writing[4] in *The Politics of Experience*, he suggests that it is through the family that the individual is first made aware of the need for co-operation with others. The family is an example of what Laing calls a nexus, a group which is essentially bound by a subjective experience of 'we'. Its characteristics are those associated with Libra. Its highest ethic, Laing notes, is 'reciprocal concern'. Its essential feature 'is that every action of one person is expected to have reference to and influence everyone else'. The family can form a means by which thee and me come to be balanced. If the balance is wrong an individual might be crippled by his upbringing and mental illness *can*, believed Laing, be the result. Equally, a family can be supportive, and he utilised family-type communities for therapeutic purposes.

Libra, like Taurus, is associated with the planet Venus. This, as might be expected, imparts a common thread of meaning to the two signs although, at the same time, there remain significant differences. Libra is less concerned with the inner turmoil of desire and obsession that marks Taurus and more to do with collective harmony, while Libran concern with lost harmony is not focused on Eden but on the sky and Classical ideas of earthly forms that correspond to some heavenly 'idea'.

We noted in an earlier chapter that Venus represents that which creates harmony and order, as in cosmos from chaos and melody from noise. It symbolises the state of grace, or what some religions call the love of God, that transforms the experience of the world as ugly or evil into one of beauty, which reflects at the societal level as a harmonious order (which can all too easily be put out of kilter by the interference of men). Libra's symbol, the scales, suggests this connection with balance and harmony, although rather than representing balance, it is more accurately described as a sign where there is a striving to restore or obtain it. Thus we have a connection with guilt, sin, contrition, confession, punishment, vengeance (getting even), which are all to do with correcting an imbalance, something perceived as wrong, unjust or evil.

A common strand of much Libran writing is the urge to bridge the gap between the real and the ideal. The following writers (all Libran Suns) are just some examples:

Eugenio Montale

At the centre of his work is an anguished recognition of the distance between man's spiritual aspiration and his actual condition bound helplessly to the wheel of life ... The prevailing images of loneliness, exhaustion and despair ... are fitfully relieved by mysterious moments of revelation, poignantly elusive intimations of grace.[5]

T S Eliot
In his earlier poems he exposes the squalor, the pretentiousness, the dreadful triviality and disenchantment of space-time experience, with haunting suggestions of the spiritual reality he was to explore later.[6]

Francesco Jovine
[Of his major work] Its outstanding quality is the perfect balance that Jovine strikes between the fable-like memory of a remote past and the presentation of an ironic, crude reality.[7]

Erik Stagnelius
Central in his system [of philosophy] was the ancient concept of matter as something which had fallen away from the idea, the divine principle, and not until matter has again identified itself with the idea, or the divine principle, will the world of creation be able to slough off its terrifying burden of evil.[8]

William Faulkner
His entire body of work, with its explicit hatred of modern life and its attendant culture, bespeaks nostalgia for an Eden which he yearns for and yet knows can hardly be regained.[9]

François Mauriac
As a novelist he was torn between his vision of things as they were and his vision of things as they ought to be.[10]

Arthur Rimbaud
[In *Le Bateau Ivre*] we find all the nostalgic longing of human nature, its aspirations and its passionate desire to escape from outworn values and to sail towards new hopes.[11]

Libra relates to collective values, what are commonly called the mores, those beliefs held in common that give order to a society and constitute, in part, its morality. Libra equates to our sense of right and wrong, and thus to our sense of justice. It relates also to things such as ethics, attitudes and standards, and to behavioural codes, where there is a commonly-held honourable and right way to act.[12] We are not talking about the universal morality of the major religions (which is symbolised in astrology by Jupiter and its signs) but something more limited and secular. Venus represents a set of values which hold for a group, but not necessarily outside of it, and may even conflict with the values of the larger matrix of which the group is a part (we think of criminal codes, for example, honour amongst thieves). We have another link here with the scales, for when we weigh something we are comparing a certain property of it – its mass – to some accepted standard. One comedian who has generated a lot of humour from the mores is Sacha Baron Cohen (a Libran Sun). His Borat character is from Kazakhstan, where the accepted and 'normal' way of behaving is (apparently) very different from what it is in the countries he visits. In America or Britain he has little idea of what is the acceptable way of acting in a given social situation.

Also related to Libra are things such as decorum, manners, courtesy, etiquette and conduct. What we have with decorum is actions that are fitting for the situation, that is, in accord with a (generally) well-established consensus about what is right. All relate to Libra because they are concerned with oiling the wheels of social intercourse. Moreover, they all relate to the fact that Libra represents the *first* step into the social world, so there is what we might call an exaggerated attempt at socialising, at fitting in, at doing what is socially sanctioned. This aspect of Libra is well captured by Rudhyar[13] when he talks of the social eagerness of the sign, and a 'vital sense of dependence upon social values'.

Values are circumscribed by time as well as place; they eventually become outmoded. The work ethic had a use when the collective task was social amelioration. The values bred in 19th century English public schools were appropriate for a nation engaged in empire building, but they are hardly relevant today. Values become outmoded, becoming at first irrelevant then often positively destructive within a society they are supposed to be sustaining. Values need to be re-evaluated, or else they become ossified idols with no power to command assent. People just stop believing in them, things fall apart and the cry 'O tempora! O mores!' is widely heard. Libran writers – perhaps Nietzsche most famously – can be noted for challenging conventional values. This is the specific way in which Librans are rebels: they question, and sometimes bring about a change, in society's attitudes and values. Laing helped change society's attitudes towards madness, and he made the treatment of it more humane. Just as another Libran Sun, A S Neill (of Summerhill), changed society's attitudes towards education and made school a happier place for children.

More Libran writing

Mario Puzo, *The Godfather*

In the character of Don Vito Corleone, the Godfather, we detect a number of traits associated with Libra. On the surface he's a gentleman, polite, gracious and courteous, and his power is rooted in his ability to charm judges, policemen and politicians. He deplores the crude methods of his eldest son Santino, who in the book is often referred to as a hothead (and is Aries in character, Libra's polar sign). Puzo's Moon is in Scorpio and in Don Corleone's strength and ruthlessness we see something of the influences of this sign. But more essentially he is Libra. He favours co-operation because he appreciates that the criminal fraternity as a whole benefits from peaceful co-existence. He is feared, certainly, yet on balance rules through Venus rather than Mars, through reverence, respect, affection, even. And he respects (and is an embodiment of) the traditions, values and moral codes of Sicily, where he was born and spent time as a boy.

Indeed, pivotal to the whole book is a moral choice: whether or not to deal in drugs. In Don Corleone's moral universe selling drugs is wrong. He is quite happy to operate gambling and prostitution rackets, which although regarded as immoral by some are in his view simply harmless manly vices. However, he is unable to adapt to changing times and circumstances. Had his judgement not been clouded by the values of his own past, he would have seen that the future of organised crime lay in the trafficking of hard drugs. But his refusal to co-operate brings about a fall from grace, war between the rival families, the death of his eldest son, and finally the effective destruction of his family.

Other Libran themes permeate the *Godfather* saga. It is about the importance of family, not just blood relationships, but the whole extended network of those who depend upon it, and whose loyalty is to this group rather than to the society of which it is a part. Ideas of justice and revenge are strong (and the point is made that Don Corleone represents justice rather than the law, which too often seems divorced from what is fair and right). But perhaps more than anything the work is the story of a decline in values.

The work begins with that very potent symbol of harmony, a wedding. At the outset, Sicilian traditions still order life to a great extent; children respect their parents and their elders, there is honour, albeit amongst murderers and thieves. The code of values by which Don Corleone lives may be flawed and circumscribed, but we can't help thinking that it shines in comparison to what follows when the ties of family and community dissolve, when brother murders brother and when even the most sacred code – Omerta, the code of silence – is transgressed.

As generations of Italians become assimilated into American life, so their traditional values are diluted and no longer have the power to bind in a cohesive and harmonious whole. And contemporary America has nothing to put in their place, or rather has only hollow values. When we think about it, the *Godfather* saga is a scarifying indictment of modern America. For the implication is that America has corrupted the Mafia, rather than the other way around.

F Scott Fitzgerald, *The Great Gatsby,*

The narrator of this book tells us that Jay Gatsby had 'an extraordinary gift for hope ... such as I have never found in any other person'.[14] His hope was to meet a woman he never stopped loving and to recapture a rare moment of enchantment they shared. We learn that Gatsby had humble beginnings but received a leg-up in life from a wealthy man. We are told of the time he rowed across the lake to the man's yacht, which to Gatsby represented 'all the beauty and glamour in the world'. It was a hint of the 'unreality of reality', and proof that 'the rock of the world was founded securely on a fairy's wing'.[15]

Gatsby joins the army and while stationed in Kentucky he meets and falls in love with Daisy. He describes a magical moment, not long before he leaves to fight in the Great War, an autumn evening, cool with mysterious excitement, when leaves were falling and the streets were white with moonlight. For Gatsby 'the world flowed with an incomparable milk of wonder', and when he kissed Daisy, his 'unutterable visions' were wedded to her. 'She blossomed for him like a flower and the incarnation was complete.'[16] Never mind, as we come to discover, that Daisy is a far from perfect human being. For Gatsby she is an enchanted object, one that haunts him and for five years he pursues his quest to be reunited with his beloved.[17]

When Gatsby returns from the war he discovers Daisy has married Tom Buchanan. This represents a dreadful loss. From that moment, we are told, his life became confused and disordered, its focus one of restoring a harmony, that state of being he experienced that Kentucky night, and a state that seems so vital to sustain Libra and whose absence leaves such a dreadful hunger. Gatsby does what he believes is necessary to recover his loss. He cultivates a certain image and attains great wealth, so that social position will not be a barrier when he and Daisy are reunited, as they are in due course. And yet almost as soon as dream and reality come together the spell is broken. For Libra it seems that it is hope itself that is paramount, almost as if it is this that forms a bridge to the air of a finer place. It is the attempt to restore, rather than the restoration, that constitutes the Libran experience. Gatsby pays the price for living with a single dream, and when he is face to face with reality:

> He must have looked up at the unfamiliar sky through frightening leaves and shivered as he found what a grotesque thing a rose is and how raw the sunlight was upon scarcely created grass. A new world, material without being real, where poor ghosts, breathing dreams like air, drifted fortuitously about.[18]

Yet the disillusionment hardly has time to seed, for Gatsby is shot by the deranged husband of Tom Buchanan's lover, in the mistaken belief he was responsible for her death.

Alain-Fournier, *Le Grand Meaulnes* (or *The Lost Domain)*
This is another work whose theme is enchantment and the search for the beloved. Set in 19th-century rural France, it is the story of a youth, Augustin Meaulnes, who skips school one afternoon, loses his way while driving a carriage, and strays into a secluded manor house, or 'domain', where something strange, but mysterious and wonderful, is happening. Like Augustin, we don't know quite what until fragmentary sights and sounds coalesce into a pattern. The domain is owned by the de Galais family and preparations are afoot for the nuptials of the son, Frantz, a romantic and fanciful young man who has ordained that all should be arranged like a palace *en fête*.

There is a delightful magical quality to this episode, one that lifts the whole book. The house is full of old and fascinating objects and theatrical costumes. Augustin dresses in the clothes of a romantic student and later sees reflected in some water another Meaulnes, 'not the collegian who made off in the farmer's cariole, but a charming and fabulous creature out of a book'.[19] There are clowns, masquerades, revelry, games, music, feasting. As in a season of misrule, it is groups of noisy, joyous children who direct proceedings. Likewise the seasons themselves seem out of kilter, for although midwinter, the days are as mild and bright as early spring. For Augustin it was two days of 'grace and marvels', of 'deep and wonderfully peaceful contentment'.

In the course of his stay Augustin meets the groom's sister, Yvonne, and the memory of this woman haunts him after he has left the domain. As with Gatsby, an ephemeral moment of perfect happiness becomes welded to the figure of a flesh-and-blood woman. We noted a similar phenomenon in the literature of the other Venus-ruled sign, Taurus, specifically in *Lolita*, but in Earthy Taurus, rather than yearning and wistful hope, we have lust and obsession. But all are expressions of Venus.

The festivities at the domain are ended by news that the marriage is not to go ahead after all. The young bride has changed her mind (and we learn later this is because she feels unworthy, because she realises Franzt sees not her, but his own idealised projection). The sounds of happy children give way to the vulgar shouts of coachmen and the cacophony of a hundred coaches preparing to leave. The gay lanterns are extinguished, and Augustin swaps the romantic garb for his shabby schoolboy attire before returning to his school, some miles distant from the domain.

Augustin's whole existence then becomes focused upon returning to the lost domain and recapturing the happiness associated with it. While still at school he spends his free time studying maps and scouring the countryside, but without success. He moves to Paris to continue his studies and here learns of the whereabouts of Yvonne de Galais, although he does not manage to meet her. However, in time, the two are reunited, at a picnic. It is not a particularly happy or auspicious occasion, for Augustin learns that the domain has largely been destroyed. He marries Yvonne, yet remains restless. He leaves their home in order to honour a promise to Frantz to help reunite him with the woman, Valentine, who jilted him, and whom, it transpires, Augustin had an affair with in Paris.

In a literary sense this is not an altogether convincing development, but it does make sense in astrological terms. It is characteristic of Libra to try to arrange others' happiness. It is also a sign where (as we have observed) it is the striving for, rather than the attainment of, happiness that is important. Augustin's yearning is rooted not so much in Yvonne as in the lost domain.[20] And not so much in the physical place as in the joy (however transitory) it represents. As he remarks:

> I am sure now that when I discovered the nameless domain I was at some peak of perfection, of purity, to which I shall never again attain. Only in death ... can I expect to recapture the beauty of that moment.[21]

In a way, by helping Frantz, Augustin is attempting to restore a lost harmony – indeed, he talks at one point of 'a great wrong' to be put right. Augustin's joyful time at the domain had to come to an end some time, but what in fact broke the spell was the change of heart by Valentine. Peace for Augustin can come in restoring the harmony by reuniting the young lovers who were responsible for it in the first place.

Arthur Miller, *After the Fall, The Crucible, All My Sons*
Arthur Miller is a dramatist whose theme is often 'unrelatedness'. Dominating the stage in *After the Fall* is a blasted stone tower from a Nazi concentration camp, a symbol of the consequences of the failure of love (in the broadest sense) and of the putrefaction that occurs in the absence in collective life of the Venus principle. The play is centred in the consciousness of one man and is an examination through flashback and memory of his attempts to relate to others. In the course of his self-analysis he becomes stripped of his illusions,

particularly regarding his own innocence in the events that have befallen his life and those of others. He is forced to conclude that each individual is ultimately to blame for the Fall and must take up the responsibility of creating anew a sacred web of relationship.

The Crucible is based on historical incidents, the persecution of those accused of witchcraft in 17th-century New England, and is also a thinly-veiled attack on McCarthyism. But it is also a play that reflects Libran themes:

1. Vengeance, which is what seems to motivate Abigail.
2. Lust disrupts the social harmony. The community is put out of kilter when someone 'sins' by committing adultery.
3. Family good is put above a greater good at a critical point of the play. Proctor has confessed to adultery and accused Abigail of being a harlot. The court seems swayed, but demands the corroboration of Proctor's wife, who is known to be an honest and truthful woman. If she confirms what is true, the hangings and the whole ghastly business will stop. The harmony will be restored. Yet rather than speaking truthfully she chooses to protect the good name of her husband.

All My Sons is likewise a play about social responsibility. It is the story of a family, and of a man who, like Elizabeth Proctor, puts what is good for his family above a greater good.

Joe Keller has built up a successful engineering business. During the Second World War he wins a lucrative government contract to manufacture cylinder heads for aircraft engines. One batch emerges from casting with hairline cracks, but, because of the pressure of wartime production, the flaws are simply masked and the heads forwarded to a fabrication plant and installed into aircraft. The planes are shipped to the Pacific Theatre, where they eventually crash, killing in all 21 pilots. Prosecution follows, but Joe's business partner gets the bulk of the blame and is sent to prison. Joe's justification not to scrap the defective batch is his family's welfare. But painful facts emerge in the course of the play that force him to acknowledge his flawed judgement.

Joe has two sons, Chris, and Larry, who is presumed dead. Chris is a man trapped by his mother's pipedream. He wants to marry his brother's sweetheart, but mother objects because she harbours the hope that Larry, whose plane was reported missing in action in the Pacific, is still alive. It is important for her to keep this hope alive, for once she accepts that he is dead she must also accept the unpalatable fact that it was her husband who killed him. Chris is also an idealist, a man sensitive to the 'rottenness' of the world. He commanded a company in the war, and saw many of the soldiers die because they were prepared to work for each other and for the common good:

> They didn't die; they killed themselves for each other. I mean that exactly; a little more selfish and they'd 've been here today. And I got an idea – watching them go down. Everything was being destroyed, see, but it seemed to me that one new thing was made. A kind of – responsibility. Man for man ... To show that, to bring that on to the earth again like some kind of monument ... then I came home and it was incredible. I – there was no meaning in it here.[22]

Thus the redemptive dream of Libra: otherness, interdependence, relatedness. Chris is rapidly disillusioned, no more so than by the capitalist system and men like his father who basically used the war for personal and selfish gain. Larry, it transpires, committed suicide when he learned of his father's role in the shipping of the engine parts. The revelation of this, more than anything, brings home to Joe that his real responsibility in the situation was not to his family, and his two sons, but to the rest of his 'sons' – All My Sons – the 21 young pilots who died.

James Clavell, *King Rat*

King Rat, set in 1945 in a Japanese prisoner-of-war camp, is a work that focuses on the contrast between individual survival and collective values. Order in the camp is kept not only by the Japanese, but also by British rules, which are founded upon British values of fair play, honour and consideration to others. The man charged with applying camp law is the twisted and much-hated Lieutenant Grey.

The other two central characters of the book, the King of the title and Marlowe, form an antithesis. The King knows nothing of fairness. Everything is fair if it allows him to live a more comfortable existence than his fellows. He buys, sells, procures and basically lives in relative affluence. He eats well, dresses well and has the best of the comforts that are available. At the same time, because of camp law that tries to prevent this sort of individualism, he is dogged by Grey. Apart from himself the only other individual the King shows any real regard for is Marlowe, an English officer. The two men are poles apart in their attitudes and yet are fascinated by one another. Marlowe is the embodiment of traditional Libran values, such as honour and fair play. He helps the King in some of his dealing (as a translator mostly) and yet feels guilt and self-disgust about making money in the circumstances. The King, an American, can not understand why the British think it vulgar to make money. For the King, everything has a price. He's proud of his money-making ability, and proud of the fact that he survives better than anyone else, because it means he's a better man. However, while people respect the King, no one really likes him.

Marlowe is a touch deluded, something of a Don Quixote struggling to keep alive civilised values, even if these are inappropriate in the barbaric circumstances. Grey is an officer but of humble origins and counters his insecurity through his role as an upholder of 'civilised' law. The King has abandoned values, because they get in the way of his survival.

Another Libran novel whose theme is men in a hellish situation, in this case the Warsaw Ghetto, is Jurek Becker's *Jakob the Liar.* It tells of a man who, by chance, overhears news of Russian troop movements and passes it on to his friends, pretending he heard it on his own radio. Soon he is pestered daily for the news that freedom is not far off. At first he feels guilty about lying, but comes to realise that false though the reports are, they are valuable because they sustain spirits. He represents hope in a hopeless situation, the faintest band of light on the dark horizon. At one point, desperate for some real information, Jakob sneaks into a German latrine to steal the squares of newspaper the soldiers use as toilet paper. As he is formulating his plan we get an insight into his motives:

> If all goes well I'll carry off a few grams of news and turn it into a ton of hope for you ... I'll do it for you my brothers, for you and myself ... for one thing is certain: I can't survive as an individual, only together with you.[23]

Libra represents the white lie, a resort to avoid confronting an individual with an unpleasant truth because we are reluctant to hurt him or her – or destroy hope. It also stands for the pipedream, a concept given memorable expression by Eugene O'Neill.

Eugene O'Neill, *The Iceman Cometh*

This play is set in 1912 in a New York waterside bar and rooming house, referred to facetiously at one point as 'The Palace of Pipedreams'. Harry Hope is the proprietor, the patrons a motley collection of failures, has-beens, alcoholics and rebellious outcasts. Most of them do indeed harbour a pipedream, which can be defined as a hope for tomorrow, but at the same time – in the case of these characters – a pining for the past, a yearning to restore a lost contentment, built upon an active role in society. Many fell from grace, either through the death of a partner, or because of a weakness for drink, or because of greed and temptation.

They sit in the bar and drink and dream, this indecisive, procrastinating collection of friends, the gang, as it is frequently referred to. It is a little world, all but isolated from the outside. It is static, complacent, irresolute, but basically content and harmonious. It is significant that any real anger is only directed towards outsiders. Within the group an outburst is almost always immediately followed by guilt and regret, and an attempt, however clumsy, to restore the harmony.

The small world of the bar has certain bridges to the outside world, people who come and go. There are three prostitutes, and there is the travelling salesman Hickey, who is the pivot of the play. The title of the work is also suggestive of this idea of a small world, distinct from yet connected to a larger sphere. The iceman in O'Neill's day occupied the same place in popular culture as the milkman or postman does today, a link between the home and what's beyond it, a source of gossip, information and sexual opportunity. The author himself has said there is an allusion in the title to the old joke:

> Husband (calling to wife): Has the iceman come yet?
> Wife: No, but he's breathing hard.

It has become a tradition that Hickey visits the bar every year on Harry Hope's birthday. It is an event much anticipated, on account of the salesman's generosity and ebullient personality. But the Hickey who arrives on this occasion is a changed man. He is not interested in drink and roistering, but appears to have undergone a kind of religious conversion. He tells them he is at peace with himself and attributes this to giving up his pipedream, 'lying hopes which nag and reproach', and which prevent a man from being at ease with himself. Now, in the spirit of friendship, he is here to help the gang give up their pipedreams. In one sense we see Hickey here exhibiting the common Libran trait of trying to arrange others' happiness.[24] We can also see him as a Nietzschean iconoclast, as he has come to shake the bar patrons from their false values and make them once more individuals capable of self-determination. But as we discover, this little community does not want to be broken up, even though the cement that binds it is based on palpable falsehoods.

The first part of Hickey's plan is straightforward. He gets the bar's patrons to do what they are always saying they are going to do. He forces the agoraphobic Harry to leave the bar to visit old friends in the locality. He enjoins others to take up old jobs and professions. They make feeble attempts – or none at all – to turn their pipedreams into reality, and then return to the bar, just as Hickey anticipated. According to his plan they should now feel free and content, because they have proved to themselves the lie of the pipedream. Yet they are not happy. Hickey has only succeeded in sowing seeds of discord.

Despite his self-assurance, Hickey's gospel turns out to be false, and it is instructive to consider why. Partly he misunderstands the nature of the pipedream. In the enclosed world of the bar the pipedream is essentially harmless; it has no consequence in the outside world, and is not tied up with the dynamic of a relationship. But in Hickey's case it is.

He does not have a pipedream as such, but experiences it indirectly, through his wife. Hickey drinks and philanders. This hurts his wife, but she forgives him, and she lives in the hope – her pipedream – that one day he will reform and they will live in marital happiness. But because she forgives so readily he is often racked by guilt, not so much because he believes the things he does to be wrong, but simply because his wife suffers because of him. Because he sins against his wife and is forgiven rather than punished, his guilt mounts and his sense of self-worth plummets. Hickey ends up murdering his wife because he believes this will end her suffering and also give him peace. It also instils in him his jaundiced view of the pipedream. The gang become convinced of Hickey's madness, and indeed his does seem to be a pathological logic.

In the eyes of the world Hickey's wife seemed perfect. Besides any physical attributes, she was loving, forgiving and supportive. Yet Hickey destroys her because, in essence, he feels unworthy.

Guilt strives for its complement, punishment, and in the end we can assume that Hickey finds contentment in the electric chair. The fact that Hickey has been deemed mad by the gang defuses him of the power to disturb the equilibrium. They take up their pipedreams once more. What O'Neill seems to suggest is that we need pipedreams, because they make life tolerable. Life with them is better than life without them, and that's their justification. Libra is a sign whose essence is a *striving* to attain something wonderful, which never turns out to be so wonderful once the hope or wish is realised.[25]

Doris Lessing, *Briefing for a Descent into Hell*

The hell of the title is not the biblical one, but rather the gross physical world as we know it. We are kept in thrall to this reality by a kind of slumber and if we can but 'wake up' we will find ourselves somewhere altogether more elevated.

The work centres on a Cambridge professor, Charles Watkins, who, apparently suffering from mental illness, is admitted to hospital and placed under the observation of two doctors. On a straightforward level the book is an account of the gradual piecing together of the patient's circumstances, and his eventual 'cure' and return to 'normal' life. But the novel also raises questions about contemporary concepts of mental illness and the way it is treated. Some of what is called mental illness today is indeed unwholesome, because it is the outcrop of a way of life that denies wholeness. Madness in primitive cultures is different. It is recognised that this state *can* be the product of great lucidity, and accordingly the lunatic is treated with a certain reverence. Charles Watkins' condition seems to accord more to the primitive concept of madness. He has slipped into a super- rather than a sub-normal state, and it is significant that neither Dr X nor Dr Y in the story can tell the difference.

In between bouts of medical interrogation the novel describes scenes of fantasy. In the first such episode a pattern of exile and redemption is quite apparent. As in *The Rime of the Ancient Mariner*, a forsaken castaway drifts on an ocean in a corrupted world. He finds his way to land, and thence to a high plateau to prepare for his redemption, which is described in the book as being absorbed by the 'crystal'. It is an evil place, this plateau, one of the familiar 'fallen' Libran landscapes; it is portrayed in strong images of atavistic rites, cannibalism, sexual frenzy and bloody childbirth. But somehow the castaway is eventually absorbed through the crystal into the keener air of an elevated reality. From here he perceives things very differently:

> It was as if the city of stone and clay had dissolved leaving a ghostly city, made in light, like an illuminated mist ... this tenuous city, which was a pattern and a key and a blueprint for the outer city.[26]

He notes the same of his body, that there was an ethereal envelope associated with the physical substance, and we can recall here the descriptions of Venus as a kind of electromagnetic core that underlies and patterns matter, and as the planetary symbol of the astral world, the realm of formative forces associated with the world of senses.

The castaway observes that planet Earth has its own aureole, which surrounds and also permeates it to some extent, shining within fissures of its solid substance like seams of metal ore. There are bridging points between the etheric envelope and the solid globe to allow the finer energy to nourish the denser. Certain individuals – artists, for example – and groups are also seen as channels where the finer air enters the Earth. Within the aureole he observes patterns of 'mind currents' moving about like coloured globules of immiscible liquid, and the overall impression of this realm is of inter-connectedness. The idea of unity and interdependence is extended as the castaway shifts his attention to the solar system itself and observes the interaction of planets and how the meshing of their aureoles can influence the Earth's field.

We are given the first clues to the real nature of Charles Watkins' condition with the introduction of the idea that the universe is being nurtured by sentient beings. In some kind of conference chamber individuals are being primed by planetary-type deities for their descent into 'hell'. The purpose of the descent, we learn, is to keep alive in any way possible the notion of humanity functioning as a whole system, and as a small chord in a greater harmony. If people forget this and are motivated instead by selfish drives then the stability of the universe is threatened – thus the concern of the celestial guardians.

Watkins appears to be one of those making the descent and his condition accords with a warning given at the briefing: 'You will wake up, as it were, but there will be a period while you are waking which will be like the recovery from an illness.'[27] His so-called mental illness is his remembering the reality from which he descended and his mission to remind others of their sleep. What seems to precipitate his recall, what unlocks the imprinted briefing, is a lengthy missive, presumably from one of his fellow missionaries. It contains a number of anecdotal accounts which mirror the details of the briefing – references to group kinships, harmony with nature, the great gulf which exists between ideals and reality – in themselves innocuous, but pieced together by the professor, they unlock the riches of his memory and catapult him into his prelapsarian state of awareness.

Many make the descent but most forget why they came, or are simply corrupted by the world. Charles Watkins comes closer than most to accomplishing his mission but in the end submits to electric shock treatment. His memory is once more erased. From the letters he writes in the last pages of the book it is apparent he is functioning as any normal professor does. Ironically, he comments in one of them: 'I seem to be in full possession of my faculties again.'

The novel has close parallels with some of Laing's ideas, specifically his notion that what we call normality is in fact a denial of a greater reality, a state of sleep brought about largely by social conditioning. He believes some mental illness is simply one of the ways in which the light begins 'to break through the cracks in our all-too-closed minds'.[28] The inner world has become so devalued in our culture, he believes, that fantasy is held to be pathological. He writes of the voyage that can be the schizophrenic experience and pleads 'can we not see that this voyage is not what we need to be cured of, but that it is itself a natural way of healing our own appalling state of alienation called normality'.[29]

Briefing for a Descent into Hell is not an immediately accessible book and indeed it can be difficult to appreciate unless there is some familiarity with what might be called the occult concepts underlying it. Certainly it is a novel that shines better for the burnish of astrological insight.

Notes

1. Dane Rudhyar, *Astrological Signs: The Pulse of Life*, Shambhala Publications, 1978, p81

2. Edward Matchett and Sir George Trevelyan, *12 Seats at the Round Table*, Neville Spearman, 1976, p44

3. The first English words learned by Monica Ali's Bangladeshi heroine in *Brick Lane* are 'sorry' and 'thank you' which captures quite well the sign's exaggerated social concern. This work is the story of a young woman, who at first accepts the role that is expected of her in her culture but learns to become more independent.

4. R D Laing, *The Politics of Experience and the Bird of Paradise*, Penguin, 1984, pp 74-75

5. *World Authors 1950-70*, ed. J Wakeman, H W Wilson, 1975, p1013

6. *Cassell's Encyclopedia of Literature*, vol 2, ed S H Steinberg, Cassell, 1953, p1771

7. *Columbia Dictionary of Modern World Literature*, ed J Bédé and W Edgerton, Columbia University Press, 1980, p414

8. Alrik Gustafson, *A History of Swedish Literature*, University of Minnesota Press, 1961, p193

9. Frederic R Karl, *William Faulkner: American Writer*, Faber & Faber, 1989, p21

10. Robert Speaight, *François Mauriac, a Study of the Writer and Man*, Chatto & Windus, 1976

11. Enid Starkie, *Rimbaud*, Faber & Faber, 1973, p445

12. Codes of behaviour are often the theme of Libran novels. Caroline Gordon and William Faulkner, for example, write of the values of the Old South. Louis Auchincloss' subject is the codes and families of New York's aristocracy. He has written of what he calls the 'organicism' of society, where the will of the individual is invested in the whole. This organicism he observes in families, in clubs, but more generally in any institution where a consensus judgement about behaviour is formulated.

13. Dane Rudhyar, *Astrological Signs: The Pulse of Life*, Shambhala Publications, 1978, p81

14. Scott Fitzgerald, *The Great Gatsby*, Penguin, 1970, p8

15. ibid, p106

16. ibid, p118

17. Don Quixote is another Libran creation who dreams of finding his beloved. He is an ageing gentleman, we are told, who loses his wits reading books about chivalry. He begins to perceive the world very differently from those around him. Instead of a windmill he sees a giant; a country inn becomes a castle; a flock of sheep warring armies; slaves gentlemen in distress. His beloved, Dulcinea, is in fact an ugly peasant girl. A clue to Don Quixote's

condition comes in a remark he makes to his companion Sancho Panza: 'I was born into this iron age of ours to revive the age of gold.' However, the chivalric age he hoped to revive existed only in legend, although it still serves to set the standard for Don Quixote. This looking back is characteristic of Libra. Like other Librans, in life and literature, Don Quixote is working to re-create a lost harmony by creating positive values in the degraded world he sees about him.

18. F Scott Fitzgerald, *The Great Gatsby,* Penguin, 1970, p168

19. Alain-Fournier, *Le Grand Meaulnes,* Penguin, 1982, p62

20. Charles Carter is one of the few astrologers to refer to this aspect of Libra. In *Essays on the Foundations of Astrology* (Theosophical Publishing House, 1978) he talks of the sense of yearning that goes with the sign: 'Libra is haunted by a sense of exile, of weeping by the waters of Babylon' (p129). He goes on:

> Always there is an undercurrent of patient endurance, the memory of an ancient wrong done or suffered. Something in the remote past that went awry, so that ever since nothing has ever been quite as it should be. Some mysterious happening that the Christian religion calls the Fall.

21. *Le Grand Meaulnes*, p148

22. Arthur Miller, *All My Sons*, Penguin Books, 1982, p121

23. Jurek Becker, *Jakob the Liar*, Picador, 1990 p75

24. In Graham Greene's *The Heart of the Matter* the central character – 'based on nothing but my own unconscious' the author notes in the introduction – is a man who is damned by his attempts to arrange others' happiness. We are told: 'he wanted happiness for others and solitude and peace for himself'. And he prays at one point: 'O God, give me death before I give them unhappiness.' He is eventually driven to suicide by the weight of social responsibility he feels. He even engineers his own death to make it appear natural, in order to prevent embarrassment to his friends and relatives. Other Libran themes are to be found in this novel, notably the awakening to the knowledge that personal action has moment in the world. (Introduction to 1971 Heinemann edition; Vintage, 2004, p174)

25. Libra is not the only idealist of the zodiac; Sagittarius and Pisces are two other signs where idealism is marked. There is common ground between the three, but also fine distinction. Both Piscean and Libran idealists aspire to something that lies beyond the tangible world, but Pisces seems more often to look forward to some imagined future which will transfigure the problems and suffering of the present, while there is something of the heroic about Sagittarius, in that it is able to embody what men dream (which is less true of Libra and Pisces). Piscean and Sagittarian writers generally conclude that we must relinquish our dreams, or at least temper them with reality. Libran writers, on the other hand, believe we need more rather than less ideal.

26. Doris Lessing, *Briefing for a Descent into Hell*, Flamingo, 2002, p89

27. ibid, p124

28. R D Laing, *The Politics of Experience and the Bird of Paradise*, Penguin, 1978, p107

29. ibid, p136

Scorpio

Writers with the Sun in Scorpio include: Margaret Atwood, Beryl Bainbridge, J G Ballard, John Berger, John Berryman, Edmund Blunden, Henri Bosco, Karin Boye, Albert Camus, Stephen Crane, Fyodor Dostoyevsky, George Eliot, David Ely, Howard Fast, Carlos Fuentes, Maggie Gee, André Gide, Jean Giraudoux, George Gissing, Nadine Gordimer, Gerhart Hauptmann, John Keats, Kazuo Ishiguro, Wyndham Lewis, André Malraux, Charlotte Mew, Naomi Mitchison, Robert Musil, Sylvia Plath, Ezra Pound, Johann Schiller, Anna Seghers, Anne Sexton, Robert Louis Stevenson, Dylan Thomas, Paul Valéry, Voltaire (François-Marie Arouet), Kurt Vonnegut, Evelyn Waugh, Peter Weiss.

Summary: Sex and death, as tradition suggests, are common themes in this sign, and Scorpio is also strongly attuned to the natural world. Light and dark within the individual, and the need to confront evil and injustice, are strong themes. The urge to remain an individual separate from the rest of humanity is fast being eroded in this phase of the zodiac, and this can form the core of a Scorpio crisis. Characters struggle against forces that work to pull a proud, isolated ego down into a kind of underworld, a common stratum of human feeling and experience. One outcome of this is the development of empathy for human suffering. Scorpio characters often have to learn that human welfare is more important than legal, religious or political dogma.

> What it comes to is that truth is not a crystal one can put in one's pocket, but an infinite fluid into which one falls headlong.
> **Robert Musil**

Scorpio is one of the autumn signs, that season when many of the visible forms of nature decay. It is a season of death, but death as a prelude to regeneration and rebirth. Decay releases a life force, which is held underground and re-emerges the following spring in Taurus, Scorpio's polar sign. As well as relating to those mysterious laws that govern the cycle of life and death, Scorpio symbolises a sub-stratum of nature, a sort of vital juice that animates organic life. This side of the sign is well encapsulated by Dylan Thomas[1] (a Scorpio Sun) in his well-known lines:

> The force that through the green fuse drives the flower
> Drives my green age; that blasts the roots of trees
> Is my destroyer.

In those strong in Scorpio there is often a marked feeling for the natural world. It is not, as with Gemini, a fascination with the visible diversity of forms, but rather this deeper awareness of an animistic energy.

Scorpio is associated with two planets, one modern and one ancient, Pluto and Mars. The Roman Mars is usually thought of as a god of war, but just as much he had a connection with nature, as Sir James Frazer makes clear in *The Golden Bough*:

> Now Mars was not originally a god of war but of vegetation. For it was to Mars that the Roman husbandman prayed for the prosperity of his vines, his fruit trees and his copses; it was to Mars that the priestly college of the Arval Brothers, whose business it was to sacrifice for the growth of the crops, addressed their petitions almost exclusively; and it was to Mars ... that a horse was sacrificed in October to secure an abundant harvest ... Once more, the consecration of the vernal month of March to Mars seems to point him out as a deity of the sprouting vegetation.[2]

Scorpio is a symbol of power, both the power of action, and in a broader sense that of a country that derives from the land itself and the resources and energies of its people. Scorpio also relates to a raw, unadorned dimension of life, where nicety and pretence are stripped away – the level of death, sex, violence and strong emotions. Sex and death are often enough themes of Scorpio writing. In Taurus sexual themes focus upon the destructiveness of lust, but in Scorpio the emphasis is on sex as a means of overcoming isolation in order to experience a sense of deep communion. The following quotations underline the concern of Scorpio writers with death:

Glen Siebrasse
My poetry has often been interpreted as a study in death.[3]

J G Ballard
[His work has] a distinctly 17th-century flavour – of the preoccupation with death.[4]

Anne Sexton
Her poems are haunted by her love and fear of death, her own above all.

It was her subject, her obsession. She considered it, tasted it, embraced it. It was her poetry.[5]

Anna, Comtesse de Noailles
[Her later work] exhibited a growing preoccupation with death and suffering.[6]

Dylan Thomas
[Of *25 Poems*] The dominant mood is still of impassioned introspection, showing an obsessive concern with death, sex, sin, and the isolation of the individual.[7]

Charlotte Mew
Obsession with death dominated everything she wrote.[8]

Patricia Beer
In all her work death is a familiar presence, referred to with intimacy and humour.[9]

Beryl Bainbridge
With the exception of *Sweet William* and *Winter Garden*, all [her] novels are centred on a death or act of violence.[10]

Sasha Sokolov
Time and memory, death and sex are major themes in all his novels.[11]

Karl Aspenström
Death is a recurring theme in [his] poetry and also in his plays.[12]

Olaf Bull
The great nothingness, death, presents an ever-renewed challenge to his genius.[13]

The fascination with death can sometimes go beyond mere writing in this sign. Suicide or early death is occasionally a price to pay for pursuing the creative life, but the burden appears to fall disproportionately on Scorpio Suns. Thomas Chatterton, the inspiration of many 19th-century romantics, took arsenic when he was only 18. Sylvia Plath, another precocious poet, gassed herself, as did Anne Sexton. John Berryman one day slipped quietly off a high bridge. Karin Boye was driven to suicide in a winter forest, and Ernst Schild took his own life, despite considerable success as a novelist. Amy Levy, a 19th century writer most remembered for her novel *Reuben Sachs*, committed suicide at 28 because, it has been said, of an incapacity for pleasure. Canadian writer Hubert Aquin shot himself when he was 47, while poet Charlotte Mew poisoned herself at the age of 58. Tadeusz Borowski wrote poems and short stories about his experiences in Nazi concentration camps and committed suicide at the age of 28. Dylan Thomas had an acute awareness of his own death and predicted he would not live beyond his fortieth year. He died aged 39 and if he didn't commit suicide in the strict sense he did drink himself to an early death.

Scorpio character

When Scorpio is emphasised in an individual's birth chart there is often a strong presence, a vital, magnetic quality. There is a desire for an intensity of living, and a corresponding aversion to the lukewarm. Often we find in Scorpio types (including characters in literature) energy, vigour, incisiveness, obsessiveness and a sharp and quick mind. Scorpio individuals respect strength and are quick to spot the weaknesses in others. They can be abrasive and dominating, even bullying and aggressive (believing that attack is the best form of defence). Scorpio types tend to harbour grudges and can be vindictive. They can be austere, severe, disciplinarian, although are just as hard on themselves as on others.

Courage and strength are Scorpionic qualities, along with the ability to act positively in a crisis. Indeed, Scorpio, like Aries, is vitalised by challenge. Scorpio types are good at abiding harsh circumstances, and can be the opposite of squeamish, finding a morbid fascination in the dark or visceral side of life. Those strong in Scorpio can appear to be shy but are actually just secretive and reticent, reluctant to reveal their feelings because to do so, they fear, can leave them exposed or vulnerable. The feeling nature is strong in Scorpio (being a Water sign) but, and particularly in men, this is often hidden behind a tough carapace. Scorpio can be a very compassionate sign, with a strong sympathy for the oppressed and, more than that, a desire to fight oppression. Scorpio is similar to the other Mars-related sign Aries in this regard. If it relishes anything more than a fight it is fighting for a cause – particularly if this relates to a legal injustice.

Pride can be strong in Scorpio types. They can often seem to retreat into an aloof and unbowed individualism. But running counter to this egocentricity is the urge to merge with others in intense emotional relationship. It is this tension that constitutes the essence of Scorpio and is often at the heart of the sign's literature.

Scorpio in essence

As stated in the previous chapter, Scorpio is part of a group of signs that symbolises the gradual assimilation of the individual into the collective, with Scorpio representing the final stage in this process. Or as Dane Rudhyar puts it: in Scorpio 'the desire to be a separate individual is being overwhelmed with dramatic intensity by the need to be more than oneself; by the urge to flow into others'.[14] In Libra, at the equinox, the demands of individual and collective are more or less balanced, but here in Scorpio the ego fights a losing battle to maintain its integrity, although it is not subsumed – an important point. Rather, what is eroded, and finally lost, in this sign is the desire of the individual to remain separate. We can see the battle in terms of the two ruling planets of this sign: the urge to maintain a strong ego (Mars) in the face of powerful disintegrating forces, Pluto, the astrological symbol of that 'power which compels all separate individualisations ... to return to their collective roots or foundation of being'.[15]

We get an insight into the tension that constitutes Scorpio through the phenomena of sleep and dreaming. Each night, to all intents and purposes, the individual dies as a conscious being. Focalised awareness is overcome by the pressure of the unconscious, where are found the regenerative forces necessary not only for health but also sanity. Through sleep both body and psyche are renewed and each morning we surface into consciousness once again. In sleep, particularly in the deep phase, the sense of being a focused, conscious being (Mars) is dissipated. You will know this to be true if you have ever been roused from a deep sleep and experienced the effort needed to focus, to literally gather yourself together. Equally, it is possible to attain a sort of consciousness in a sleep state. Lucid dreaming entails being aware of a dream as it is being dreamed, and is characterised by images much sharper than in a normal dream. In this state we experience the same sense of 'I amness' of waking life, although at the same time maintain the knowledge that we are asleep.

The central crisis in a Scorpio life (and which often forms the theme of its literature) can involve a 'fall', or a transition from a position of aloof isolation to a state of common being. Something is lost in the process, but something gained too. Pride, ruthlessness, strength and vigour are tempered and in their place come a deeper sense of being rooted in life and a blossoming of the feeling nature. The experience can be described as subscendence (rather than transcendence). It is breaking through a shell *into* a new world, in contrast to Cancer, the previous Water sign in the zodiac, which represents a breaking *out* into a wider sphere.

In the calendar sequence of I Ching hexagrams it is number 23, 'Splitting Apart', that relates to Scorpio. Wilhelm[16] tells us that 'splitting apart' also means decay, and a good deal of the meaning of the hexagram relates to the death/renewal aspect of the sign. The structure of the hexagram shows one light (yang) line on top of five dark (yin) ones. Moreover, 'The dark lines are about to mount upward and overthrow the last firm, light line by exerting a disintegrating influence on it'.[17] In other words, the proud ego is about to have the ground pulled from under its feet. Perhaps, as we will see shortly with Raskolnikov in *Crime and Punishment*, what triggers the descent into the underworld are unregenerate forces within. Or perhaps, as with the mythical Persephone, innocence itself is enough to attract the Plutonic forces of dissolution. The image associated with the hexagram is of a mountain resting *on* the earth:

> When it is steep and narrow, lacking a broad base, it must topple over. Its position is strong only when it rises *out* of the earth broad and great, not proud and steep.[18] (My emphasis)

Again, this is suggestive of descent to a common, but deep, perhaps mystical, level of being.

The hexagram's judgement reads 'It does not further one to go anywhere', which alludes to the inevitability of the processes of life, death and rebirth. Nothing in the world of form lasts forever, so when the time comes we have to submit to physical death, or perhaps simply the death of an old self. The judgement can also be interpreted as meaning that Scorpio is a sign where one must grasp the nettle. If there is evil abroad, confront it; if there is danger, fight rather than flee. And put faith in your self and your resources rather than in some distant redeemer. This facet of the sign emerges regularly in literature.

Scorpio and mythology

Some of the Greek myths relating to the Underworld can help us understand the nature of this sign. We should not regard this Underworld as a physical place but rather as a psychic state. Most of us spend some time here, but those strong in Scorpio will be more familiar with it. It can be a place of suffering caused by jealousy, frustration, futility and powerlessness. One resident of the Underworld was Tantalus. He was condemned to stand in water underneath a bough laden with fruit. But when he tried to eat and drink, both water and fruit receded, so that the torment of hunger and thirst was intensified by having what he desired close at hand yet infinitely out of reach (hence 'tantalise'). This idea of desire immediate enough to tempt but impossible to satisfy, a tormenting state beyond mere frustration, tells us something about the specific quality of Scorpio pain.

Another character in the Underworld was Sisyphus, who was made to push a heavy boulder up a hill. When he reached the top, the rock rolled back to its original position at the bottom, and he was forced to begin again. Once more this describes a quality of

Scorpio suffering: endless cycles of frustration made the more intense because the objective seems so close to being achieved.

Albert Camus (a Scorpio Sun) uses the character to illustrate his so-called absurdist philosophy. The enormity of Sisyphus' punishment is that it is eternal. But, insists Camus, the knowledge that it is for ever is at the same time a salvation. Sisyphus must abandon hope. There is no hope. He can not evade or escape the situation, as many of us try to do when faced with something challenging or unpleasant. He can not stand outside his fate, nor insulate himself from it through the knowledge that at some point in the future things will improve. Sisyphus has no alternative but to accept the pain and frustration. In so doing, however, by fully entering into his situation, he is redeemed. He lives life as it is, not some abstraction of it. There is no awareness of anything but the moment. All else is meaningless to him and irrelevant to his situation.[19]

More Scorpio writing

Fyodor Dostoyevsky, *Crime and Punishment*

This is the story of a student, Raskolnikov, who brutally murders two women. His crime is not motivated by gain or passion. Rather, his intention in killing the malevolent old pawnbroker (the death of the second woman is a 'mistake') is to substantiate his theories about 'supermen', an intellectual elite whose actions need not be trammelled by conventional morality. The murders trigger a battle within Raskolnikov, between an arrogant self and the darker forces within his subconscious.[20] As the book progresses he becomes increasingly schizoid.[21] Selfishness and compassion alternate, and shortly after the murders he gives away his last rouble to a destitute family. He battles against the irrational forces within that make him court detection, until finally he is overcome and confesses his crime to the astonished authorities.

Crime and Punishment is essentially the story of one man's purification, with penal servitude in Siberia forming a kind of Underworld. Raskolnikov has to learn that the life of a wretched old woman is worth more than all his abstract notions of superiority. At first he shows no remorse for his crime, only regret that his experiment failed. It is only toward the end of his first year of captivity, and perhaps largely through the devotion of his lover, Sonia, who has followed him to the tundric wastes, that the process of regeneration really begins. He is opened up to a new level of being:

> He could not think for long together of anything that evening and he

> could not have analysed anything consciously; he was simply feeling. Life had stepped into the place of theory.[22]

He is struck by the vividness of his environment. It is as if he had been asleep all his life and woken up for the first time. More significantly, though, he finds himself able to communicate meaningfully with others.

It is made clear that his awakening – which is accompanied by illness and apocalyptic dreams – is only the start of the process of renewal. Trapped in Siberia, Raskolnikov still has many trials to overcome. But Dostoyevsky tells us, in the last few sentences of the book, that these do not belong in this work:

> He did not know that the new life would not be given him for nothing ... that it would cost him great striving, great suffering. But that is the beginning of a new story – the story of the gradual renewal of a man, the story of his gradual regeneration, of his passing from one world into another, of his initiation into a new unknown life.[23]

Scorpio writing is full of characters that undergo this same kind of regeneration by being immersed in the deeper wellsprings of life, what Keats (a Scorpio Sun) termed 'fellowship with essence'. The hero of Robert Musil's *Young Törless* experiences Dionysian states and discovers 'that a darker, richer, and entirely separate mystical dimension resides within the human psyche but can not be encompassed by the rational mind'.[24] The nameless narrator of Margaret Atwood's *Surfacing* undergoes a cleansing madness and a deep insight into self in the Canadian wilderness. Michel in André Gide's *The Immoralist* likewise undergoes this same subscendence:

> There was an increase, a recrudescence of life, the influx of a richer, warmer blood which must of necessity affect my thoughts, touch them one by one, inform them all, stir and colour the most remote, delicate and secret fibres of my being ... I remember shouting aloud, as if calling could bring him to me: 'A new self! A new self.'[25]

Albert Camus' short story, 'The Adulterous Woman', tells of an itinerant merchant and his wife, Janine, who peddle wares about a circuit of Algerian desert towns. Her life seems arid and unfulfilled, but one night she leaves her husband's bed and makes her way outside, where she experiences a profound resurgence, an intimate and mystical union with the desert night:

> Janine opened a little more to the night ... After so many years of mad, aimless fleeing from fear, she had come to a stop at last. At the same

> time, she seemed to recover her roots and the sap again rose in her body ... Then with unbearable gentleness, the water of night began to fill Janine, drowned the cold, rose gradually from the hidden core of her being and overflowed in wave after wave, rising up even to her mouth full of moans.[26]

In the same collection of stories is 'The Growing Stone', which is set in a rain forest in Brazil, where 'blood and seasons mingled', and where 'life was flush with the soil'. The central character d'Arrast likewise experiences a deep emotional experience:

> he felt rising within him a surge of obscure and panting joy that he was powerless to name ... With eyes closed, he joyfully acclaimed his own strength; he acclaimed once again, a fresh beginning in life.[27]

As well as a tale about regeneration and 'fellowship with essence', 'The Growing Stone' is also a paradigm of Scorpionic agnosticism, a plea for the intensity of life over religious abstraction.

Another tale of a split personality, and of an individual being drawn down into purifying and regenerating depths is Camus' *The Fall.*

Albert Camus, *The Fall*

The 'fall' of the title relates to the central figure Clamence's descent from a life as a successful lawyer to the role of 'judge-penitent' amongst the working classes of Amsterdam. The short novel takes the form of an extended confession in which Clamence describes the transition.

The self-centredness and emotional isolation of his life as a fashionable lawyer becomes evident. 'I was always bursting with vanity. I, I, I is the refrain of my whole life,'[28] he notes at one point, and he also confesses to a 'congenital inability to see in love anything but the physical'.[29]

Clamence specialises in bleeding-heart defences, and while this suggests a humanitarian nature, he admits such cases only served to fuel his self-esteem. When the verdict was 'innocent' he fed off the tears of gratitude, and if 'guilty' then he merely shrugged his shoulders as the judge condemned and the victim was taken down. For all his rhetorical pleas he was not essentially involved in the brute reality of the situation.

Clamence's determination to avoid any real involvement in life is made plainer in other parts of his confession:

> Those supreme summits, the only places I can really live. Yes, I have never felt comfortable except in lofty surrounds. Even in the details of daily life I needed to feel above ... in the mountains I used to flee the

> deep valleys for the passes and plateaux. Coal bunkers, ship-holds, subways, grottoes, pits were repulsive to me.[30]

In Scorpio, as in the polar sign Taurus, there is a paradox. Taurus has to learn that you can only possess by letting go. In Scorpio the paradox is that you have to go down to go up. It is as if one is prevented from advancing by an umbilical cord tethered firmly in the depths and only by descent can one sever it. We are reminded of the *I Ching* imagery, where the mountain rises out of the earth, rather than rests upon it.

Despite his revulsion of the depths, Clamence is pulled under. A number of incidents precipitate his fall, but most significantly an occasion in which he fails to assert himself against an aggressor, after which he finds himself plotting revenge out of all proportion to the event. He does not carry it out but does come to realise that co-existing with his refined, intellectual self is an altogether darker nature.

He moves to Amsterdam where he finds some vital communion with the city's underclass. He becomes what he calls a judge-penitent, and acquires the ability to be with a person, in the therapeutic sense. He becomes both siphon and receptacle for the poison of others, neither condemning nor judging the darkness that issues forth. The city is portrayed as a kind of underworld. Flat featureless land, grey seas and sky merging into one, mists and rain create an impression of gloomy uniformity. Foghorns wail like lost souls, and the city's concentric structure is compared to Dante's purgatory.

As in *Crime and Punishment*, the writer stops short of the central character's regeneration. Scorpio novels tend to focus on the initial opening of the enclosed ego to cleansing and revitalising waters.

Kurt Vonnegut, *The Sirens of Titan*

Vonnegut is a Scorpio writer who believes we should focus our energies on the here and now. 'Our brains are two-bit computers,' he has written:

> and we can't get very high grade truths out of them. But as far as improving the human condition goes our minds are certainly up to that. That's what they were designed to do.[31]

Scorpio in essence is agnostic rather than atheist, holding that if there is a moving intelligence in the universe then man is not capable of comprehending it, and rather than directing our love skyward, there is a more pressing need for it closer to home. In a number of his books we see Vonnegut's concern with human welfare to the fore, and he has said in interview that he sees the re-establishment of human community as the most pressing need of our time. He is not usually a writer compared to Camus but in *The Sirens of Titan* we have an eloquent expression of the latter's philosophy of the absurd. It also tells the story of the purgatorial trials of one man.

Winston Niles Rumfoord, one of the book's central characters, does not exist in a particular place at a particular time, but rather at any number of places on a pulsing spiral bounded by the sun and Betelgeuse. Rumfoord materialises wherever a planet intercepts his spiral of being, although at the same time he has a permanent existence on Titan, one of Saturn's moons.

His delocalised existence, among other things, means he has knowledge of the future and this coupled with a vast earthly fortune provides him with considerable power. He uses this to manipulate a war between Earth and Mars. The army of Mars – actually inhabitants of Earth kidnapped and brain-washed – fails abysmally in its invasion, largely because of Rumfoord's connivance. When the army has been wiped out the reason for his scheming becomes clear. The Martian army was only ever intended as a sacrifice. In the face of common adversity – the invasion – the people of the world unite. And upon a widespread feeling of remorse for the butchered invaders a new religion is founded, with Rumfoord at its head. It is called 'The Church of God the Utterly Indifferent', and its basic tenet is an absurdist one: we delude ourselves if we believe God cares about, or takes a hand in, the lives of individuals.

But the climax and ultimate irony of the novel are yet to come. It takes place on Titan, the home of Rumfoord, and also Salo, a machine-creature from Tralfamadore, a highly advanced civilisation from a distant galaxy (whose technology served as the means for Rumfoord's end). Salo is an ambassador from his world. He carries a message to the limits of the universe, a sort of goodwill gesture on the part of his people, but he has become stranded on Titan with engine failure and awaits a spare part. It transpires that the history of humankind served no greater purpose than the delivery of this spare part. (It is finally delivered, inadvertently, by another character, Malachi Constant, who is absorbed into the Tralfamadorian will pattern, and whose story is basically one of suffering and purification.) Salo was able to gauge the progress of his rescue through certain historical landmarks. The Great Wall of China and Stonehenge were no more than coded messages sent from Tralfamadore via Earth to let Salo know that things were in hand. So a half-baked rescue mission turns out to be the meaning of life. The message that was so important? One word – greetings!

Rumfoord himself is sacrificed as the terminals of his spiral shift and diffuse his existence more widely through the universe. His Church, we assume, lived on, with its followers much happier as individuals devoting their energies to human wellbeing rather than heavenward.

Karin Boye, *Kallocain*

Kallocain, first published in Sweden in 1940, is in essence a work about different types of communion: one the state attempts to force from without, and one that grows organically from within.

Kallocain is a drug, named after Leo Kall, a scientist who lives and works in Chemistry City No 4, in Worldstate. It is essentially a truth drug and is seen at first as a valuable tool for strengthening the power of the state over the individual. In some respects Worldstate resembles George Orwell's dystopia in *Nineteen Eighty-Four.* The state intrudes on every aspect of personal life. An individual's free time is pared down to a minimum. Leisure activities must be group- and state-oriented. Laws are framed to prevent any deep bonds between individuals, in order to strengthen the individual–state bond. Families are broken up when children are young, couples chaperoned in their own homes, and surveillance cameras in the bedroom make sex more a matter of procreation than bonding.

In the course of the drug's test programme it is discovered Kallocain's capacity as a truth serum is only incidental. More fundamentally what it does is to unlock innermost feelings, and sometimes a person's dark and evil side. At the same time the experiments seem to suggest that the reality that Kallocain exposes contains the seeds of a deeper level of being, one where 'pulses are being driven by a heart in the cosmos'. What Kallocain does, in effect, is resolve the struggle that besets Scorpionic characters, by eroding the will to remain separate.

Kall, like the majority of individuals in Worldstate, is a fearful, self-controlled, suspicious person who can not connect with others and does not *feel* a sense of unity with the state. Communion implies giving as well as taking. Simply forcing individuals together with laws in a cumbersome social structure does not create a *feeling* of unity. Yet there is within him a thirst for something deeper, although, as most of us do, he fears what he most yearns for.

Kall admires 'strength, superiority, power', and despises his boss, Rissen, who exemplifies none of these qualities. Indeed Rissen is not aloof and cold like those others in the book who occupy positions of power, but shows kindness toward the experimental subjects, and generally seems taciturn and more preoccupied with an inner world. He remarks at one point:

> I wanted so to believe there was a green depth in the human being, a sea of undefiled growing power that melted all dead remnants in its crucible and healed and created an eternity.[32]

The first volunteer to be injected with Kallocain speaks of a 'moment of lofty bliss' he once experienced. Kall envies him this, but finally comes to taste the deeper waters and, like Raskolnikov, to feel rather than think. He concludes: 'I was released from one communion which was choking me and was delivered into a new obvious, simple one which supported but did not bind.'[33]

Naomi Mitchison, *The Blood of the Martyrs*

In an address at Oxford University Mitchison once remarked: 'We want to get into a community. We are bored with being individuals and separate in our loves and hates and jealousies, our own overwhelming fears.'[34]

In the same vein a biographer notes:

> [she believed] individual relations were the bricks out of which a more communal intimacy and sharing could be built. This is a theme that runs through almost everything that Naomi wrote.[35]

One of Mitchison's best known works, and one in which the above theme shines through, is *The Blood of the Martyrs*, which is set in ancient Rome, when Nero was emperor, although most of the action takes place among slaves and poor people. Particularly the focus is on the growth of a Christian cell. What characterises this community is people's feeling for each other, which expresses itself in kindness and helpfulness. People feel a sense of connectedness with one another. The time in which the book is set was an epoch of unifying. Rome was its height. Its empire united large portions of the earth under a single language and a single polity. But it was held in place by military might, Roman law and Rome's sense of its own imperial mission. Even amongst high-placed Romans there was no sense of participating in a common level of being. Indeed, as two converts in the book observe, people live separated by their fears, hatreds and possessions:

> These two men were convinced that there was a kind of relationship between people ... which was worth everything else in life. When people were in this relationship, they loved and trusted and understood each other without too many words, they were no longer separated by fear and suspicion ... it was not possible for the rich to enter into this relationship, because their possessions put up a barrier of envy and greed between them and their neighbours.[36]

The Christian community in this work is bound by quality of experience rather than coercion or shared ideals. And they enter into their new world through a baptism to ritually cleanse them of the fears and hatreds that had hitherto prevented them from communing with their fellows. Some seem to experience the Scorpio subscendence that was mentioned above. At one point the slave Argas is dipped three times into the dark, winter waters of the Tiber and undergoes a death-like ritual. But when he emerges, finally, and is taken home, he feels different, sees things in a different light:

> The grains of coarse salt were each separate beings; the texture of the bread was beautiful. For a moment he did not want to eat; what did this new person he had become want with eating?[37]

Albert Camus, *The Plague*

This novel caused Camus much labour and some despair. He began it in 1942 while stranded in France by the war, beset by anxieties about the wellbeing of his friends and relatives in his native Algeria. It was published in June 1947, and sold very well: 100,000 copies by the autumn of that year, 360,000 by 1955.

The Plague is a multilayered work. On a straightforward level it is an account of an outbreak of bubonic plague set in the Algerian town of Oran. On another level some commentators have taken it to be an allegory of the Nazi occupation of France. But more fundamentally the novel is about breaking down the barriers between individuals and is another expression of Camus' abiding concern with the absurd, which, to reiterate, is a philosophy that puts the challenging or human demands of reality before abstractions of one sort or another.

In the book the physical plague symbolises two main things. One is the ruthless use of power, particularly when this is wielded in the name of some ideal or dogma; the second is for something within the human condition – a 'poison' – that prevents people coming together in empathic relationship.

There are some powerful descriptions of death and dying but for the most part the novel focuses upon the living, particularly on the experience of an extended quarantine. As the plague begins to spread the gates of the city are locked, and it is decreed that without exception nobody may leave. There is also a ban on mail being sent, for it is feared this might spread infection, and the telephone lines are open only for emergencies. For most of the city's inhabitants the real trial of the plague if one of forced separation. Many of them have loved ones outside the city, but even inside, and despite the common adversity, people are being forced apart.

Such communities as exist – barracks, nunneries and so forth – are disbanded, to minimise the risk of contagion. So too are families forced apart. When the plague strikes a particular home the victims are transferred to a fever hospital, and the rest of the family confined to the house. And throughout the city friends and neighbours are divided by a barrier of fear and suspicion, for:

> ... Though they have an instinctive craving for human contacts [they] can't bring themselves to yield to it, because of the mistrust that keeps them apart. For it is common knowledge that you can't trust your neighbour; he may pass the disease on to you without your knowing it.[38]

There is no escape from the ever-present and real danger of the plague. Nor does the future offer any immediate hope and comfort, for no one can say when the plague will end. The town becomes a kind of purgatory where suffering can not be avoided. At first these conditions create a sense of detachment and unreality, with many of the inhabitants reduced to an abstracted limbo, 'wandering shadows that could have acquired substance only by consenting to root themselves in the solid earth of their distress'.[39] However, as the plague continues many begin to do just that.

Two of the novel's central characters, Rieux and Rambert, have wives beyond the city. The former's reaction to the circumstances is to put his wife from his mind and work resolutely to fight the plague. He establishes so-called sanitary squads, groups of individuals who work with disinfectant and fire to contain the plague. Work in these squads naturally increases the chance of contagion and death. Nevertheless, the squads attract many volunteers, people who wanted to 'root themselves in the solid earth of their distress'. Rambert volunteers only after much soul-searching. At first the yearning for his absent wife is so strong that he attempts to leave the city. His escape is arranged through a clandestine network, but he decides that it is his duty to stay and work with the sanitary squads to help combat the plague. 'It does not further one to go anywhere,' counsels the I Ching. Rambert is in harmony with the Scorpionic times.

So too is the priest Father Paneloux. At first he tells his congregation that the pestilence has been sent by a wrathful God and must be accepted in humility, but as the plague intensifies and the deaths and agonies multiply his attitude changes. He concludes that salvation must be worked out in the shadow of the plague. The priest joins the sanitary squads, where he sprinkles disinfectant rather than holy water, and rewrites his sermons. 'Who would dare to assert,' he preaches, 'that eternal happiness can compensate for a single moment's human suffering.'[40]

We get another insight into what Camus meant by 'plague' through the character Tarrou, who functions as a sort of chronicler. In an extended monologue Tarrou talks of his childhood, and notably of his father, who was a state prosecutor. He recalls an occasion when he visited the court to watch his father in action. It was a murder case and, as was his duty, the prosecutor was demanding the accused be executed. The spectacle of his father pressing for the death of a pathetic, frightened human being remained with Tarrou and came to symbolise a fundamental flaw in the human condition. This remoteness that could treat human life so casually, this ruthless application of the abstract over individual suffering, represented a kind of poison, a 'plague'.[41]

Tarrou goes on to recount his resolve to combat 'plague'. Like Camus himself, he joins political organisations only to discover that in their use of violent means to bring about dogmatic ends they are equally as 'plague' ridden. Fighting plague, he discovers, is like fighting the Hydra: you think you are winning when in fact you are only creating more infestation. Tarrou is forced to conclude that there are few, very few, individuals who can directly overcome evil. The best most of us can do is guard against bringing more into the world.

In one sense the buboes, or bodily eruptions, of plague are the body's way of casting out poisons. So too when the collective body becomes diseased it generates its own noxious discharge in phenomena such as Nazism. There is something about Nazism, the Holocaust in particular, that relates to Camus' ideas of abstraction, plague and evil. The situation where seemingly normal human beings could murder six million Jews on the basis of theories of race supremacy was a terrifying manifestation of 'plague' and Raskolnikov's folly on a scale Dostoyevsky could not have imagined. In one sense, then, *The Plague* is about the Nazi domination of Europe, but the connection is at a deeper level than mere allegory.

Notes

1. Dylan Thomas, *Collected Poems (1934-1952)*, J M Dent, 1972, p8
2. Sir James Frazer, *The Golden Bough*, Macmillan, 1963, p578
3. *Contemporary Poets*, ed James Vinson, Macmillan 1980, p1388
4. *Contemporary Novelists*, ed James Vinson, St James Press, 1976, p90
5. Katinka Matson, *Short Lives*, Picador, 1981, p301
6. *Columbia Dictionary of Modern European Literature*, ed J Bédé and W Edgerton, Columbia University Press, 1980, p568

7. John Ackerman, *Dylan Thomas: His Life and Works*, Macmillan, 1991, p62

8. *An Encyclopaedia of British Women Writers*, Garland Press, eds P & J Schlueter, 1978, p321

9. *Dictionary of British Women Writers*, ed Janet Todd, Routledge, 1989, p49

10. *Contemporary Novelists*, 7th edition, St James Press, 2001, p54

11. *Contemporary World Writers*, St James Press, 1993, p483

12. *Dictionary of Scandinavian Literature*, ed Virpi Zuck, St James Press, 1990, p30

13. ibid, p93

14. Dane Rudhyar, *Astrological Signs, The Pulse of Life*, Shambhala, 1978, p90

15. Dane Rudhyar, *An Astrological Triptych*, ASI, 1968, p282

16. *I Ching*, Routledge & Kegan Paul, 1975, p500

17. ibid, p93

18. ibid, p94

19. Voltaire's *Candide* is another work that embodies anti abstraction and 'absurdist' ideas. The work is perhaps best remembered for the character Pangloss, a philosopher who, despite all evidence to the contrary, propounds the view that, 'we live in the best of all possible worlds. What we regard as evil will, if rightly considered, be found conducive to the good of some other creature.' But in *Candide* the characters, through a catalogue of suffering, achieve some sort of redemption by realising the worthlessness of Pangloss' optimism and learning to live for the moment.

20. This theme of conflict between dark and light forces intermingled in the human psyche is common in Scorpio. Perhaps the best known example is R L Stevenson's *Dr Jekyll and Mr Hyde*. We observe it also in the fiction of Henri Bosco, notably in his novel *The Dark Bough*. The central character is engaged in a similar conflict to Raskolnikov, with one level of himself, one that represents the darker traits of human nature, attempting to rise and dominate the other.

21. We can note that in Russian the root of the name Raskolnikov – *Raskolot* – means 'to split'.

22. Fyodor Dostoyevsky, *Crime and Punishment*, Bantam, 1981, p472

23. ibid, p472

24. *Columbia Dictionary of Modern European Literature*, ed J Bédé and W B Edgerton, Columbia Univ Press, 1980, p556

25. André Gide, *The Immoralist*, Penguin, 1981, p52

26. Albert Camus, 'The Adulterous Woman,' in *The Exile and the Kingdom*, Penguin, 1979, pp28-29

27. Albert Camus, 'The Growing Stone', in *The Exile and the Kingdom*, Penguin, 1979, pp 151-52

28. Albert Camus, *The Fall*, Penguin, 2000, p37

29. ibid, p44

30. ibid, p19-20

31. Kurt Vonnegut, 'The Playboy Interview', reprinted in *Wampeters, Foma and Granfalloons*, Panther, 1974, pp214-215

32. Karin Boye, *Kallocain*, Madison, 1966, p176

33. ibid, p168

34. Naomi Mitchison, paper read to the English Club, University of Oxford, 1930; cited in Jenni Calder, *The Nine Lives of Naomi Mitchison*, Virago, 1997, p74

35. ibid, p186

36. *The Blood of the Martyrs*, Canongate Classics, 1998, p29

37. ibid, p72

38. Albert Camus, *The Plague*, Penguin, 1981, p 160

39. ibid, p 61

40. ibid, p183

41. In Stevenson's *Weir of Hermiston* a similar observation is made by Archie Weir regarding his father, Adam, when he condemns a man to death. The acerbic elder Weir is a good example of a certain face of Scorpio character.

SAGITTARIUS

Writers with the Sun in Sagittarius include: Louisa May Alcott, Jane Austen, John Banville, Louis de Bernières, William Blake, Heinrich Böll, Howard Brenton, John Bunyan, Samuel Butler, Erskine Caldwell, Thomas Carlyle, Joyce Cary, Willa Cather, Noam Chomsky, Arthur C Clarke, Joseph Conrad, Noel Coward, William Cowper, Philip K Dick, Emily Dickinson, Joan Didion, Maurice Duggan, Zoe Fairbairns, Gustave Flaubert, Ford Madox Ford, Jean Genet, Rumer Godden, Peter Handke, Joel Chandler Harris, Horace, Eugene Ionesco, Laurence Lerner, Carlo Levi, Claude Lévi-Strauss, C S Lewis, Jose Lezama Lima, John Milton, L M Montgomery, Michael Moorcock, Mary Norton, Edna O'Brien, John Osborne, Frederic Pohl, Laurens van der Post, Anthony Powell, Rainer Maria Rilke, Christina Rossetti, George Santayana, Isaac Bashevis Singer, Alexander Solzhenitsyn, Baruch Spinoza, Laurence Sterne, Randolph Stow, Jonathan Swift, James Thurber, Joanna Trollope, Mark Twain, Lope de Vega, Sylvia Townsend Warner.

Summary: One characteristic of the sign is the production of cycloramas, sequences of connected novels – as many as 20 or 30 – in which the individual works are sufficient in themselves yet taken together add up to something more. Sometimes a writer's focus is on the contrast between man's animal nature and his spiritual potential. Sagittarian writers will also lament the loss of the spirit in an overly-secular world, and there is a strong tendency to be didactic. Disenchantment is a major theme, the tendency for idealism to founder on the rocks of reality.

> There was a mean trick played on us somewhere. God put us in the bodies of animals and tried to make us act like people. That was the beginning of trouble.
> **Erskine Caldwell**, *God's Little Acre*

Sagittarius of all the signs is the most opinionated and the most outspoken; not only are the opinions strong, but there is the compulsion to express them, and this often spills over into literature. A common criticism, one levelled almost exclusively at Sagittarian Sun writers, is of a habit of preaching. There is a tendency to trammel work with a moral or political message so that the content of a play or novel is determined to a greater or lesser extent by a point to be made or a message to be put across. This is generally transparent and is often, but not always, to a work's detriment. Not every Sagittarian writer is prone to this trait, but at the same time it is not difficult to build up a list of some who are:

Mulk Raj Anand
Like many writers impelled by social motive, however worthy, whose attitude to life is too patently dominated by theory, he has a habit of preaching at the reader... The defect which restricts his real creative capacity is the habit of allowing his moral and social purpose to become separate from the actuality of the fiction.[1]

John A Williams
[Author] I think art has always been political and has served political ends more graciously than those of the muses. I consider myself to be a political novelist and writer ... The greatest art has always been social-political, and in that sense I could be considered striving along traditional paths.[2]

Katherine Pritchard
Her political convictions ... insured that her critics frequently over-praised or dismissed her for ideological rather than artistic reasons.[3]

John Bale
John Bale, Bishop of Ossory, was the first English writer to use the drama for polemical purposes.[4]

Rewi Alley
Propagandist of the Chinese revolution ... Alley has the broad vision of the poet with few of the niceties of the craft ... can turn out political verses that are mere lists of slogans.[5]

Ludwig Anzengruber
It was his ambition to be a true teacher of the people and a strong didactic vein runs through all of his works.[6]

David Caute
His novels are written out of a deep ideological commitment to Marxism.[7]

G A Henty
Henty's books have been seen as ... the epitome of the values of British imperialism, and powerful weapons in the transmission of its ideology.[8]

John Bunyan
The impulse which originally drove him to ... write was purely to celebrate his faith and to convert others ... to treat literature as a means to an end.[9]

Francis Clifford
He is in fact, sometime so concerned to point a moral that his endings

fall a little flat; and plot sometimes suffers at the hands of cleverly concealed polemic.[10]

Herman Heyermans
[His] dramas generally are tendentious pieces.[11]

James Agee
In his short stories, too, Agee frequently preached. Or if he did not preach, he tried to put into the stories messages more or less hidden, about religious and philosophical problems.[12]

Manlio Argueta
As with many of his generation, Argueta saw literature as a weapon which acted directly within society; the literary skills he cultivated were those of direct, forceful expression, put at the service of a political aim.[13]

Alexander Solzhenitsyn
In exile, Solzhenitsyn has devoted his prodigious energies and literary gifts to deliberately programmatic works, significant more for its political and historical substance than for its artistic merit, even when cast as fiction.[14]

Louisa May Alcott
[Of *Little Women*] The novel has a strong didactic tone throughout.[15]

Howard Brenton
Believing that all drama is political, Brenton declares that his plays are written 'unreservedly in the cause of socialism'.[16]

Frances Ridley Havergal
The quality of her work is uneven. Too much of it tries too hard to teach a lesson.[17]

Spider Robinson
His storytelling is often marred by a coarse and sentimental didacticism.[18]

Grace Paley
To speak out is a basic theme in Paley's stories, and it reflects her own life and political principles ... This intermingling of politics and art brought [her] mixed reviews.[19]

John Milton
The moral of other poems is incidental and consequent; in Milton only it is essential and intrinsic. His purpose was ... to vindicate the ways of God to man, to show the reasonableness of religion, and the necessity of obedience to the Divine law.[20]

Maxwell Anderson
He enunciated as rule number one the necessity of having a central idea or conviction that can not be excised without killing the play ... Though his convictions changed markedly during his career, the use of the stage to express them did not ... He presented each new certainty with as much strength as the one before.[21]

Edgar Mittelholzer
[His] work at its worst descends to obsessively haranguing the reader to accept an extreme and warped vision of the world.[22]

Sagittarius is a sign of dogmas, conviction and certitude, of truths unconditional and absolute. 'Uncompromising' is a word applied to Sagittarius more than to any other sign. Sagittarius (and its associated planet Jupiter) symbolises the urge within a person to surrender to the dictates of a higher order, be this a spiritual doctrine, a religion, a political idea, or simply some principle or cause.[23] The urge to proselytise, the attempt to get everyone to believe in one thing, likewise comes under Sagittarius. It also stands for the prophet, in the original sense of the word, one who voices the divine will (as opposed to predicting the future), and for those generally who purport to dispense a higher truth.

Sagittarius relates to what Sorokin[24] terms the ideational mentality, one which looks beyond the visible world to some unchangeable ultimate reality. Jupiter and Sagittarius represent theocratic or ideological cultures, where life to a large degree is subservient to (or guided by) some over-riding principle or dogma, and to the idea of a transcendent unity and the urge within the individual to become part of this. The religious vein in Sagittarius can manifest both positively and negatively. It can produce high-minded and moral individuals whose life is guided by spiritual principles. Indeed, we find these characters in Sagittarian literature and usually their moral fastidiousness is tested by the hard edges of reality.[25] But equally it can manifest as bigotry, self-righteousness or zealotry.

Dane Rudhyar captures the essence of this sign very well with the following descriptive metaphor. Sagittarius represents

> ... the age of great adventures into the vast uncharted realms of generalisations. It is the time of crusades and pilgrimages burning with the intensity of the quest for God, the quest for eternal values valid anywhere and at any time, the quest for absolutes. It is the age of social movements and fanaticism, of martyrdom and intolerance; when men lose the sense of the earth, the narrow feelings of self preservation and security, the will to personal happiness – and soar on the wings of self-denial toward distant social or mystical ideals, for which they are glad to die.[26]

In the Western world we no longer live in religious times, but the human need for the numinous, for something greater, more perfect and more powerful than ourselves has not disappeared. It has, however, taken a perverse turn. Instead of aspiring to the infinite we make gods out of mortals. We inflate, glamorise and worship actors, sports champions and musicians, those who not so long ago were considered servants, artisans or even (in the case of actors) beyond the pale. This phenomenon of elevating the ordinary to the extraordinary is a quality of Jupiter and Sagittarius. It is a quality that emerges at the individual level in two basic ways. The mantle of hero or king seems to fall most easily on those strong in Sagittarius (or with a strong Jupiter). Equally, the Sagittarian type can have a more than average tendency to idealise and hero-worship. It is not always as extreme as kings, gods and heroes. It is sometimes just a case of being a focus for undue hope and expectation, or of being celebrated. A Sagittarian musician, actor or writer may be good, but not as good as the claims made on their behalf by the adoring masses.[27]

Sagittarian writers will usually assert the value of an imaginative reality in a world that tends to deny it, and they will vaunt the supremacy of spiritual/moral values over pragmatic or material ones. Sagittarians will trace the shortcomings of a society to the absence of a higher principle, often speaking out against *over*-secularisation in a society, when the focus swings too far from the spirit (ideal) to worldly things (real). In Europe in the 18th and 19th centuries, when the trend towards secularisation was accelerating, a number of such commentators emerged, among them Samuel Butler, Thomas Carlyle, William Blake and Jonathan Swift, who were all Sagittarian Suns.

Butler was alarmed at the alacrity with which his contemporaries made a secular dogma of Darwin's work and he focused a good deal of his critical writing on this. He perceived that no good could come of a creed that held man to be a chance mutation as opposed to a meaningful part of a spiritual whole. Carlyle wanted a society that reflected man's higher nature, and warned that over-reliance on mechanism had produced a sick fabric of society. William Blake saw in the advancing materialism of the Industrial Revolution a Britain becoming increasingly 'satanic', that is, divorced from the spirit. The lines of *Jerusalem*, for example, lament this fact. The squalid industrial landscapes springing up throughout 'England's green and pleasant land' at the time he lived were the consequence of men's eyes turning from the sky to earth (and materialism). The greater part of Blake's writing and painting was devoted to revealing a spiritual reality that lay beyond external appearances, a reality which could not be proved by argument or experiment, but only perceived directly by what he called the imagination. In his conviction that the world of appearances is only a projection of an underlying spiritual reality, and in his dedication to restoring to mankind the consciousness of infinity, Blake embodied the essential nature of Sagittarius.

In each of these writers the emphasis is upon wholeness and

the warnings are against the errors of turning from the spirit. Swift was another who focused not so much on the spirit but more generally upon what happens when men lose sight of the bigger picture. He lived at a time when the world view in Europe was undergoing significant change. It was coming to be believed that truth could be discovered by breaking things down into component parts and then examining these parts and the way in which they interacted. This so-called mechanistic paradigm has proved to be a very valuable way of looking at the world, at least with regard to utilising it to improve our material condition. Yet it grew beyond this to become a touchstone of truth, and it is only in more recent decades that its limitations have come to be widely accepted. Yet even as this world-view was being born the perceptive Swift was pointing out how incomplete a picture it provided.

He addressed himself to an intellectual polarity, to what happens to our understanding if we become too small or fragmented in our thinking. *Swift's Anatomy of Misunderstanding* is one text that examines this aspect of Swift's writing in some detail. Its author describes *Gulliver's Travels* as 'a demonstration of the art of making mistakes behind a screen of accurate empirical measurement'.[28] She goes on to note that at the end of his travels Gulliver has all the facts and very little knowledge, as Swift satirises 'how doggedly scientific minds go wrong confusing facts and the sorting of facts with the understanding of them'.[29]

There are many instances when Gulliver or those he encounters misinterpret sense data. The Lilliputians, Swift tells us, 'see with great exactness but at no great distance'. At one point they examine Gulliver's belongings, cataloguing in great detail, yet not understanding, indeed misunderstanding, what it is they have before them. As readers we can see at one point they are examining a watch but we can only do this by bringing non-empirical faculties into play. We have a preconception of the object in its entirety which the Lilliputians do not. They have never seen a watch before and their meticulous observations and ridiculous conjectures lead them nowhere.

Facts of themselves can be arranged into any number of patterns, in the manner of a kaleidoscope. The fact that we are able to form a pattern is no proof that we have discovered the truth of a situation, and indeed, the most elegant of theories can be wide of the mark. It seems, rather, that truth must act as a sort of seed crystal about which facts may cohere. Truth is a balance of whole and parts and over-reliance on one or the other simply produces opinion. Confusion of opinion and truth is at the root of intolerance and bigotry and has spawned some of mankind's darker deeds. The Lilliputians go to war over a difference of opinion as to how an egg should be broken, just as Swift's contemporaries fought bloody wars about the 'right' way to worship the same God. Opinions are like truth resolved into component parts. The true picture resides not in any one part, but in a distillate of them all. And it seems the smaller minded we are, the more vigorously we cling to our partial view.

A zodiac sign's glyph (or symbol) can sometimes give a clue to its meaning. Sagittarius is usually depicted as a centaur, a mythical creature with the body of a horse and the torso and head of a man, about to loose an arrow. This gives rise to a number of ideas. Both the horse and the bow extend the individual's range of power. The man on horseback or armed with a bow becomes a more formidable person, either in hunting or in battle. Almost every version of the glyph, whatever the era, shows the bow bent and the arrow about to be released. This alludes to the nature of Sagittarius as a sign pregnant with possibility, of potential to be made actual through the arrow of time.

The glyph has almost always been depicted as a hybrid of man and beast, generally a horse; but there are a number of examples of medieval sculpture[30] where Sagittarius is depicted as a Pan-bodied bowman, with goat legs. This all suggests a specific aspect of the sign's duality. Man has a god-like nature, but also a bestial side, and a challenge in this sign is to recognise this divide and aspire to live in one's higher nature.[31] This is an important strand in Sagittarian literature, as later examples will show. The same idea is suggested in some of the ancient myths surrounding Zeus/Jupiter. He was an Olympian, the chief of the gods, yet at the same time a lusty seducer, forever taking on animal forms in order to sate his desires with mortal women. And it is significant that no good ever came of the liaisons. The hapless partners invariably incurred the wrath of a jealous wife, and the offspring were often cursed in some way. In Sagittarius virtue is often its own reward, while moral lapse can bring a heavy price.

Sagittarius relates to ideas of abundance, expansion and wholeness. In human life it represents that feeling that we exist as a kind of under-inflated ball and are able to become greater or better than we are. It represents opportunity and the opening up of possibility (although while those strong in Sagittarius often have a great sense of possibility their sense of what is practically possible is much poorer). Sagittarius stands for growth in the sense of things becoming fully expressed. Ludwig van Beethoven had both his Sun and Moon in this sign and one thing he excelled at was improvisation, expressing a musical theme in many different ways. In the *Diabelli Variations,* for example, he produced 33 variations on a simple waltz tune and these endure today as proof of his ability to expand through elaboration. He was also a great expander of musical form. The piano sonata was a form used by many Classical composers in the late 18th century. Beethoven wrote 30-odd himself, but in so doing exhausted the form of its possibilities. It became a worked-out vein and comparatively few were written after his death. And certainly there are those who argue that he brought the symphony to its apogee.[32]

In literature the expansive nature of Sagittarius emerges in a number of ways. The writers of this sign can be very productive, although the output is often of an uneven quality, and because the faculty of discrimination is at its weakest in the Jupiter signs there can be difficulty in distinguishing between what is good work and what not so good. Another way the expansive principle manifests is the production of cycloramas – novels written as part of an ongoing process, often complete in themselves and yet building to something more. These sometimes monumental creations draw together space and time to produce a panoramic picture that reveals that events occurring at different times or places can in fact have closely related implications. The Sagittarian world view is simultaneous rather than linear, and the cyclorama is able to reflect this with more fidelity than single novels. Equally, these long chains of individual works may simply be concrete variations on a single theme. Sagittarian Sun writers who have produced in this mode include:

Hervey Allen: *Anthony Adverse*, 9 volumes
Carl Almquist: *Book of the Wild Rose*, 17 volumes
Mulk Raj Anand: *The Seven Ages of Man*, 7 volumes
Poul Anderson: Technic Civilization Series
Upendranath Askh: *Cetan* cycle, 5 volumes
Ford Madox Ford: *Parade's End*, 4 volumes
Thomas Haliburton: *Sam Slick* series
Joel Chandler Harris: around ten volumes of *Uncle Remus* stories
C S Lewis: *The Chronicles of Narnia*, 7 volumes
L M Montgomery: *Anne of Green Gables* series, 9 volumes
Mary Norton: *The Borrowers*, 5 volumes
Patrick O'Brian: Aubrey/Maturin naval fiction series, 20 volumes
Claude Ollier: *Le jeu d'enfant*, 8 volumes
Anthony Powell: *A Dance to the Music of Time*, 12 volumes
Jose Sionil: *Rosales* saga, 5 volumes

Laurence Sterne: *Tristram Shandy*, 9 volumes
Henry Williamson: *A Chronicle of Ancient Sunlight*, 15 volumes

The French author Paul Adam wrote a number of sequential works, including *Le Temps et la Vie Napoleonic.* The production of multi-volumed work is not a particularly common literary device – genre writing aside, perhaps – but it is even less common outside of Sagittarian Sun writers. When it does occur there is more often than not a strong Sagittarian element somewhere in the writer's chart. The following writers, for example, have either Moon or ascendant in Sagittarius, or Jupiter conjunct the Sun:

Honoré de Balzac: *La Comédie Humaine*, 11 volumes
Pío Baroja: *Memoirs de un Hombre de Accion,* 22 volumes
Marcel Proust: 10 parts of *Remembrance of Things Past,*
Jules Romains: *Les Hommes de Bonne Volonté*, 27 volumes
Emile Zola: *Les Rougon-Macquart* series, 20 volumes

Sagittarian themes

To recap before considering some more examples of the sign's writing. The major Sagittarian literary themes can be summarised as follows:

1. A sacred/profane dualism, with work that focuses on the divide between man's god-like and bestial nature – the centaur symbolism.
2. An ideal-real dualism, where the focus is on an imbalance that exists between the two frames of reference. There are two variations:
   a. Too little 'ideal', where the faults of a society are traced to the absence of or turning away from some higher principle.
   b. Too much 'ideal'. The ideal here is not spirit, but grandiose delusion. Sagittarian writers often seek to deflate or disenchant, perhaps juxtaposing a stark reality against an idealised view. Sagittarian characters must often learn to distinguish between ideal and reality. Sagittarius is a sign famed for its love of truth. Capricorn is another sign concerned with truth, but in a significantly different way, best illustrated at this point by saying that Capricorn distortion of truth we call hypocrisy, while the Sagittarian guilty of the same is more likely to be called a myopic or romantic dreamer.

Carlo Collodi, *Pinocchio*
Pinocchio is a moral fable and a tale of upward aspiration, of a wooden puppet who wants to become a flesh-and-blood little boy. He eventually realises his goal by obeying the moral dictates of his Good

Fairy conscience, and by living the human virtues of truth, goodness and self-sacrifice. This sign seems to incorporate the idea that moral choice rests with the individual, and that there are no half-measures; one must choose to walk with the gods, or necessarily degenerate to the level of a beast. This is certainly the experience of Pinocchio. He strays often from his course, and whenever he does seems to suffer for it, at one point, literally turning into a beast, a donkey. In Sagittarius the need is to associate with the higher rather than lower nature, and to abandon the path of righteousness is to be damned. This same theme of a tightrope of righteousness is the crux of Bunyan's *The Pilgrim's Progress*, and of much of the writing of Isaac Bashevis Singer – one foot from God and we plunge into the abyss, is how he puts it.[33] It occurs too in Conrad's popular work, *Heart of Darkness*, and in Swift's *Gulliver's Travels*.

Joseph Conrad, *Heart of Darkness*

The pivotal character in *Heart of Darkness* is Kurtz, an ivory trader who establishes a base deep in the Congo. His business is successful but he is feared and despised by his colleagues because his methods are 'unsound'. He seems to hold a messianic sway over the tribes of the interior and he is known to have committed atrocities. Also we are told, 'he lacked restraint in the gratification of his lusts'.

But Kurtz had not entered Africa such a man. Far from it. We are informed that at one time he was one of the most civilised of men, admired for his culture and intellect, respected for his idealism. Indeed, we learn that before setting out for the Congo he had been entrusted to further the work of 'The International Society for the Suppression of Savage Customs'. In the 19th century central Africa was believed to be a satanic place (in the sense that Blake uses the word), and these black holes in the sea of faith acted as magnets to Christian missionaries. Kurtz sets out with the best of intentions, but once in the heart of primitive Africa he appears to abandon his humanity and succumbs to his animal nature. Though not strictly so, for animal savagery is for the most part instinctual and survival oriented, and in Kurtz what we seem to get is the worst of both worlds, an unhappy amalgam of reason and instinct whereby the darker drives are simply enhanced and given greater scope by the ingenuities of mind – in essence, a distorted outcrop of Sagittarian duality.

In one sense Kurtz personifies the colonial powers that occupied Africa in the 19th century and in some cases behaved abominably (particularly Belgium in the Congo). But beyond that, *Heart of Darkness* can be interpreted as a parable of the human condition.

Our civilisation may not be perfect but in its churches and cultural institutions it embodies something of the higher nature of man. If we reject it, as Kurtz does, then we court the abyss. By rejecting his higher nature Kurtz chooses his own mortal corruption and discovers too late 'the horror'. As with other Sagittarian writers the message seems to be: there are no half measures; reach for the stars, or be damned.

Woody Allen *Crimes and Misdemeanours*
Perhaps Allen's most thoughtful film, *Crimes and Misdemeanours* is an examination of contemporary morality. Judah, the central character, is a successful and wealthy ophthalmologist, happily married and a pillar of his community. But he also has a mistress and she threatens to reveal their two-year affair to his family. When he can not persuade her otherwise, he has her killed by a professional hit-man. Afterwards he suffers considerable emotional turmoil. Contrary arguments are put through various characters, some stating that the world is a moral place and God sees everything and punishes the wicked, while others dispute this and say the expedient act is justified, particularly if you get away it. Judah does, and comes to be at peace, despite being an accessory to murder.

A second strand of the film belongs to Cliff (played by Woody Allen). He's an idealist who values artistic integrity above all else. He wants to make serious films about weighty subjects. He despises Lester, a vain and shallow (but successful and wealthy) producer. Cliff's moral fastidiousness catches on the edges of reality. He loses not only the woman he worships but his faith is badly shaken when the philosopher he admires commits suicide. The film is rather depressing in its conclusion: cheats, charlatans and murderers seem to prosper, while the only high-minded character in the film is doomed to penury and obscurity. This runs against the grain in that generally in Sagittarius those who morally transgress come to a bad end.

Steven Spielberg, *Close Encounters of the Third Kind*
The essential thrust of this film, which Spielberg wrote and directed, is the human urge to experience something wonderful, superhuman or god-like, something more than the prosaic world of the senses. In this case that something is benign space aliens from a superior civilisation. Cable repair man Roy Neary's thirst for the extraordinary is ignited by an epiphany while he is about his work (an encounter of the second kind). He becomes obsessed by an image he can't understand, grows more dissatisfied with the everyday world of his job and family and finally abandons both to pursue his quest. He

infiltrates the elaborate government operation that has been established to land an alien spaceship in Wyoming, and ends the film boarding the alien craft, where, we assume, he lived happily ever after in a distant galaxy.

Jonathan Swift, *Gulliver's Travels*
Gulliver's sojourn in Houyhnhnmland forms another example of the reason-instinct theme. In this place, by some strange inversion, horses have come to be the dominant species. The word 'Houyhnhnm', we are told, means a horse and signifies in its etymology 'the perfection of nature'.[34]

They are noble creatures, these horses, possessed of all those qualities that are regarded as the best in human nature. Indeed, Gulliver wishes they might be sent to Europe to teach some of the inhabitants there 'the first principles of honour, justice, truth, temperance, public spirit, fortitude, chastity, friendship, benevolence, and fidelity'.[35] The horses value truth so highly that there is not even a word for 'lie' in their vocabulary.

In the same land Gulliver discovers a second species called Yahoos. Physically Yahoos are human-like but temperamentally they are brutish, motivated only by their primitive wants. They are feared by Gulliver and despised by the horses, who use them as beasts of burden and tether them in sties. A Houyhnhnm and a Yahoo stand sundered, at opposite ends of a dipole. One is incapable of acting like the other. But Gulliver is different. Physically he is not far removed from a Yahoo, and, as an individual, he is a reasonable being and close to the horses. But Gulliver's species – humankind – is another matter. The horses are shocked to hear of the appalling deeds of Gulliver's European contemporaries. Humankind has the potential to be as the horses, and yet it chooses not to use it (and we are reminded that Swift once described mankind as a 'pernicious race of odious little vermin'). Once more, what we have is a perversion of the reason-instinct polarity.

Gulliver is eventually expelled from Houyhnhnmland, but the memory of the virtuous horses stays with him. He is unable to adjust to a prosaic life in his own country, but suffers a divine discontent, haunted by possibilities of what might be, pricked by unlived potential. At the same time Gulliver perhaps learns most from this, the last of his voyages. He is reminded that men have the power to be godlike. The memory of the Houyhnhnms seems to act as an ideal and an inspiration, a focus of aspiration in a gross world.

One variation of the ideal-reality theme might be titled disenchantment. Characters in Sagittarian novels can fantasise excessively. They believe themselves to be something they are not, and particularly to be something more glamorous, noble or important than in reality they are, but usually they end up disenchanted. When characters such as Thurber's Walter Mitty and Twain's Tom Sawyer fall to earth the result is generally harmless and comic. In the case of Conrad's Lord Jim and Flaubert's Emma Bovary, however, the outcomes are tragic.

In *Lord Jim*, the eponymous central character is an incorrigible romantic unable to live up to the idealised image he holds of himself. The following analysis of his character, taken from a critique of the novel, supports this view. He is described as a man:

> ... whose will is valiant and whose behaviour is craven, who is bravely active in his intentions and disastrously passive in his deeds, whose ideal aspirations are courageous and whose real conduct in a crisis is ignoble. He is a man who pursues a glamorous dream at the same time as he flees from an ugly fact. In him the *best and basest* of human motives are ominously interwoven.[36] (My emphasis)

Jim's heroic self-image is shattered when the ship on which he is first mate threatens to sink. Dream and reality are brought face to face and he has a chance to be a real hero. But he fails to meet his destiny, and instead of being a hero he flees ignominiously. The ship does not sink after all so his behaviour comes to official attention. He is disciplined by an enquiry but the greater punishment comes from disenchantment. He is forced to face up to the fact that he is not heroic, but all too human. In effect he loses his foothold in the bright world of the spirit and is condemned to a life he finds grey, ordinary and meaningless.

However, the opportunity for redemption comes his way. He finds himself in a remote and untamed Asian province, and through his own efforts he establishes some sort of moral order in what had been a 'satanic' community. He wins the respect of the people, becoming in their eyes Tuan Jim, 'the visible tangible incarnation of unfailing truth and unfailing virtue'. He becomes something heroic, but only by establishing a creative equilibrium between ideal and reality, and only, finally, by devotion to something bigger than himself.

Gustave Flaubert, *Madame Bovary*

Emma Bovary is characteristically Sagittarian in that she finds it impossible to abide a prosaic life. She yearns for something exalted and extraordinary, some transcendent splendour. She is a woman of passion, in the sense that her first lover describes passion, as 'the only beautiful thing there is on earth, the source of heroism, enthusiasm, poetry, music, art, of everything'. She is Romantic with a capital R, attuned to the exotic or, more generally, things remote from everyday life. However, as much as Emma reaches for the stars she fails finally to extricate herself from the swamps of provincial dullness and mediocrity.

Emma is raised on a farm, and at due age attends a convent school, where she is drawn to music and literature, and to religion, perhaps sensing in its mystery that something exalted she so craves. Her teacher-nuns are pleased with her piety, and are hopeful that Emma might join them in the sisterhood. However, she does not embrace the Church. At the same time she does not abandon religion and whenever her dreams are most violently shattered she finds some solace in God.

On her father's remote farm few eligible men would have come into Emma's life so it is quite credible that she marries the first one who does, Charles Bovary, a simple country doctor. She enters marriage with high hopes but even the morning after the wedding night we perceive disappointment. The consummation produces in Charles a giddy air, but Emma seems unmoved. We can imagine that whatever Charles' prowess as a lover, he could not possibly live up to his wife's high expectations. When sex fails to transport her, as it did the heroines of the romantic fiction she imbibed in her youth, the first seeds of disappointment are sown.

Throughout the book, and with increasing intensity, Emma suffers the chill of disenchantment (the inevitable shadow of high hopes). The marriage falls far short of her inflated expectations, and she broods on lost possibility, on what might have been and the life she might have led:

> Everything in her immediate surroundings, the boring countryside, the imbecile petit bourgeois, the general mediocrity of life, seemed to be a kind of anomaly, a unique accident that had befallen her alone, while beyond, as far as the eye could see, there unfurled the immense kingdom of pleasure and passion ... Other people's lives, however drab they might be, were at least subject to chance. A single incident could bring about endless twists of fate, and the scene would shift. But in her life nothing was going to happen. Such was the will of God! The future was a dark corridor and at the far end the door was bolted.[37]

Emma comes to loathe Charles, both for what he is and what he is not. He is not the Byronic lover of her imaginings. He's a simple country doctor making a meagre living. He examines his patients' excrement, bleeds and purges them. He is decent, devoted and hardworking, but dull. He has no dreams, no ambition, simply a bovine contentment:

> Charles's conversation was as flat as any pavement, everyone's ideas trudging along it in their weekday clothes, rousing no emotion, no laughter, no reverie.[38]

Charles, for his part, adores his wife. To him she is a source of pride and pleasure, something she seems to resent. His solid but unexciting qualities do not register with Emma. She would prefer it (at least in her imaginings) if he were a poet struggling in a garret. Charles' father, however, accords more with her idea of what a man should be: he is an old soldier, something of a roué, the wrong side of respectable, and yet colourful, romantic, a man of the world with stories to tell.

And then there is the Marquis's father. In gratitude for medical services rendered by Charles, he and Emma are invited to a ball at the Marquis's country home. At table she listens enthralled to the stories surrounding the Marquis's father. He is probably the most unattractive man in the room. He is old, has bloodshot eyes, and sits dribbling gravy from his lips. Yet he had led a tumultuous life. Here was a man who had moved in the court circles of a glittering age. Here was a man who (it was said) had slept with Marie Antoinette. Emma is plainly captivated by this aristocratic world, and the occasion is one that leaves a profound impression. In her eyes the people here – like the Parisian high society she worships – were as Olympians:

> Extravagant as kings, they were full of idealistic ambitions and wild enthusiasm. They lived on a higher plane, between heaven and earth, among storm clouds, so sublimely. As for the rest of the world, it was nothing, it was nowhere, it scarcely seemed to exist.[39]

Charles on the other hand is completely out of place at the ball; he spends the evening somewhat bemused, and watching the card games. Certain she has discovered what she yearns for, Emma awaits anxiously for the next invitation. But it never comes.

There is an episode when it seems the couple might be reconciled. At the suggestion of a friend, and encouraged by Emma, Charles attempts to cure the village ostler of his club-foot using a new and untried operation. Emma sees possibilities: if her husband cures the man, fame will follow and the name of Bovary will spread throughout France. Clients will beat a pathway to their door and wealth and luxury will follow. It seems at first that the operation is a success and for a short time Emma treats her husband as a hero.

But there are complications and the ostler loses his leg. Humiliation rains down on Charles, while Emma's scorn for him returns intensified. As the novel progresses Emma becomes more gripped by fantasy. She takes lovers, surrounds herself with luxury, believes herself an aristocratic lady of leisure. But she finds in adultery the same emptiness she found in marriage. It is a touch ironic: Flaubert's contemporaries found his book shocking, by and large because his heroine did not regret or repent her adultery. And yet, as so commonly with Sagittarians, it is this moral lapse that precipitates Emma's final calamity. A common Sagittarian failing is extravagance and Emma is no exception. Reality catches up with her in the form of unpaid bills and the threat of the bailiffs, and rather than disgrace she chooses death.

Even in her death we sense disillusionment. Her suicide has something of cheap fiction and grand gesture about it. She takes poison, and in her fervid imaginings no doubt saw a peaceful falling asleep, friends and family constellated about the bed in tearful poses, flowers and incense, and the mournful intoning of the priest. But in reality she dies surrounded by hysteria and incompetence, writhing in agony and vomiting black liquid.

In part Emma Bovary might be a victim of her time and circumstances, yet only rarely, and with little conviction, does she complain at being a woman (when pregnant she hopes for a son, for example, acknowledging that men had more freedom to pursue adventure). She is more a victim of temperament. She would have been dissatisfied anywhere. She never visits Paris, yet idealises the city. Had she been raised in Paris, in its reality, she would have craved some imagined rural idyll, with pastures, shepherds and rustic innocence.

Essentially Emma Bovary is unable to formulate what it is she craves. There is throughout the book a certain vagueness about her fantasies, because she is unable to translate them within the world of her own limited mind. There is harmony in balance, and Madame Bovary is an unbalanced being. In astrological terms there is too much Fire, not enough compensating Earth. A contemporary astro-therapist would have advised her to work on this imbalance: cherish your dreams, but come to terms with reality.[40]

In this same way Charles and Emma form an antithesis. They are literally poles apart. Charles can not contemplate the majestic heights to which his wife aspires. Charles' world to Emma is at best vague and shadowy, at worst sordid. Charles is unbalanced himself, so that too much Earth makes him stolid and unimaginative. But he achieves a measure of balance through his wife. He feeds off her

Fire. When she dies he deteriorates rapidly and likewise dies before his time.

Notes

1. *Contemporary Novelists*, ed James Vinson, St James Press, 1976, p49
2. ibid, p1495
3. *World Authors 1950-70*, ed J Wakeman, J W Wilson, 1975, p1169
4. *Reference Guide to English Literature*, Vol 1, ed D L Kirkpatrick, St James Press, 1991, p199
5. *Contemporary Poets*, ed James Vinson, Macmillan, 1980, p28
6. *European Authors 1000-1900*, V Colby and S Kunitz, H W Wilson, 1967
7. *Contemporary Novelists*, ed James Vinson, St James Press, 1976, p254
8. *Great Writers of the English Language: Novelists and Prose Writers*, ed James Vinson, Macmillan, 1979, p572
9. *Encyclopaedia Britannica*, Vol 4, 1942, p414
10. *Contemporary Novelists*, ed James Vinson, St James Press, 1976, p283
11. *Cassell's Encyclopaedia of Literature*, Vol 2, ed. S Steinberg, Cassell
12. *American Writers*, Charles Scribner's Sons, Vol 1, 1974
13. *Contemporary World Writers*, St James Press, 1993, p26
14. ibid, p493
15. *Great Women Writers*, ed Frank Magill, Robert Hale, 1994, p8
16 *Dictionary of Literary Biography*, Vol 13, Gale Research, 1982
17. *An Encyclopaedia of British Women Writers*, ed Paul & June Schlueter, Garland Press, 1988, p221
18. *St James Guide to Science Fiction Writers*, St James Press, 1996, p785
19. *Great Women Writers*, ed Frank Magill, Robert Hale, 1994, p394
20. Samuel Johnson, *The Lives of the Poets*, Vol 1, ed Roger Lonsdale, Oxford University Press, 2006, p283
21. *Reference Guide to American Literature*, ed Thomas Riggs, St James Press, 2000, p25
22. *Encyclopaedia of World Literature in the 20th Century*, Vol 3, ed Steven R Serafin, St James Press, 1999, p275
23. We can also note that in the Tree of Life the prime virtue associated with Chesed/Jupiter is obedience.
24. P A Sorokin, *Social and Cultural Dynamics*, American Book Co, 1937
25. See, for example, *The Flint Anchor*, Sylvia Townsend Warner, and *The Last Puritan*, George Santayana
26. Dane Rudhyar, *Astrological Signs, The Pulse of Life*, Shambhala, 1938, p96-97
27. See Paul Wright, *Jupiter & Mercury an A to Z*, Flare Publications, 2006
28. Frances Deutsch Louis, *Swift's Anatomy of Misunderstanding*, George Prior, 1981, p124
29. ibid, p18

30. For example, on the north porch of the west front of Amiens Cathedral, dating from the 13th century. See Frederick Goodman, *Zodiac Symbols*, Brian Trodd Publishing House, 1990, p111

31. This aspect of the sign is not often mentioned in astrological texts, but Charles Carter's observation is an exception: 'Perhaps the Centaur Sagittarius stands for the alternatives: further growth in the company of gods or reversion to a sub-human state.' (*Essays on the Foundations of Astrology,* Theosophical Publishing House, 1978, p128)

32. We find this capacity in other Sagittarian Sun musicians. One critic has noted of Jimi Hendrix, for example:

> undoubtedly the most adventurous and daring electric guitarist of the Sixties, Hendrix *enormously expanded the possibilities* of the instrument, masterfully manipulating devices such as the wah-wah pedal, fuzz box, uni-vibe and tape-delay mechanism to produce sounds sometimes gentle and melodic, but more often loud and psychedelic, even extraterrestrial and aquatic. (Brock Helander, *The Rock Who's Who*, Schirmir Press, 1982, p244. My emphasis).

33. We can note the following observation of Singer: 'No other writer mirrors so clearly man's urge towards the sacred and yielding to the profane.' (*American Writers*, Vol 4, Charles Scribner's Sons, 1974, p7)

34. Jonathan Swift, *Gulliver's Travels*, Penguin, 1981, p281

35. ibid, p343

36. Tony Tanner, *Studies in English Literature 12, Conrad: Lord Jim*, Edward Arnold, 1963, p7

37. Gustave Flaubert, *Madame Bovary*, Penguin Classics, 1992, p49

38. ibid, page 31

39. ibid, page 46

40. Bovarism (or Bovaryism) is a recognised psychological syndrome, described in one text thus: 'Holding an unreal, glamorised conception of the self to the extent that one fails to distinguish between romance and reality. (*Encyclopaedia of Psychology,* vol 1, eds H Eysenck and R Meili, Search Press, 1972)

Capricorn

Writers with the Sun in Capricorn include: Matthew Arnold, Isaac Asimov, Nina Bawden, Julian Barnes, Peter Barnes, Pio Baroja, Robert Bly, James Bridie, Alejo Carpentier, Wilkie Collins, Nigel Dennis, John Dos Passos, Umberto Eco, Ronald Firbank, Theodor Fontane, E M Forster, Alasdair Gray, L P Hartley, William James, Jennifer Johnston, Robinson Jeffers, Juan Ramón Jiménez, Rudyard Kipling, Fritz Leiber, Jack London, Henry Miller, A A Milne, Timothy Mo, Molière, Kyle Onstott, Joe Orton, Alan Paton, Edgar Allan Poe, Simon Raven, J D Salinger, Wilbur Smith, Susan Sontag, Henrietta Stannard, J R R Tolkein, Alan Watts, Dennis Wheatley.

Summary: Writers of this sign are the enemies of hypocrisy, and are often concerned with a shift from outer values to some inner world reflective of the genuine self. Capricorn writers seem attuned to Earth energies and more than other signs lament the impact of technology and civilisation on the Earth. Another major theme is caste or class systems, specifically a resigned understanding that no good comes of defying these artificial but very solid structures.

> But Man is an odd, sad creature as yet, intent on pilfering the earth, and heedless of the growths within himself.
> **E M Forster**

> The goat is noted for hardness outwardly and weakness within.
> **I Ching**

A good encapsulation of the essence of this sign is found in J D Salinger's *The Catcher in the Rye*. This is a straightforward tale of a few days in the life of a teenager, Holden Caulfield. He is expelled from his boarding school but rather than go home right away to face his parents he spends some days in New York in a kind of aimless limbo. In the final chapter we learn that a new school has been arranged for the following term.

Beneath the surface events, the book is about sham and teenage ennui. Holden fails his exams not because he is unintelligent but because he finds the school objectionable and is not able to apply himself. As he tells his sister: 'It was one of the worst schools I ever went to. It was full of phonies. And mean guys.'[1] The mean guys he goes on to describe are guilty of snobbishness, a failing Holden ranks second only to phoniness, or hypocrisy. In this novel 'phoney' is a word that occurs frequently in Holden's judgements, and we soon discover he values people in inverse proportion to their propensity for this trait.

The main component of Holden's ennui is a strong awareness of the falseness of much modern life. His crisis revolves around the desire to be genuine, to avoid in any way being a hypocrite. In a heart-to-heart with his sister he talks about his future role in life, for such decisions are being demanded of him. He considers law but rejects this because in his eyes it is a profession where form and appearance seem more important than anything else:

> Lawyers are all right, I guess ... I mean they're all right if they go around saving innocent guys' lives all the time, and like that, but you don't *do* that kind of stuff if you're a lawyer. All you do is make a lot of dough and play golf and play bridge and buy cars and drink martinis and look like a hot-shot. And besides. Even if you did go around saving guys' lives and all, how would you know if you did it because you really *wanted* to save guys' lives, or you did it because what you *really* wanted to do was be a terrific lawyer ... How would you know you weren't being a phoney? The trouble is, you *wouldn't*.[2]

As we will see in the course of the chapter, Capricorn relates to the idea of a shift from the objective to the subjective, a turning away from the outer world to something person-centred. As far as I am aware, it was the astrologer and psychologist Liz Greene who first established the essential meaning of Saturn, Capricorn's ruling planet, as this same polarisation:

> Saturn is connected with the educational value of pain and with the difference between external values – those which we acquire from others – and internal values – those which we have worked to discover within ourselves ... By denying a component which ordinarily comes from the environment, Saturn's influence forces an individual to create that missing component himself if he is to have any peace. He must gradually withdraw identification of the value with the external world and find its reality within himself as part of his own psyche.[3]

Just such a shift is at the heart of Holden Caulfield's crisis. Social roles no longer seem important to him. The only thing he wants to *be* is the 'catcher in the rye' – something which has no objective reality at all, but is a figment sparked in his imagination by a Robert Burns poem. Importantly, though, it is of the heart and internal, not something sanctioned from without.

This idea of a deviation between outer form and inner meaning explains why a common theme among Capricorn writing is hypocrisy, as the following quotes taken from critics' analysis suggest:

> **Pío Baroja**
> All his books rise out of a characteristic view of life which changed little through the years. He saw sham and falsity in nearly everything around him and hated them with a remarkable intensity.[4]
>
> **James Bridie**
> An intense loathing of hypocrisy and humbug.[5]
>
> **Calder Willingham**
> An enemy of hypocrisy who turns its lies and pretences back on themselves.[6]
>
> **Nina Bawden**
> [Her] best novels ... are about the central characters' efforts to achieve honesty to self, to separate the genuine from the hypocritical or convenient motive.[7]
>
> **Joe Rosenblatt**
> My ... verse and prose poems ... attack the human condition and society with its crass materialism and phoney value-structure.[8]

Molière's character Tartuffe has become synonymous with the word 'hypocrite'. Orton's plays have given rise to the expression 'Ortonesque' to describe a dissociation between what a character says and what he does. It is interesting to note that some ancient zodiacs have used the amphibious crocodile, rather than the goat-fish hybrid, as a symbol for this sign. There may be a connection here with the expression 'crocodile tears', weeping for show, rather than to express genuine sorrow. The peculiar sigil that commonly represents Capricorn suggests a contrast between the watery inner world of feeling, and the outer rocky domain of the mountain goat.

According to Rudhyar, Capricorn is the phase of the zodiac where the collectivising force is at a maximum. This, he tells us:

> impels the individual to seek an ever deeper identification with ever larger collectivities. It brings to men the generalisations and discoveries of civilisation, whose development binds together generation to generation, racial group to racial group, individual achievement to individual achievement until personalities discover themselves to be but

> relatively insignificant cells in the vast organism of human society. Tribal groups and smaller nations ultimately disappear. The days of the Empire have come ... Capricorn symbolises thus any typical state organisation encompassing large territories and various racial groups, and all that goes with such an organisation.[9]

We witnessed the collectivising process in action in the twentieth century with the transformation of Russia and (to an extent) China from essentially feudal societies to powerful nation states. It seems significant that in each case it was masterminded by men – Stalin and Mao – who were Capricorn Suns. Nasser too, who did much to modernise Egypt, was a Capricorn Sun, as was Konrad Adenauer, who led the reconstruction of a modern German state following the Second World War.

However, this does not mean that Capricorn writers champion the state in the same way that Cancer writers do the individual. At best they are ambivalent, recognising that socialisation has a dark as well as a bright side. It may protect and expand the scope of the individual, but at the same time it dehumanises and enslaves. Yet Capricorn more than most is aware of the shortcomings of smallness, the parochialism, self-interest and blind subjectivity that is the negative side of the Cancer coin. Capricorn is capable of thinking big, of operating on a vast scale, and transcending boundaries to embrace ever larger frames of reference, from personal to national, international and cosmic. In Capricorn's polar sign, Cancer, the collectivising force is at a minimum, and one outcome of this was an ill-defined fear of totalitarianism, particularly an abhorrence of distant rules or laws that trammel the idiosyncratic expression of the individual. Big Brother was the nightmare of Cancer, a vague bogey in that sign that becomes the actualised state in Capricorn.

The fulfilment of a sign's meaning involves a reorienting towards the polar horizon, a tempering, as it were, of the pure sign meaning in terms of a distant potential. Capricorn, then, is not in essence the all-encompassing state, or the avid pursuit of wealth and position, although it commonly enough produces those who embody these traits. Rather, it is the beginning of a change, because a certain mode of development has culminated. This expresses in Capricorn writing in a number of ways. There can be a focus upon the deviation between outer form and inner meaning – themes of hypocrisy, as we noted earlier. Or the concern is with the impact the structures of the social world have on the individual. And Capricorns can write about the attempt to reconnect with some inner spiritual core. Capricorn is an Earth sign so 'spiritual' can be taken broadly to embrace the kind of nature spirit symbolised by figures such as Pan and Dionysus (and we note a similarity with Virgo, another Earth sign). Related to this, the concern of some Capricorn writers is the impact of civilisation on the natural world, as the following critical observations suggest:

> **Douglas Livingstone**
> Preoccupied with the disrupting effect of Western civilisation upon primitive peoples and traditions.[10]
>
> **A B Guthrie**
> Again and again, Guthrie returns to this theme: desirable – and necessary – though progress and civilisation may be, they come at the cost of terrible and irreversible changes in a way of life, and in the world itself.[11]
>
> **Alan Paton**
> [His writings are] powerful modern renderings of ... the contrast between the beauty of the natural world as man found it and the ugly place that his greed and narrow-mindedness have made of it.[12]
>
> **Robinson Jeffers**
> [His] twenty or so books of verse interpret man as depraved and disgusting compared with the wild integrity of nature.[13]
>
> **Allen Planz**
> [Author] Recently I've come to think of my best work as discovery – discovering again the ancient relations between man and earth.[14]
>
> **Rudyard Kipling**
> His imperialism ... at least constituted a serious call to return to the instinctual morality of corporate face-to-face groups in place of the hypocritical moral absolutes of depersonalised society ... [he restored] a balance to over-urbanised over-intellectualised society by linking it in service with the under-developed world and renewing it spiritually, by fresh contact there with nature and otherness.[15]
>
> **Barry Lopez**
> Lopez has made it his life's work to reveal the vast wonder of the natural world – its majesty, beauty and terror – to a culture that he believes is rapidly losing this knowledge[16]

The I Ching hexagram related to Capricorn is number 24, 'The Turning Point', or 'Return' and its theme is, once more, this idea of turning away from the outer world to an inner light. 'Return is small yet different from external thing',[17] notes the text, emphasising that we are dealing with a turning *point*, with the germ of something different from externality. We could say Holden Caulfield's 'germ' is the catcher in the rye which, however nonsensical, stands for something fundamentally different from the values of his school, parents and society.

In the text appended to the hexagram Wilhelm remarks:

> The light principle returns: thus the hexagram counsels turning away

> from the confusion of external things, turning back to one's inner light. There in the depths of the soul, one sees the Divine, the One. It is indeed only germinal, no more than a beginning, a potentiality, but as such clearly to be distinguished from all objects. To know this One means to know oneself in relation to the cosmic forces. For this One is the ascending force of life in nature and in man.[18]

The beginning of the sign Capricorn corresponds to the winter solstice. We look upon this time – around about 21 December in the northern hemisphere – as the beginning of winter, and yet equally it corresponds to a turnaround. In astronomical terms the winter solstice represents the limit of the sun's southerly declination. It will stand directly overhead at the Tropic of Capricorn, 23 degrees south, while in northern skies it will culminate as near to the horizon as it ever gets (in polar latitudes below the horizon). However, and very slowly at first, this culminating point rises higher each day, so that the days grow longer and warmer, until, eventually, it reaches a maximum at the summer solstice, the first point of Cancer.

To primitive peoples, particularly those who dwelt in high latitudes, the winter solstice was recognised as a special time and solstitial festivals celebrated the renewal of life through the return of the sun, or more generally embodied the idea of a turnabout. A good example of the latter was the Roman Saturnalia, celebrated between 17 and 23 December. (Saturn, we are reminded, is the planet ruling Capricorn.) Sir James Frazer describes the Saturnalia as:

> An annual period of licence, when the customary restraints of law and morality are thrown aside, when the whole population give themselves up to extravagant mirth and jollity, and when the darker passions find a vent which would never be allowed them in the more staid and sober course of ordinary life.[19]

What was remarkable about the Saturnalia, notes Frazer, was the inversion of the social order which took place at this time. For the period of the festival masters and slaves changed roles, and this focus upon the social order is characteristically Capricorn.[20] We can note also that the celebration was in honour of Saturn, a fabled king who, it seems, presided over the first communist state. In the age of Saturn there was no slavery or private property, for like Stalin he collectivised agriculture. But Saturn's reign, like Stalin's, also had a shadowy side, with human sacrifice and bouts of Dionysian revelling. Not so much of the latter in the former Soviet Union, although vodka was a problem and fly agaric the rage in the Tundra, but plenty of the former with hundreds of thousands of lives sacrificed to the state machine.

Capricorn is traditionally held to be a cool, hard-headed, somewhat sceptical sign. There is certainly some truth in this, as there is in its association with the scientific temperament. And yet it is not by any means a sign wholly given to rationalism, for as much as setting limits on experience, according to the dictates of scientism, it seems just as intent on transcending these limits to explore – albeit in a detached scientific way – modes of being beyond our immediate ken.

So we find with Capricorn Suns people like Isaac Newton, who was as much interested in alchemy and theology as physics and mathematics, and William James who turned his scientist's eye to religious and drug-induced experience. Another Capricorn Sun was Carlos Castaneda, an anthropologist who recorded in a number of volumes his experiences under the tutelage of a Mexican Indian shaman he called 'Don Juan'. Sceptical but open-minded, with notepad and pen in hand, he too ventured beyond the boundaries of the rational to explore a mysterious stratum of reality, what might be called the forces of the living Earth, embodied in the flora, fauna and terrain of Mexico.

John C Lilly, also a Capricorn Sun, worked in a variety of scientific disciplines – biophysics, neurophysiology, neuroanatomy – and became well known for his work on communicating with dolphins. He also gained a certain cult status for his book *The Centre of the Cyclone*, a title which relates to the still point at the heart of the storm, to that

> rising quiet central low-pressure place in which one can learn to live eternally. Just outside the centre is the rotating storm of one's own ego, competing with other egos in a furious high-velocity circular dance.[21]

This is Lilly's perception of the emergence of the germinal Day Force, that inner seed which is different from external things.

The book recounts some of the extraordinary experiences he underwent in the course of exploring inner worlds, experiences induced by a variety of techniques including ingestion of LSD, sensory deprivation, combinations of the two, and, as he became more adept, a variety of less drastic spiritual techniques. Lilly's accounts of non-ordinary reality give an insight into a number of Capricorn concepts, not least the horror of a totally objective universe. The following description arises in the chapter titled 'A Guided Tour of Hell':

> Suddenly I was precipitated into what I later called 'the cosmic computer'. I was merely a very small programme in somebody else's huge computer ... I was being programmed by other senseless programmes above me and above them others. I was programming smaller programmes below me. I was meaningless. This whole computer was the result of a senseless

> dance of certain kinds of atoms in a certain place in the universe, stimulated and pushed by organised but meaningless energies. I travelled through the computer as a programme that floated through other programmes ... Everywhere I found entities like myself who were slave programmes in this huge cosmic conspiracy, this cosmic dance of energy and matter which had absolutely no meaning, no love, no human value. The computer was absolutely dispassionate, objective and terrifying.[22]

This then was Lilly's experience of Saturn/Capricorn as the symbol of impersonality and objectivity. Everything is external, mechanical, devoid of meaning or life.[23]

Capricorn and boundaries

Capricorn in traditional and contemporary astrology has much to do with boundaries, more specifically perhaps, as they relate to function and control within organised society. The following observation about Kipling tells us something about this side of Capricorn:

> Foremost in Kipling's mind was always the apprehension of danger without, and the agencies that must be used for protection against such perils – the Law and the Wall. It is a fundamental demand for strong government, an almost atavistic demand for security. His law is the Law of Civilisation and of progress ... the Wall ... became symbolic in Kipling's mind of the preservation of the Law. Once a breach is made in the Wall by the barbarian without, the Law is in danger. At all costs it must be held against the forces of anarchy and rapine.[24]

We think also of things like the Pale in 16th and 17th century Ireland, a region of variable size centred upon Dublin, which marked the extent of effective English rule. Beyond the Pale (and hence the phrase) wild Irish manners prevailed. Related to boundaries and a recurring theme in Capricorn novels is transgression of the social order, and the destructive consequences that are invariably the outcome.[25] The breach is generally plugged, but only after the damage has been done, usually to an individual of a lower social order. Three Capricorn writers in which this is evident are L P Hartley, Jack London and E M Forster.

L P Hartley, *The Go-Between*

This novel is set for the most part in late-Victorian England and tells the story of 12-year-old Leo Colston and the summer holiday he passes at the home of a school friend. Away from the protective confines of home and school for the first time he is forced to cope with the unfamiliar world of adults. It proves to be an experience that marks him for the rest of his life.

Capricorn is a very controlled sign and this manifests in a number of ways. One is the cultivation of a public image. The individual presents to the world only what he or she wants to reveal. It is often a well-behaved face, one that conforms to social norms, but it can also be a role the person acts out, something he decides he wants to be, and which may bear some or no resemblance to what he actually is. On the whole those strong in Capricorn can, over time, learn to function very well in public life. However, Leo Colston is probably too young to have cultivated this polished veneer. It is made plain that he feels very self-conscious amongst his so-called betters, terrified of doing the wrong thing, or appearing foolish. The first thing he discovers in his sojourn at the Hall is the importance of dress. He arrives with a totally inappropriate wardrobe, something which distresses him:

> Hitherto I had always taken my appearance for granted; now I saw how inelegant it was compared with theirs; and at the same time, and for the first time, I was acutely aware of social inferiority. I felt utterly out of place among these smart rich people.[26]

He is sent with Marian, his school friend's older sister, on a trip to Norwich to buy new clothes, and learns from her that outfits are worn for effect, for the impression they make on others, rather than for their feel. And he remarks later that his pride in his new outfit had altered his outlook on the world, and his relation to it.

At the heart of *The Go-Between* is the transgression of those invisible but rigid and formidable boundaries that structured social life in Victorian and Edwardian England. Leo's friend, Marcus, and his family are of a high social standing. Their home, Brandham Hall, exists in a more-or-less feudal relationship with the nearby village. The biggest social snob, or at least the most overt, is Marcus himself. There are a number of occasions where he can not disguise his contempt for the villagers. Being so young he has not yet learned that it is bad form actually to speak one's superiority; it is enough to assume it.

However, there is an occasion in the Brandham year when the normal social restraints are relaxed. At the annual cricket match between Hall and village, and at the concert afterwards, commoner and gentry can compete and socialise more or less on equal terms, although there is still deference and difference, and there is form to be followed. The fact that at no other time can there be this familiarity and co-mingling forms the thrust of the story.

Marian has a passion for a tenant framer, Ted, and in secret trysts they pursue an illicit and carnal affair – illicit, because public opinion will not allow such a liaison. Marian is betrothed to one of her own class, Hugh, the Viscount Trimingham, whom she no doubt likes and respects, and accepts that it is her duty to marry. But she does not love him, and one imagines the relationship has little of the animal passion that is generated between she and the earthy Ted. Indeed, we can imagine his vitality and simplicity are what attract Marian. Even when she is old, she never regrets the relationship, despite the fact that it destroyed or tainted a number of lives. At the end of the book, when Leo, now an old man,[27] meets up with her, she still maintains the value of the relationship, as something genuine, a union of 'happiness and beauty' that stood in sharp contrast to the formality of the Hall and its arranged marriages and well-ordered behaviour.

Leo is the messenger, a go-between bridging the two classes with the letters he carries from one to the other to arrange their trysts. It is a role he accepts willingly at first, because he is won over by the charm of Marian and feels flattered that she is interested in him at all. He innocently assumes the messages concern business, but when he discovers the relationship is more than businesslike he is less keen to act as messenger. There are a number of reasons why what had been a pleasure becomes an onerous duty. In the first case there is some sense of betrayal, for he likes the Viscount, Marian's fiancé. But something deeper baulks too. At heart, perhaps unconsciously, Leo approves the social order. He judges the relationship to be wrong, feels people should keep their place. In the cricket match, largely thanks to Ted's spirited batting, it seems as if the village side will prevail, which possibility disturbs Leo. But in the end it is his own action – a good catch that dismisses Ted – that saves the match and, as it were, maintains the social stability.

Perhaps what is the hardest thing for Leo to bear is the realisation that people speak one thing with their mouths, another with their hearts. At first, innocently, he takes Marian's interest in him at face value, as friendliness, kindness, even affection. But he comes to realise that she had an ulterior motive, and that her affection was somewhat contingent on his complaisance. The expedition to Norwich turns out to be not so much thoughtfulness as opportunist, a chance to be with her lover for an hour. Buying Leo a bike for his birthday simply meant he could deliver the messages more efficiently.

In the end the relationship is discovered, Ted commits suicide, and Marian, pregnant, marries the Viscount. Leo, probably feeling himself partly responsible for the tragedy, undergoes an emotional breakdown. He recovers and yet we are left in no doubt that the whole episode has indelibly marked him, made of him a 'cindery creature' who, as he put it, spent his life in a dusty room cataloguing books instead of writing his own. He seems to dwell in a limbo, cut off from his imagination but equally reluctant to enter the adult world with its false face of hypocrisy and its demands to achieve.

Jack London, *Martin Eden*

Martin Eden is the story of one man's burning ambition to better himself, and of the emptiness he discovers once his ambition is realised. The eponymous hero is a sailor and adventurer who one night rescues a young man from a drunken gang. Out of gratitude Martin is invited to the man's family home for dinner, where he passes a self-conscious evening amongst people he regards as his social superiors. At the same time, he is captivated by their cosmopolitan manners and resolves to be like them. He also falls in love with the young man's sister, Ruth.

In what is very much an attraction of opposites the relationship develops and they become engaged. Ruth is stirred by the vigour and earthy masculinity of Martin, while he is moved by her refinement and learning. Ruth's parents collude with what is happening, not because they approve the match, but because they believe Martin will serve the purpose of awakening Ruth's romantic nature so that when the time comes it will be easier to pair her off with a more suitable partner.

Ruth is cool, conventional, snobbish, sterile, and almost wholly attuned to appearances. When she agrees to help Martin in his programme of self-education she begins by working on his diction, believing how you speak is more important than what you say. At university she was taught what to think, not how to, so when it comes to debate she sides with authority:

> She did not weigh Martin's words, nor judge his arguments by them. Her conclusion that his argument was wrong was reached ... by a comparison of externals. They the professors were right ... because they were successes. Martin's literary judgements were wrong because he could not sell his wares.[28]

As poverty and failure accumulate about Martin, the engagement is broken off, but once he is a success – measured by publication and dollars – she is prepared to renew it. Martin undertakes a gruelling regimen to improve his mind and financial position. He takes up writing because this seems to him an easy and efficient way of making money.

In the end after much hard work and experiencing much failure he does achieve success. His books sell and are critically acclaimed, and he makes a lot of money. Yet he is far from happy. He appreciates that he is not being valued for himself, but because in the world's eyes he is a success.

Other Capricorn characters in fiction, and indeed in life, often come to the same conclusion. In Fontane's oeuvre, *Effi Briest*, for example, the detached, able, hard-working and ambitious Innstetten discovers too late the emptiness of his worldliness:

> I've lost all pleasure in everything. The more distinctions I earn, the more I feel that it's been valueless. I've made a mess of my life and so I've been thinking to myself I ought to have nothing to do with ambition.[29]

Martin Eden's pursuit of success cuts him off from his life source. Like Leo Colston, he ends up 'a cinder of a man', neither one thing nor the other. He does indeed 'shake off the incubus of his working class station', but in the process he swaps a personality for a persona, and only later realises his folly. It is also another example of a novel where transgressing social barriers leads to no good, for in the end he kills himself.

E M Forster, *Howard's End, A Passage to India*

Howard's End contrasts three families – the Wilcoxes, the Schlegels and the Basts. Henry, the head of the Wilcox family, is a successful businessman. Like his children he is unimaginative and conventional, and we discover in the course of the work that little seems to lie beneath a strong outer crust.

The Schlegels on the other hand are cultured, bohemian even. They take up Leonard Bast who, although of different social background – a menial clerk in an insurance company – is a sensitive and intelligent man. He is brought into contact with them through his pursuit of culture and (like Martin Eden) seems over-awed and self-conscious in the drawing-rooms of the well-to-do intelligentsia. Yet social distinctions do not seem to concern the Schlegels (as they do the snobbish Wilcoxes), for they value content more than form, seeing a man for what he is rather than who he is.

Despite the contrast in the families, Margaret Schlegel is attracted to Henry, particularly to his worldliness, his achievements and competence in business. As she remarks at one point to her sister:

> There is a great outer world that you and I have never touched – a life in which telegrams and anger count. Personal relations that we think supreme are not supreme there.[30]

Although Henry and Margaret agree to marry, the different worlds they represent do not really coalesce. It seems to be a common note in Capricorn novels that social barriers are very difficult to breach, and even when they are breached no good comes of it, as in *Howard's End*, when Leonard Bast dies, almost for his presumption. Capricorn is a sign that more accurately represents the first stirrings of the urge to transcend boundaries, or to substitute content for form, but the process is not brought to completion.

The concerns of *Howard's End* are found in other Forster novels, not least in *A Passage to India*, a work set in British India in the early part of the last century, when the Empire was still at its height. It centres about the arrival in the (fictitious) town of Chandrapore of two English ladies, Adela Quested and Mrs Moore, and an experience they later undergo in some local caves. Forster once said in an interview that even before he wrote a word of the novel he knew something was going to happen in the Marabar Caves and that it would represent the pivot of the novel.

An expedition to the caves is arranged by Dr Aziz (a Muslim). It comes about because he is anxious to court the company of his social superiors although at the same time is too ashamed to take them to his home, which he thinks not grand enough. But also because the women inform him they wanted to see 'the real India', the one that lay beyond the colonial compound. It's a wish that is fulfilled on the picnic, although not in the way they can have imagined.

In the course of the outing Aziz and Adela become separated from the main party, and then Adela is left alone in one of the caves. Something happens to her, the nature of which is ambiguous, but the outcome is she flees in a panic. Upon the return of the main party to the town Aziz is accused of assaulting Adela, arrested and imprisoned. Later at his trial he is acquitted because the young woman admits in clear-headed confession that an assault could not have taken place. The fact that Mrs Moore experienced a similar reaction to the caves seems to substantiate the confession.

The mythic Pan throws some light on the Marabar incident. Forster understood something of Pan, and indeed writes about him in a short story.[31] In one guise Pan symbolises those pagan and elemental earth forces that are given such vivid exposition in Castaneda's early writing, but which increasingly are being buried under concrete and tarmac as man 'civilises' his planet – something often lamented by Capricorn writers, as we noted earlier.

In another guise Pan represents fear, fear of what lies beyond the limit or the protective wall. Joseph Campbell has discussed this side of the god:

> ... this dangerous presence dwelling just beyond the protected zone of the village boundary ... The emotion that he instilled in human beings who by accident adventured into his domain was panic, fear, a sudden groundless fright. Any trifling cause then – the break of a twig, the flutter of a leaf – would flood the mind with imagined danger, and in the frantic effort to escape from his own aroused unconscious the victim expired in a flight of dread.[32]

Thus the word 'panic'. Although an ancient figure, Pan is no stranger to the modern world. Writer and statesman John Buchan, for example, recounts in his autobiography an encounter with the goat-footed god in an Alpine wood. His peasant guide was the first to react:

> suddenly he began to run, and I ran too ... terror had seized me also, but I did not know what I dreaded ... we ran – we ran like demented bacchanals, tearing down the glades, leaping rocks, bursting through thickets, colliding with trees, sometimes colliding with each other.[33]

Buchan concludes that his guide had seen Pan, and goes on to describe the similar experience of a friend climbing in Norway when 'the terror of space and solitude came upon him'.

Jack London is another who writes of 'the terror of space and solitude':

> Nature has many tricks wherewith she convinces man of his finity ... but the most stupendous, the most stupefying of all, is the passive phase of the White Silence. All movement ceases, the sky clears, the heavens are as brass ... and man becomes timid, affrighted at the sound of his own voice. Sole speck of life journeying across the ghostly wastes of a dead world ... Strange thoughts arise unsummoned, and the mystery of all things strives for utterance. And the fear of death, of God, of the universe comes over him.[34]

I think the goat-footed god is also at work in the panic reactions that sometimes result from mind-altering drugs, for these in their way represent stepping beyond the village compound of 'normal' reality to a vaster sphere of experience. To what Campbell terms 'the sacred zone of the universal source', or to Faerie, as Tolkein calls it, and warns that it is a perilous land with 'pitfalls for the unwary and dungeons for the overbold'. I can recall one such experience myself when what had been a blissful state was overtaken, for no apparent reason, by fear and a yearning for the dull but familiar reality of everyday. I retreated – in panic – but only to some black-hole of a place reeking of fear and isolation, and from which vantage the universe seemed a dark and hostile place promising only despair and hopelessness. Recalling the experience helped me understand something of Lilly's hell, London's white silence, and perhaps also the Marabar echo. For it was the cave's echo that proved most disturbing to the two English ladies, and which perhaps distilled for them 'the terror of space and solitude', or the experience of universal impersonality that diminishes the sense of self to one of insignificance in a meaningless void.

The fear induced by Pan is a subjective one, and this is shown in the different reactions of the two women. Mrs Moore does not panic, but seems able to put her experience into a cosmic perspective. Nevertheless, even she is not the same after her encounter. That Adela at first interprets her experience as attempted rape reflects not only the poverty of her own imagination but also the crass and unfeeling prejudices of her peers, who like most colonials harboured the view that all dark-skinned men are savages who will jump on a white woman given half a chance.

It is through the women's experiences in the caves that we begin to understand something of the way of the ruling Anglo-Indian caste, particularly the reliance on boundaries or defences. In primitive countries such as India (and Castaneda's Mexico) man lives closer to the earth, and civilisation, such as it is, stands in an uneasy truce with the wilderness. 'The inarticulate world is closer at hand,' observes Forster, 'and readier to resume control as soon as men are tired'.[35]

Although to an extent the 'muddle' of India was ordered by British administration, and its wildness trammelled by law and technology, Forster makes us aware throughout the book that this is a precarious order. A constant vigilance is necessary to prevent the chaos encroaching beyond the defences. 'Men try to be harmonious all the year round,' he writes, emphasising the mad-dog mentality of the conquering white man and the gulf between the artificial patterns of the ruling elite and the cycles of nature:

> and the results are occasionally disastrous. The triumphant machine of civilisation may suddenly hitch and be immobilised into a car of stone, and at such moments the destiny of the English seems to resemble their predecessors', who also entered the country with intent to refashion it but were in the end worked into its patterns and covered with its dust.[36]

We referred to Kipling (a Capricorn Sun) earlier but can note again that he was a man who approved of and appreciated the roads, cities, laws and bureaucracies that imposed shape on what in his day was a primitive sub-continent. The heroes of Kipling's writing are the soldiers, clerks and administrators who faithfully carried out their duty as cogs in the machine of Empire.[37]

For the ruling British, with their undeveloped hearts (as Forster put it), incapable of treating their 'inferiors' as human beings, the chaos and mystery of India was to a large extent embodied in its volatile people and consequently barriers were erected to exclude them from the colonial compound. Social intercourse was restricted as far as possible to token and formal interchange – the so-called bridge party (which had nothing to do with cards). An expedition organised by an Indian involving two English ladies was most unorthodox and from the outset it was discouraged by their peers. Newly arrived, the women are not tainted with the colonial creed. They are not pukka. It is definitely not pukka to want to venture beyond the compound to experience the 'real India'. The whole episode comes to be regarded as a lapse in vigilance, and the consequence was a breach in the defensive wall that allowed the 'muddle' of India to encroach and undermine British rule. That these Capricornian fears have some substance at least is born out by the carnage that followed independence in 1947, when, as J K Galbraith put it, 'all the pent up lawlessness of a century was suddenly released'.[38]

A Passage to India, then, goes beyond the politics of British India. It touches on more profound matters, and at this level we see Forster's astrological signature clearly reflected. Once more the picture of Capricorn that emerges is of a contrast between inner and outer, subjective and objective, and the difficulty in reconciling these. At the end of the book the boundaries remain as solid as ever, between British and natives, and between Hindu and Muslim. The impersonality of the outer world proves stronger than the intimacy of personal relationship, and when a barrier is breached – the Marabar incident – once more, no good comes of it.

Notes

1. J D Salinger, *The Catcher in the Rye*, Penguin, 1982, p174
2. ibid, pp178-79
3. Liz Greene, *Saturn, a New Look at an Old Devil*, Samuel Weiser, 1976, p10 and 22
4. *Concise Encyclopaedia of Modern World Literature*, ed Geoffrey Grigson, Hutchinson, 1963, p45
5. Winifred Bannister, *James Bridie and his Theatre*, Rockcliff, 1955, p9
6. *Contemporary Novelists*, ed James Vinson, St James Press, 1976, p1513
7. ibid, p106
8. *Contemporary Poets*, ed James Vinson, Macmillan, 1980, p1239
9. Dane Rudhyar, *Astrological Signs, the Pulse of Life*, Shambhala, 1978, p106
10. *Contemporary Poets*, ed James Vinson, Macmillan, 1980, p927

11. *Fifty Western Writers*, ed F Erisman & R Etinlain, Greenwood Press, 1982, p166

12. *Contemporary Novelists*, ed James Vinson, St James Press, 1976, p1066

13. *Twentieth Century Writing*, ed K Richardson, Newnes Books, 1969, p327

14. *Contemporary Poets*, ed James Vinson, Macmillan, 1980, p1192

15. Eric Stokes, 'Kipling's Imperialism', in *Rudyard Kipling, The Man, His Work and his World*, ed John Gross, Weidenfeld & Nicolson, 1972, p96

16. *Reference Guide to American Literature*, ed Thomas Riggs, St James Press, 2000, p532

17. *I Ching*, Routledge & Kegan Paul, 1975, p504

18. ibid, p505

19. Sir James Frazer, *The Golden Bough*, Macmillan, 1963, p583

20. The spirit of the Saturnalia lives on to some extent in our own Christmas celebrations, not least in the office party, where exists a certain sanction for the insulting of superiors and the release of pent-up lusts. That most office parties are not bacchanalian riots is beside the point. The fact that it is a popular and enduring image I think substantiates the connection. In the same vein we have Saturday (Saturn's-day) night, where high spirits are released at the end of a working week of restraint and discipline.

21. John C Lilly, *The Centre of the Cyclone*, Paladin, 1974, p7

22. ibid, p94

23. We note a comment by Jacob Bronowski (a Capricorn Sun) on his own work, *The Identity of Man*. The central theme is: 'the crisis of confidence which springs from each man's wish to be ... a person, in the face of the nagging fear that he is a mechanism.' ('A machine or a Self' in *The Identity of Man*, Heinemann, 1966, p8). We can also note the following observation regarding Robert Bly's poetry: 'His poems are efforts to regain that lost sense of a vital universe in which selfhood is only an atom, though a necessary and participatory one.' (*Reference Guide to Modern American Literature*, ed Thomas Riggs, St James Press, 2000, p90

24. Lord Birkenhead, *Rudyard Kipling*, Weidenfeld & Nicolson, 1978, p227

25. *The Ruling Class* by Peter Barnes (a Capricorn Sun) appeared as a play in 1968 and as a film in 1972, with Peter O'Toole in the lead role. Its subject is indeed the British class system, but there is more to the play than that. The Gurney family, which uses a literal translation of the Bible to buttress its position of power, is alarmed when the incumbent earl, Jack, declares himself a living Christ, a god of fun, humour and love. In other words, he embodies the spirit, rather than the letter of Christianity. However, his power-hungry family subject him to treatment that realigns him with the outer trappings of religion rather than its inner content. He becomes once more a cog in the machine of political power.

Some interesting connections in this vein emerge from the work of Maurice Nicoll. Writing in *The New Man* he applies the contrast between outer and inner to Christianity and suggests that in part at least Christ's mission can be seen as the transformation of the literal or 'stone' truths of the Commandments, to a living inner truth. The figure of Christ has a connection with Capricorn through his symbolic birthday, 25 December, close to the winter solstice. His greatest enemies were the Pharisees, who were attuned to the letter rather than the spirit of religion. It is a word, Pharisee, that has come to be synonymous with hypocrite.

26. J P Hartley, *The Go-Between,* Penguin, 1997, p38

27. Saturn and Capricorn are traditionally connected by astrologers with old age. I don't believe they indicate the number of years a person will live, but those strong in Capricorn in my experience often take time to mature and remain creative into old age, and this is as true with writers as with other categories of individuals. Theodor Fontane's first work was published when he was 59, and his magnum opus appeared when he was 76. L P Hartley was 50 when his first full-length novel appeared, Umberto Eco 48, Alan Paton 45, Henry Miller 43, Cyrus Colter 62 (all Capricorn Suns). Ramon Guthrie's (born 14 January 1896) most important work, *Maximum Security Ward,* appeared when he was 74. An analysis of the ages at which those listed in *Contemporary Novelists* (St James Press, second edition) first published tells the same story. Of all those who were not published until their fortieth year, a notably high proportion – about 30 per cent – after adjusting for relative numbers – were Capricorn Suns. Those strong in Capricorn and its associated planet, Saturn, who do start out young, tend to continue for a long time, and there are many examples of evergreen personalities in the sports and entertainments arena.

28. Jack London, *Martin Eden,* Penguin, 1984, p253

29. Theodor Fontane, *Effi Briest,* Penguin, 1981, p259

30. E M Forster, *Howard's End,* Penguin, 2000, p41

31. E M Forster, 'The Story of a Panic', *Collected Short Stories,* Penguin, 1980

32. Joseph Campbell, *The Hero with a Thousand Faces,* Princeton University Press, 1963, p81

33. John Buchan, *Memory Hold the Door,* Hodder & Stoughton, 1940, pp135-136

34. Jack London, *Son of the Wolf,* Panther, 1964, p15

35. E M Forster, *A Passage to India,* Penguin, 2000, p215

36. ibid

37. We are reminded too of Kipling's epigraph to 'In the House of Suddhoo'

> 'A stone's throw out on either hand
> From that well-ordered road we tread
> And all the world is wild and strange'

38. J K Galbraith, *The Age of Uncertainty,* BBC/Andre Deutsch, 1977, p127

Aquarius

Writers with the Sun in Aquarius include: William Harrison Ainsworth, Paul Auster, Paul Bailey, Iain Banks, Brendan Behan, Richard Brautigan, Bertolt Brecht, George Douglas Brown, Robert Burns, William Burroughs, Robert Burton, Lord Byron, Lewis Carroll, Kate Chopin, Paddy Chayefsky, Anton Chekhov, J M Coetzee, Colette, Len Deighton, Charles Dickens, Roy Fuller, Lewis Grassic Gibbon, Germaine Greer, John Grisham, Susan Hill, Russell Hoban, E T A Hoffmann, Anthony Hope, B S Johnson, James Joyce, Charles Lamb, Sinclair Lewis, Norman Mailer, W Somerset Maugham, George Meredith, James A Michener, Toni Morrison, John O'Hara, Thomas Paine, Boris Pasternak, Ruth Rendell, Mordecai Richler, Romain Rolland, John Ruskin, Georges Simenon, Muriel Spark, Wallace Stegner, Gertrude Stein, Stendhal (Marie-Henri Beyle), August Strindberg, Angela Thirkell, Keith Waterhouse, Beatrice Webb, Simone Weil, Edith Wharton, Virginia Woolf.

Summary Under this sign fall a well-defined sub-group of acknowledged literary radicals who work to minimise the constraints of form, and maximise the effects of spontaneity and randomness. Aquarius also produces excellent social commentators, with a keen sense of history as it is being created. Freedom, the worth of the ordinary person, the struggle against all forms of authority, and the cause of liberty are likewise strong themes.

Watching him, it seemed as if a fibre, very thin but pure of the enormous energy of the world had been thrust into his frail and diminutive body ... it was as if someone had taken a tiny bead of pure life and decking it as lightly as possible with down and feathers, had set it dancing and zig-zagging to show us the true nature of life ... One is apt to forget all about life seeing it humped and bossed and garnished and cumbered so that it has to move with the greatest circumspection and dignity.
Virginia Woolf *The Death of a Moth*

The labels 'rebel' and 'radical' are often applied to those strong in Aquarius, and certainly the sign produces more than its share of literary radicals, as the list above testifies. However, a more typical expression of Aquarius is tension between independence and conformity. Rather than outright iconoclasm there is progressive improvement – or the fleshing out of the skeletons of state structures 'through inventions, social improvements and the glorification of special social virtues', as one writer put it.[1] Another way the tension manifests is in what might be called differentness within a peer group, so that the individual is in some ways quite singular yet is still very much defined by the group, of which he or she is a part. We think of former High Court judge Christmas Humphries, a man of the establishment but probably the only one of his hoary profession who also practised Zen Buddhism. In a similar vein was the priest Andrew Greeley who wrote a good deal of fiction and non-fiction that was provocative and challenging to the Church.[2]

A good illustration of this dichotomy in fiction is Jean Brodie, the creation of Muriel Spark. Miss Jean Brodie is an unorthodox and independent individual, but it is made plain that this is relative:

> It is not to be supposed that Miss Brodie was unique at this point of her prime; or that (since such things are relative) she was in any way off her head. She was alone, merely, in that she taught in a school like Marcia Blaine's. There were legions of her kind during the nineteen-thirties, women from the age of thirty and upward, who crowded their war-bereaved spinsterhood with voyages of discovery into new ideas and energetic practices in art or social welfare, education or religion. The progressive spinsters of Edinburgh did not teach in schools, especially in schools of traditional character like Marcia Blaine's School for Girls. It was in this that Miss Brodie was, as the rest of the staff spinsterhood put it, a trifle out of place. But she was not out of place amongst her own kind.[3]

Jean Brodie tells us why she was eager to teach in such a school:

> It has been suggested again that I apply for one of those progressive schools, where my methods would be more suited to the system than they are at Blaine. But I shall not apply for a post at a crank school. I shall remain at this education factory. There needs must be a leaven in the lump.[4]

This last sentence encapsulates what is a fundamental part of Aquarius: the need to vivify the soulless structures of society, or an organisation, with culture and progressive vision. At the heart of much of Virginia Woolf's writing is the question: how might spirit illumine a society without being extinguished by its inertia?

Meaning of Aquarius

The essence of Aquarius can be summed up quite simply: it always works to overcome the laws and limitations of space, time and matter. From this one principle stems a number of related concepts and phenomena such as evolution, social amelioration, technology, democracy, internationalism, common language, universalism, speed, freedom, rebellion and libertarianism.

Aquarius works to break down divisive barriers, thus creating the conditions where what is separate can come together and move towards one end. It breaks down class and caste systems to bring about democracy, and national barriers to create a unified body of humanity. One of the things that have helped create an international world is speed. Trains, automobiles and aircraft all overcome man's inherent immobility and have catalysed the intermixing of the separate races of the world. Travel was once a major undertaking, slow, hazardous and expensive so that interchange between nations was necessarily limited. E F Schumacher has pointed out that immobility creates isolation and leads to frontiers, the main structural element of world organisation. But since the advent of motorised transport, he notes: 'Everything and everyone has become mobile. All structures are threatened and all structures are vulnerable to an extent they have never been before.'[5]

The Aquarian capacity to transcend barriers of time and space reflects in literature, where we often find writers whose work appeals to different generations, classes and nationalities. It is neither wholly simple nor sophisticated but a combination of the two that strikes at some common level in human beings everywhere.[6] Dickens, Maugham, Hope, Byron, Burns and Carroll were Aquarian Suns whose work demonstrates this universal quality. Carroll's *Alice* books have been translated into forty or more languages and are among the most widely read and quoted in the literary spectrum. They are enjoyed in the nursery, yet are pondered over by scholars. They are at once simple stories and yet it can be said that Carroll's experiments with language anticipated Joyce, and his vision of Wonderland Einstein. The creator of *The Simpsons*, Matt Groening, is likewise an Aquarian Sun. Homer Simpson is an Aquarian figment only in the general sense – he stands as an everyman, a representative of ordinary humankind. But *The Simpsons* as a phenomenon also reflects the sign's universal nature. It became the most popular prime time television programme of all time, has been translated into many languages, appeals to young and old, to simple and sophisticated tastes and is also quietly subversive. Georges Simenon (who created Maigret) and Jules Verne were others who gained a huge popularity outside of their own country and across a wide readership, while three internationally acclaimed dramatists are also Aquarian Suns – Brecht, Strindberg and Chekhov. While not Aquarian Suns, H G Wells, Robert Louis Stevenson, Rider Haggard, J B Priestley, John Buchan, Rudyard Kipling and Arthur Conan Doyle all have a strong Aquarian element in their charts and all exhibit the same sort of cross-barrier popularity.

The Aquarius-Leo polarity of the zodiac has a particular relationship to evolution. This was discussed in the chapter on Leo, a sign that relates to the idea of self-conscious individuals who can act as the live end of an evolutionary spiral. But here in Aquarius the emphasis is on the evolution of mankind. Aquarius symbolises the urge to improve life, to create and sustain those conditions in which human potentiality can flower, and a more inclusive, ultimately more spiritual life can evolve.

Accommodating the contrasting dictates of spirit and matter is a dilemma that faces the self-conscious individual. Man is, whatever else, a physical creature with material needs that must be attended to. At the same time, too great an involvement with the world of affairs stifles spiritual impulse, so that the work of refinement can not even begin. If life is survival-oriented, with all the narrowness and repetitiveness that this implies, then the opportunity for mankind to evolve is very limited. In Third World countries the majority of the population still leads a primitive agrarian lifestyle where existence revolves about the plough, the gathering of fuel and water, and a variety of other menial tasks. There is little energy to be directed towards inner growth. India, for example, may be a religious culture, but for the most part this is at a primitive level, more geared towards making peace with nature and ancestors, or soliciting supernatural favours, than toward spiritual growth in a wider evolutionary sense. I've no doubt that there are spiritually advanced Indians, but these are an exception, and indeed in many cases these individuals can only follow their course because they are supported by charity or the generosity of followers, and are thus free from the burden of material survival.

If evolution were a case of first past the post then terrestrial existence might have ceased long ago. Rather – and this is what Aquarius represents – it is a case of the whole field having to finish, of the raising of the entire species. The problem is then: how might the mass be relieved of the burden of material survival? In the past some societies sought a solution by making slaves – or women – perform the drudgery, but a more encompassing solution has been scientific technology. It has made the processes of labour hyper-efficient and has to a significant extent liberated us from the burden of productive toil. Technology has been the means of social amelioration, which is a necessary *first* step towards a more spiritualised humanity.

That technology has proved double-edged can not be denied. At the same time I believe much of the destructive side stems from the fact that most have lost sight of the end to which it is a means. We can detect here something of the perverse or contrary nature that is often associated with Aquarius, for in order to be loosened from the bonds of matter it has been necessary for the past two centuries or so to become deeply engrossed within it. Evolution implies a spectrum, a movement from the materially dense to the spiritually refined. It just so happens that the majority of mankind are lodged at the former end so it has been necessary for the evolutionary impulse to manifest in a material way at this stage of our history – hence technology.

Also central to the meaning of Aquarius is a conflict between force and form, or structure. By force we mean the creative evolutionary spark that improves life, refines it, carries it forward to something more enlightened than it was. This force-form relationship can be likened to that between the explosive energy of petrol and a combustion chamber. One is no good without the other. An engine lies inert and useless without an explosive charge to drive it. Equally, without the containing walls of a chamber and the mechanisms of an engine, explosive energy is simply dissipated without doing any useful work. Form channels force, gives it duration in time. But at the same time it also checks it, deprives it of dynamism and freedom. Form is death to the creative spark.

This side of the relationship is reflected in an ancient Greek myth associated with this sign, where Cronos (Saturn) at the instigation of his mother (Earth) castrates his father, the sky god Ouranos (Uranus). The planets Saturn and Uranus are both associated with Aquarius[7] and a challenge in the sign seems to be to hold the two – force and structure – in a dynamic balance, so that life becomes a matter of process, thus something capable of evolutionary change, rather than something fixed and crystallised.[8]

The avant-garde side of Aquarian literary expression seems to be a reflection of this dynamic interplay. This is why writers such as Joyce, Johnson, Burroughs and others abandon the accepted literary formats, and why the likes of Stein, Woolf and again Joyce utilise the so-called stream-of-consciousness approach. What these writers seek is a 'live prose', that is, one that is not subordinate to the dictates of established form, logic, grammar or even the dictionary meaning of words.

We might say that compared to Joyce's writing conventional prose is emasculated. Carroll invented portmanteau words, and in other ways deviated from convention to give full expression to his creative impulse. In the cross-column and cut-up techniques of early Burroughs' works we see the principles of randomness and chaos at work. Nothing is fixed. The work is created in situ. What it seems these writers are attempting to do is to hold suspended the creative impulse rather than let it be smothered by the restrictions of the conventional written format.

The principle of randomness also underlies B S Johnson's work *The Unfortunates*, which is not bound in the conventional manner but is presented loose-leaf in a box so the chapters can be arranged in any order the reader chooses. In the introduction to his work, *See The Old Lady Decently,* Johnson states that it is not important to follow the book through in a linear fashion. 'It is not part of my intention,' he notes, 'to provide a continuous narrative ... my purpose is to reflect the reality of the chaos, what life really seems to be like.'[9] Paul Bailey's *Trespasses* and *A Distant Likeness* both adopt a technique of intricate cross-cutting between fragmented monologues that demands imagination from the reader to piece them together. Harry Mathews in *Tlooth* uses faked documents, diagrams and word puzzles. Henri Pichette uses visual devices in his books in an attempt to 'smash the barriers between man and language'.[10] All Aquarian Suns.

Aquarius is a sign, then, in which those bonds, circumstances or conditions which check human life must be loosened and that which is crystallised at least begin to melt. As such, we find the theme of freedom is a major concern with the writers of this sign, who will often champion those who are in some way enchained. The tyrant, with a monstrous ego and a disregard for his subjects, is the nightmare of Aquarius, which is in a sense the darker side of Leo (Aquarius' polar opposite in the zodiac).

Freedom is not the soul preserve of Aquarius, although where it is a theme in other signs, it takes on a different guise. In Gemini, for example, freedom is tied up with self-determination and the denial of possibilities through the act of commitment. In Sagittarius, freedom equates with surrender to the dictates of some religious, spiritual or political dogma. In Libra, freedom is the right to challenge the mores or the conventional wisdom. As we will see in the next chapter, Pisces is quite tolerant of outer bondage, so long as there is an inner freedom, one based upon the assent of the individual soul.

The I Ching hexagram related to Aquarius is number 19, 'Approach', whose meaning is summarised as:

> The Superior man is inexhaustible
> In his will to teach
> And without limits
> In his tolerance and protection of the people.[11]

The latter part suggests this sign's concern with the welfare of humanity. The first two lines relate to another important aspect of the sign, that is, Aquarius as educator. It's a sign that seeks to teach and enlighten (which is what motivated Jean Brodie). There can be a didactic vein, though it is not as marked as it is in Sagittarian writers, and generally there is no moral overtone. Rather, the underlying urge is to enlighten, to awaken understanding (and this rather than simply impart knowledge) and the sign produces writers who seek to popularise an abstruse subject, make it comprehensible to the ordinary person. We can cite people like Desmond Morris, Jules Verne, Ernst Haeckel, who introduced Darwin to a wider audience, Havelock Ellis and John Ruskin, who saw his mission as lighting the dark materialism of the Victorian age with education and art. Ruskin was characteristically Aquarian with his regard for his fellows – he coined the phrase 'social affection' to describe the respect we owe to others – and in his urge to create enlightenment and culture within the framework of his society.[12]

There is a strong vein of humanity about Aquarius, a love of mankind.[13] A number of signs are associated with what might be called a social conscience, but what characterises Aquarius is detachment. It does not seek to immerse itself in the flesh and blood of humanity to the extent, for example, that Scorpio and Pisces do. Aquarius wants to elevate the poor and downtrodden to his level, rather than be subsumed in theirs. Aquarius will cry freedom and equality in an attempt to awaken others to the plight of those enchained by unnatural laws and denied the right to express their humanity. Brotherhood is another keyword traditionally associated with Aquarius, which manifests on the behavioural level as sociability and friendliness. 'Cool but friendly' is a phrase often used to describe those strong in the Air sign Aquarius.

The following quotes bear out something of the above.

Brendan Behan
Brendan loved humanity; he believed heart and soul in its causes.[14]

Lewis Grassic Gibbon
Basically he was a revolutionary idealist, tormented by the thought of man enchained, burningly conscious of human needs, and haunted by the dream of a more kindly world ... The Community of Men was his dream of the future.[15]

James A Michener
His theme again and again is a variation on the Quaker belief in the literal brotherhood of man ... In book after book his interest seems to centre on freeing mankind from illiberal attitudes.[16]

Romain Rolland
Rolland will be remembered as one of the most active and determined defenders of human dignity and freedom and as an eager advocate of a more just and humane social order.[17]

Theodor Plievier
His youthful feeling of revolt never diminished but was transformed into an intense belief into man's right to individual liberty and freedom from want.[18]

René Guy Cadou
Nature and love for mankind are predominant themes in his poetry.[19]

Bertolt Brecht
His is an uncommon sort of belief in the common man.[20]

Ferenc Kormendi
I seem to have an inborn aversion to heroes; my interest has been focused on the life of the common man.[21]

Sadiq Hidayat
A sincere and sensitive author who writes about the common people and uses their language.[22]

John O'Hara
I have an instinct for what the ordinary guy likes.[23]

R C Hutchinson
He seems to say again and again, that in spite of a very evil world in which we live, there is an essential goodness about the ordinary man and woman which is ineradicable[24]

Jóhn Úr Vör
His main concerns remain the same: the right of ordinary people to live their simple, everyday lives in peace and justice.[25]

More Aquarian writers

Charles Dickens Even in his own lifetime Dickens was an international figure and a century and more after his death remains one of Britain's greatest literary exports. Like many Aquarians, he was attuned to his society and his sensitivity to the forces at work within it made him a great chronicler of his times.[26] Some critics have remarked he was not just a creative writer but a history book.

What Aquarians are able to capture is the history of a time even as it is being created, its quality rather than its outline, and particularly the quality of ordinary life, a living history.

Dickens wrote for the ordinary man, not just the intelligentsia, and despite being a literary lion he consistently attacked the society that fed him, and campaigned for humanitarian reform. He created some of the most enduring characters in the English language and one of them, Ebenezer Scrooge, reflects the twin nature of the sign as it sometimes manifests in individuals. There are those strong in Aquarius who reflect the Saturn side of the sign, with its melancholy and cold misanthropy. Indeed, a not uncommon pattern is for the young Aquarian to be rebellious or humanitarian, only to become cold and reactionary in later years. Age hardens Scrooge. As a young man he was gregarious and enjoyed life. The elder Scrooge, it seems, is incapable of human warmth or a charitable thought. At what is traditionally a time of joy his attitude is 'bah humbug'. But in the course of the story, through encounters with supernatural agents, he is transformed into the more positive representation of the sign – humane, philanthropic and concerned for the welfare of his fellow man. Aquarius becomes whole by embracing the qualities of its polar sign Leo, with its abundance of human warmth.

Lord Byron Byron fits the traditional image of Aquarius with his eccentricities and determination to stand beyond the pale. The heroes of his poems, mirrors of himself – the likes of Childe Harold, Don Juan and The Corsair – were solitary outsiders, rebels who despaired at the lack of liberty in the world. And his work was universally popular, read not just by a refined elite but by ordinary people, as the following quote from a biography suggests:

> Byron's influence was singular, beyond all predecessors and successors in the wideness of its range. He was read by everybody. Men and women who were accessible to no other poetry were accessible to his, and old sea captains, merchants, tradesmen, clerks, tailors, milliners, as well as the best judges in the land, repeated his verses by the page.[27]

Thus Aquarius, the great democrat of the zodiac.

Colette (Sidonie-Gabrielle Colette): Colette wrote 18 novels, almost all set amongst the *demi-monde* of turn-of-century France. One of her most acclaimed works is *La Vagabonde*, in which the central figure is 'a lonely woman holding tenaciously to her personal liberty', and yet whose life is restricted by the exigencies of the theatrical milieu in which she chooses to work. This interplay of freedom and bondage is a characteristic theme in Aquarian novels. The following biographical observation is also very suggestive of the sign:

> Perhaps the first word that comes to mind in thinking of Colette is the word liberty. Not that Colette enjoyed more liberty than other women of her generation, but she took advantage of that liberty that was hers, a liberty to be what she was ... The story of Colette's life is the story of a fight for freedom, not a political, social or economic freedom, but a personal freedom – that freedom which has most meaning in terms of an individual human existence.[28]

Havelock Ellis Ellis was a doctor and a pioneer of sexual enlightenment. His 7-volumed *Studies in the Psychology of Sex* pre-dated Freud and was one of the first modern objective (as opposed to moral) treatments of the subject. It was controversial in its day and no doubt the guilt-ridden Victorians and Edwardians found his words liberating. (In a similar way was *The Joy of Sex*, written by Aquarian Alex Comfort, liberating to a later generation.) The following description of Ellis chimes well with Aquarius:

> (He) regarded himself as one of the band of intellectual and spiritual pioneers who in every age overthrow the *idées recues* inherited from previous generations and reformulate the constant truths of humanity in a new and dynamic form, while at the same time driving forward the frontiers of knowledge ... the epitome of the New Man interested in all the rapidly emerging sciences ... his life work was a selfless devotion to humanity.[29]

W Somerset Maugham Maugham was another whose work possessed universal appeal and which has been widely translated. His theme is often freedom: his magnum opus, *Of Human Bondage*, focuses on a struggle between autonomy and enslavement, while his first book, *Liza of Lambeth*, is about entrapment by poverty and relationship. It is worth quoting biography at length on this point:

> As the title indicates, *Of Human Bondage* is about enslavement and liberation, primarily emotional bondage but also a variety of forms of physical, economic, intellectual and philosophical constraints. In his final years the author confessed to an interviewer that the 'main thing I've always asked from life is freedom. Outer and inner freedom, both in my way of living, and my way of writing.' The course of his long life was indeed a succession of attempts to find complete freedom – not merely physical liberty, but true independence of spirit. The freedom meant more than mere escape from duties and obligations, financial dependence, or the restraints of time and place. These were only the surface of a search for deeper liberation – intellectual freedom and

emotional detachment. In one way or another almost everything Maugham willingly did was motivated by this vision.[30]

Robert Burns Burns is Scotland's bard, but unlike Shakespeare is a popular voice, loved and admired by the ordinary person. He wrote in his commonplace book that he 'had an unbounded good-will to every creature'. He was an Aquarian mix of rebellion and conformity and, as one critic notes, 'a bitter satirist against all forms of religious and political thought that condoned or perpetuated inhumanity'.[31] At the same time he had a respect for the intelligent classes and despite his humble origins moved in the genteel circles of Edinburgh's literati. He was anxious for their approval and would sometimes write what he believed they wanted to read.

But perhaps Burns' main creative focus was upon the heart and soul of his country. In effect what he did was to breathe new life into old forms, thus preserving and carrying forward something of the past (and in this there is Aquarius). He spent a good deal of his short life collecting old songs and poems, which he refined, or reworked, or used as the basis for new pieces. This was how that great anthem to friendship, *Auld Lang Syne*, came into being. He worked in conjunction with two publishers, but accepted no payment, considering the work a service to Scotland.

Burns is another embodiment of Aquarian universality, a man admired the world over and whose appeal spans social barriers.

Another novel whose theme is a man enchained is **Edith Wharton's** *Ethan Frome.*

Albert Camus in a discussion of freedom referred to the man who had spent a week in the little-ease, the medieval torture cell too low for a person to properly stand, too short and narrow to lie down. The man released from here learns the simple fact of freedom. So too, we might opine, does Ethan Frome, the eponymous hero of Wharton's short novel.

The book is set in the Massachusetts countryside around the turn of the 19th century and tells the story of a man trapped by economic necessity, a dead-in-life community, and a stultifying marriage. Ethan is healthy and intelligent. He attended college as a young man and harboured hopes of becoming an engineer. But his studies were interrupted by the death of his father and the need to nurse his mother and run the family farm. We are told Ethan did not learn enough to be of any economic value, yet enough to feed his fancy that there was a better, freer, way of life.

A cousin, Zeena, comes to live at the farm, to help nurse the mother and to keep house. When his mother dies Ethan is frightened of being alone, so asks Zeena to marry him. However, from being a companion and helper she becomes a burden, a hypochondriac eating into Ethan's meagre resources with her demands for doctors and medicines. Only 28, she is old before her time. With her misanthropic mien and her gaunt, bloodless features, she casts a chilling presence over the household. Ethan's chance of a decent life, of money, education and self-expression, and his taste for the cosmopolitan life, are all sacrificed because of his wife. A countryside frozen and dead in the depths of a harsh New England winter forms the backdrop for the book and seems to mirror the joyless hopelessness of Ethan's life.

Yet hope springs. There comes another woman into his life, again a distant relative, Mattie, who is summoned to be a housekeeper. In stark contrast to Zeena she is reckless, gay and an affirmation of life. Sugar to Zeena's vinegar. It is not long before something stirs in Ethan. It is not love or lust, but something more refined and dispassionate. When she arrived at the farm, 'it was like the lighting of a fire on a cold hearth'.[32] She awakens in him 'a slumbering spark of sociability', and he was 'warmed to the marrow by friendly human intercourse'.[33]

Mattie is an emblem of the joy of life and of human fellowship, and for a time she leavens Ethan's leaden existence. There is one particular night, while Zeena is away visiting a doctor, when they share a happy but perfectly innocent evening in the warmth of the kitchen, and Ethan is allowed to believe, just for a time, that this is what life could be like. But circumstances change again, and Mattie is told she must leave. A new girl is coming to look after Zeena. Ethan is mortified. He protests, but when he can not break the will of his wife, he resolves to run away and marry Mattie. But yet again he is thwarted. He has no money, and also enough human feeling not to abandon his wife, who could not survive without him. He is essentially paralysed, 'handcuffed like a prisoner'.

He sees one way out, however. He decides death, real death, is preferable to the death-in-life without Mattie. He takes her sledging on a steep slope, and steers into a tree.

Neither is killed, but both are badly injured. In a cruel irony, the attempt to escape only worsens his condition. Ethan's body is twisted and broken in the crash, his lameness 'checking each step, like the jerk of a chain'.[34] Mattie suffers spinal injury, but worse, becomes as dead in life as Zeena. The creature that warmed the Frome kitchen becomes embittered by infirmity and the three are left to live out their lives huddled from the harsh winters in the loveless home. As a neighbour comments: 'I don't see's there's much difference between the Fromes up at the farm and the Fromes down in the graveyard.'[35]

Jules Verne *Twenty Thousand Leagues Under the Sea*
The 19th-century French writer Jules Verne embodied many Aquarian traits, both in his character and his writing. In life he was a singular mix of conservatism and progressiveness: on the surface a solid member of the bourgeoisie – a stockbroker, a member of the Academy, seemingly in complete harmony with the time in which he lived – but underneath a utopian, a man of radical views, and one who cherished independence more than anything.

Like H G Wells he was a man conscious of the power of science and technology to better mankind. He celebrates technology in his early works, its power to improve social conditions, but in his later writing, the vision has crystallised into vistas of industrial complexes, and cities that entrap rather than free the spirit of man. Like other Aquarians, Verne wrote of his times, and what he chronicled was the modern industrial world coming into being. He was an extremely popular writer, and, moreover, universal in his appeal. It is said in fiction sales he is exceeded only by Shakespeare.

One of the more enduring figments of Verne's fiction is Captain Nemo in *Twenty Thousand Leagues Under the Sea*, the story of the kidnap of a naturalist and his two colleagues and of their journey of discovery aboard a submarine around the oceans of the world. From the observations of the naturalist, Professor Aronnax, we learn that Nemo is a brooding, intense, secretive man, as well as ruthless, vengeful, authoritarian and courageous – traits better described by Scorpio, which is the sign of Verne's Moon. However, in other ways Nemo is notably Aquarian. He is a rebel, a man who has excluded himself from society. He remarks at one point: 'I am not what you call a civilised man! I have done with society entirely, for reasons which I alone have the right of appreciating. I do not therefore obey its laws.'[36] Nemo flies the flag of anarchy. The sea for him is freedom. Aboard his vessel he is beyond the laws of any country. 'The sea does not belong to despots,' he remarks to Aronnax:

> Upon its surface men can still exercise unjust laws, fight, tear one another to pieces ... But at thirty feet below its level their reign ceases ... Ah! sir, live – live in the bosom of the waters! There only is independence! ... There am I free.[37]

Beneath Nemo's cold, authoritarian facade we find a humanitarian nature. He plainly cares about his crew, who live bound by a strong sense of community and common purpose.

Their nationalities are secondary; they have abandoned the countries of their birth and speak instead an invented language.[38] And Nemo is a man prepared to support the 'oppressed races of the world', for example supplying the inhabitants of Crete with gold salvaged from wrecks to help them in their struggle to throw off the yoke of the Turks.

Sinclair Lewis *Babbitt*

Sinclair Lewis was a writer praised for the breadth of his vision. Critics have noted that he was the first American writer of any significance to shun regionalism and successfully embrace his country's huge variety to capture an essence of her people and places in his novels. Perhaps in recognition of this he became the first American to win the Nobel Prize for literature. His most acclaimed works are *Main Street* and *Babbitt,* and the latter forms an excellent example of Aquarius as Civic Man.

Dane Rudhyar has described Aquarius as a releasing agent, a sign that at some level expands or glorifies what has been built in the previous sign, Capricorn, or else tends to destroy or transcend it. George Babbitt, the central character of Lewis' novel, inclines to glorification. Rudhyar also describes Aquarius as 'The Test of Discontent':

> There must come at the very zenith of an era individuals who refuse to be bounded by the social limits of a standardised attainment and satisfied with the official contents of the human type bred by their society and culture. In them burns the fire of 'divine discontent' ... [they] pursue relentlessly, or perhaps subtly, their crusades against a stultified sense of plenitude and surface social harmony.[39]

This is essentially the experience of Babbitt. The book is a story of one man's rebellion, but also one of rejection of rebellion in preference for the comforts of conformity and fellowship. Basically it is the story of one man's failure to pass the test of discontent.[40]

The novel is set in affluent Middle America in the pre-Depression Twenties, and written at a time when it was not common to mock, however mildly, the American dream. George Babbitt is a family man and the owner of a real estate business. This is a profession he idealises somewhat, for he looks upon himself as 'a seer of the future development of the community', and 'a prophetic engineer clearing the pathway for inevitable change'.[41] We detect here the forward-looking conservatism of Aquarius.

Babbitt is a cosmopolitan who fully appreciates the benefits his affluent society provides. He loves his city, Zenith, and is proud of the fact he contributes to its prosperity through his business. He is a pillar of his church but feels his real religious duty is 'to serve my fellow men, to honour my brother as myself, and to do my bit to make life happier for one and all'.[42] He is a gregarious soul, at home in the type of societies where like minds of the merchant and professional classes meet to talk shop and swap favours, and where friendship is expressed in the hale-heartiness of defused insults and jocular back-slapping. Cool Aquarius, noted for its broad humanity but discomfort with feeling, seems to thrive in such an impersonal atmosphere of effusive but generalised bonhomie.

Babbitt sometimes addresses meetings at his clubs. He tells one gathering:

> It's the fellow with four to ten thousand a year, and an automobile and a nice little family bungalow on the edge of town, that makes the wheels of progress go round.[43]

He is, of course, talking about himself, the ideal and successful citizen in his mid-American utopia.

But he is not happy. He tires of the dullness of his life, admits that it has become incredibly mechanical, and rebels. What he does seems innocuous – he falls in with a bohemian crowd, and expresses lukewarm support for a local union agitator – but it is enough to have him ostracised by his club and the business community, and to be regarded as a crank by his friends. Babbitt achieves the personal freedom he desires but at a price, and one he decides he does not want to pay. He enjoys his city, and the company of his friends, and comes to realise these are more important to him than the right to pursue his individualistic impulses. A domestic crisis precipitates the end of his rebellion and he welcomes the opportunity to flee back to conformity.

However, his thoughts of independence and rebellion do not quite die. His son marries on impulse, resulting in a tide of consternation and reproof from most of the elders involved in the situation. But Babbitt takes his son aside, not to upbraid him, but to congratulate him on having the courage to disregard convention. The burden of Babbitt's rebellion had passed on to a new generation.

Notes

1. Dane Rudhyar, *Astrological Signs, The Pulse of Life*, Shambhala, 1978, p115

2 Another Aquarian Sun regarded as a touch eccentric by his peers was Henry Frederick Thynne, 6th Marquess of Bath. He was an aristocrat with a

common touch, the first to open up his stately home to the public. He once said: 'I believe that all men are the same. I'm much happier in these modern days when men are equal.' (Quoted in *The Guardian* obituary, John Ezard, 1.7.1992)

3. Muriel Spark, *The Prime of Miss Jean Brodie*, Macmillan, 1972, p7

4. ibid, p52

5. E F Schumacher, *Small is Beautiful*, Abacus, 1978, p 57

6. One critic has noted: 'It is Brecht's unique achievement that he has reconciled two traditions in German literature ...In Brecht the rough, plebeian, popular tradition and the sophisticated, academic, refined, respectable tradition have come together.' (Martin Esslin in *European Writers*, vol 11, Charles Scribner's Sons, 1985, p2108)

7. Like any good discipline, astrology incorporates new discoveries into its framework of knowledge. The planets Uranus, Neptune and Pluto were only recognised in relatively modern times, and they have since acquired a body of symbolic meaning in the way the ancient planets have.

8. By way of illustration we can think of a waterfall, or a vortex: two phenomena whose form wholly depends on movement, on a constant flow of water – images used by Aquarian Fritjof Capra in his book *Web of Life* (Flamingo, 1997 pp 164-165). Capra recognises process – along with structure and pattern – as a key criterion of life. The paintings of Aquarian Bob Venosa, with their images of transcendent spirit-matter, are a good illustration of this facet of the sign. (See *Manas Manna*, Big O Publishing)

9. B S Johnson, *See the Old Lady Decently*, Hutchinson, 1975, p13

10. *World Authors 1950-70*, ed J Wakeman, HW Wilson Co, 1975, p1135

11. *I Ching*, Routledge & Kegan Paul, 1975, p79

12. Biographer Peter Quennell has written of Ruskin's anxiety to 'instruct and enlighten', and his 'passionate desire to establish some genuine communion with his fellow human beings'. (*John Ruskin, the Portrait of a Prophet*, Collins, 1949, p196)

13. Again, the *I Ching* dwells on this aspect of Aquarius: 'the sage is inexhaustible in his readiness to teach mankind ... [he] sustains and cares for all people and excludes no part of humanity.' (p80)

14. *World Authors 1950-70*, ed J Wakeman, HW Wilson Co, 1975, p137 (Behan's brother quoted)

15. Ian S Munro, *Leslie Mitchell: Lewis Grassic Gibbon*, Oliver & Boyd, 1966, p134

16. *Contemporary Literary Criticism*, Vol 1, Gale Research, 1973, p214

17. *Columbia Dictionary of Modern European Literature*, ed J Bédé and W Edgerton, Columbia University Press, 1980, p676

18. *Dictionary of Literary Biography*, Vol 69, Gale Research, 1988, p243

19. *Columbia Dictionary of Modern European Literature*, ed J Bédé and W Edgerton, Columbia University Press, 1980, p134

20. Eric Bentley, *The Playwright as Thinker: A Study of Drama in Modern Times*, Reynall & Hitchcock, 1946, p68

21. *World Authors 1950-70*, ed J Wakeman, HW Wilson Co, 1975, p813

22. *Cassells Encyclopedia of Literature*, Vol 2, ed S Steinberg, Cassell, 1953, p1828

23. Quoted in *Twentieth Century Authors*, Kunitz & Haycraft, HW Wilson Co, 1956, p1045

24. *Contemporary Novelists*, ed James Vinson, St James Press, 1976, p696

25. *Dictionary of Scandinavian Literature*, ed Virpi Zuck, St James Press, 1990, p301

26. We note the following about the Scandinavian writer Anders Bodelsen: his 'ability to evoke the essence of his own time is unsurpassed in modern Danish literature, and his straightforward, often ironic style makes him one of today's most popular and accessible authors'. (*Dictionary of Scandinavian Literature*, ed Virpi Zuck, St James Press, 1990, p72). The German author Theodor Plievier was another who excelled in his depictions of major historical events of the 20th century, perhaps most notably the Battle of Stalingrad. In his novel *Stalingrad* he adopts a realistic documentary account common in Aquarius, a cross between journalism and fiction, and focuses on the point of view of the ordinary soldier. Norman Mailer likewise developed a style of writing that became known as New Journalism, again a cross between reporting and fiction, and a subjective accounting of history as it was being born. As a young man the Aquarian Mailer was a voice for radicalism and an inspiration for the rebellious students of the late Sixties. As he grew older, however, he mellowed. His relationship to his society became more harmonious and he favoured the approach of gradual change from within, rather than breaking down from outside.

27. André Maurois, *Byron*, Constable, 1984, p197

28. Elaine Marks, *Colette*, Secker & Warburg, 1961, p10

29. Arthur Calder Marshall, *Havelock Ellis*, Rupert Hart-Davis, 1959, p115

30. Robert Calder, *Willie, The Life of Somerset Maugham*, Heinemann, 1989, p29

31. David Daiches in *British Writers* Vol 3, Charles Scribner's Sons, 1980, p313

32. Edith Wharton, *Ethan Frome*, Virago Press, 1997, p26

33. ibid, p44

34. ibid, p11

35. ibid, p103

36. Jules Verne, *Twenty Thousand Leagues Under the Sea*, J M Dent, 1993, pp 45-46

37. ibid, p50

38. Those who advocate or formulate common languages are often strong in Aquarius. Swedenborg, Ampère and Arrhenius were all Aquarian Suns, while Dr Zamenhof, who invented Esperanto, was an Aquarian Moon.

39. Dane Rudhyar, *An Astrological Triptych*, ASI, 1978, p183

40. This chapter in *Triptych* is very pertinent to Babbitt as a man who prefers

simply to enjoy the rewards of social living rather than lead others upward. 'Having thus played the game and attained,' writes Rudhyar,

> will he [Aquarian Man] be able to lead others toward freedom of the spirit? Or will he not have carried the mask so well, that underneath it his own discontent will have died and he too will conform and bask in respectability, even though he might occasionally utter grand words about spiritual values and individual creativeness in order to soothe his numbly aching soul and hide the tragic, perhaps unconscious, emptiness of his success. [p 184]

41. Sinclair Lewis, *Babbitt*, Jonathan Cape, 1973, p49
42. ibid, p203
43. ibid, p178

Pisces

Pisces writers include: Kobo Abe, Douglas Adams, Edward Albee, Walter Allen, W H Auden, Sybille Bedford, Georges Bernanos, William Boyd, Elizabeth Barrett Browning, Anne Brontë, Anthony Burgess, John Burnside, Morley Callaghan, Jim Crace, Richard Condon, Gabriele D'Annunzio, Peter de Vries, Lawrence Durrell, Ralph Ellison, D J Enright, James T Farrell, Gabriel García Márquez, Hugh Garner, William Godwin, Herbert Gold, Kenneth Grahame, Alex La Guma, Patrick Hamilton, James Herlihy, Victor Hugo, Henrik Ibsen, John Irving, Nikos Kazantzakis, Weldon Kees, Jack Kerouac, Elizabeth Langgässer, Mike Leigh, Siegfried Lenz, Robert Lowell, Stéphane Mallarmé, Anaïs Nin, Ben Okri, Caryl Phillips, Philip Roth, Arthur Schopenhauer, Irwin Shaw, Alan Sillitoe, John Steinbeck, Kylie Tennant, Walter Tevis, John Updike, John Wain, Christa Wolf, Tom Wolfe.

Summary More than any other sign, Piscean writers demonstrate compassion for the unfortunates of this world, the poor – the despised, the sick or oppressed. And a common theme is of individuals learning to resist forces that press upon them from all around, and particularly a need to reclaim identity from false identities forced on them by others. Piscean novels sometimes centre on disillusion, deceit, self-denial, dashed hopes and wishful thinking.

Castles in the air – they're so easy to take refuge in. So easy to build too.
Henrik Ibsen *The Master Builder*

A novel that gives a good flavour of Pisces is James Herlihy's *Midnight Cowboy*. It is set mainly in a New York netherworld of social outcasts, criminals and prostitutes and focuses on two characters who dream of escape. Texan Joe Buck fancies himself a stud. He gives up his menial job and travels to New York, where he imagines scores of wealthy women with jaded sex lives will queue up to pay him for sex. He is rapidly disillusioned, runs out of money, and is forced to live on the streets, where he meets Ratso Rizzo, a cripple and petty thief. It is an unlikely match, but a strong friendship develops as the two men help each other survive a harsh, homeless New York winter. Joe pursues his ambition, but far from sharing the beds of rich ladies, he is forced to earn a living as a male hustler. Ratso, who is a sick man, dreams of the day when he can leave New York for the sunshine of Florida, where he believes an idyllic existence awaits him.

It is a story of compassion, self-denial and of individuals struggling to survive on the fringes of society while dreaming of escape to a better life. And Joe Buck shares a failing with many other Piscean characters: he lives a lie. He is not essentially a stud. Rather, this is a role he has drifted into and which he has taken on through the power of suggestion. There's the girlfriend who told him he's the best lover she ever had, and the grandmother who raised him who tells him he's 'the handsomest cowboy in the parade' (and, we can assume, first dressed him in cowboy clothes). But Joe is not a cowboy at all – he works as a dish-washer. Nor is he really suited to being a stud, because he's far too decent a person. He cares about other people, is easily moved by their problems.

As Ratso's health worsens Joe finds the money to take his friend to Florida. This represents a sacrifice on Joe's part, for he was starting to have success finding women prepared to pay him for sex. And yet it is on the journey south that he realises he has been living a lie. He admits he was never really cut out to be a stud, and that once in Florida he is going to find a job working on the land. Ratso dies on the coach, just as his cherished dream is about to be realised.

Pisces and compassion

Probably the most positive quality of Pisces is an innate empathy with those who suffer. Some other zodiac signs move in the same area, but the emphasis is different in each case. In Pisces the concern is the degrading aspect of poverty with the emphasis on sympathy, pity and succour, as opposed to social amelioration (Aquarius), or confronting – and fighting – the perceived causes of social ill or injustice (Aries and Scorpio). There is resistance in Pisces, but generally just the beginnings, or an aimless thrashing about at ill-defined targets. It is true that in some Piscean individuals compassion can emerge inverted as self-pity, but of all the signs Pisces remains the most easily moved by suffering and the most forgiving (sometimes exasperatingly so). Pisces' world view is one of wholeness and inter-connectivity and its compassion is rooted here. The Piscean individual feels the pain of others because at a deep level he perceives himself to be of the same essential substance as the rest of humanity.

W H Auden's description of a pivotal event in his own life forms a good example of this side of the sign. Auden, a Pisces Sun, tells of an ordinary summer night, sitting on a lawn with friends discussing everyday things, when he felt himself invaded by an irresistible power and knew for the first time in his life – because he was doing it – what it was like to 'love thy neighbour'.

> I felt [the friends'] existence as themselves to be of infinite value and rejoiced in it. I knew that so long as I was possessed by this spirit, it would be literally impossible for me to deliberately injure another human being.[1]

He recalls that the experience did not last long, and in the days and months following it he lapsed into non-Christian ways. The difference now, he recounts, was that when he did behave uncharitably he felt guilty about it and could not deceive himself about his behaviour.

It is quite easy to find among critical texts Piscean writers who have been singled out for their compassion.

John Steinbeck
[He had] an all-embracing love of every variety of life undistorted by any ideas of what should or should not be: a love which could look with equanimity at human freaks and social outcasts.[2]

Hugh Garner
His sympathies for the underdogs of our society – the poor, the unemployed, the immigrant, the North American Indian, the itinerant worker – are always readily apparent.[3]

B Traven
He passionately defended the underdog.[4]

Morley Callaghan
An unsentimental compassion for life's misfits and rejects.[5]

Paul Green
A great compassion for society's underdogs.[6]

Peter Jilemnický
Most of [his] works are marked by his compassion for the poor and oppressed.[7]

Bengt Lidner
He quite deliberately proceeds to wring every sad tear of sympathy for the unfortunate ones of this world.[8]

George Birimisa
His major themes are the pain of human isolation and its economic and social roots ... his plays are filled with compassionate rage against human suffering.[9]

D J Enright
To Enright's acute, compassionate eye, the great enemy is indifference

to suffering ... 'Simply, he was human, did no harm and suffered for it' is his epitaph for the poor and oppressed.[10]

Raul Brandäo
His works are marked by a fascination with the life of the poor and destitute ... these people are misfits, dreamers and human wrecks who tenaciously struggle against the seemingly cosmic forces that beat back any attempts by them to overcome or make sense of their nightmarish existence.[11]

Alex La Guma
Most of his heroes are men made criminals by the environment. Underdogs, perpetual losers, victims of circumstances and unjust laws, they nevertheless possess a stubborn courage and a will to resist the forces that push them to the bottom.[12]

James Herlihy
Herlihy is fascinated by society's rejects, by men and women whose lives seem doomed by their emotional needs and their longing, but who struggle to maintain some shred of human dignity in a world which seems remorseless in its devices for destroying the self.[13]

Ivar Lo-Johansson
Both in fiction and in reportage he is the champion of the underdog.[14]

Pier Paolo Pasolini
His passionate sympathy for the poor.[15]

Paul Wilhelm Kyrklund
(His work) The mood is pessimistic, but there is almost always sympathy for the humble and oppressed.[16]

Ben Okri
His vision of social squalor and human degradation is ... unflinching and ... compassionate.[17]

Victor Hugo
[Hugo] always shows warm compassion for all that is weak, lonely, sorrowful ... in the poems of Victor Hugo there constantly occur those notes of love for fallen women, for the poor who are crushed by the cogwheels of society.[18]

Robert Lowell
While he shows compassion for the dispossessed of this life, he is nevertheless seized with horror by a life that imposes so much wretchedness on human beings.[19]

Pisces and illusion

One aspect of illusion that reflects in the writing of this sign is the notion that truth is a product of wholeness. The partial perspective is ambiguous and what is true at a particular time and place is not necessarily true generally. We can use the analogy of a train. We can be sitting in a stationary carriage and believe we are moving if a train is passing our field of vision. There needs to be another reference point (or a different perspective), say from outside of the carriage, if the confusion is to be resolved. Piscean writers are quite often concerned to view the same events through different eyes, or with the benefit of hindsight. Like the other Jupiter sign, Sagittarius, although not to the same extent, they employ the cycloramic method to provide a complete and dynamic view of life. Lawrence Durrell, Anthony Burgess, James T Farrell, Jack Kerouac and John Updike are some who have done so.

What is considered real and what illusory varies from time to time and place to place. The contemporary Western world view has it that the sensible world of appearances is real. However, in other systems of thought appearances are held to be deceptive, mere reflections of a unitary state underlying the sensible world. Modern science dismisses the world of gods and myths as fantasy, superstition and delusion. The Hindu sage, on the other hand, regards as illusion or *maya* the fragmented, ever-changing flux of events – epitomised by newsprint, and flickering TV images – that passes for reality in our secular age.

The dichotomy between truth and appearance also emerges in other ways so the sign is associated with things like deception, ambiguity and delusion. The faculty of differentiation is weakest in Pisces (strongest in polar Virgo) so there can be a difficulty in distinguishing between what is self and what not-self, and a tendency then to absorb identities impressed from without. There can be a protean aspect to Pisces. Those strong in the sign do not so much cultivate roles or images as absorb them and reflect what others want to see (and to reflect different things to different people). There can be a slippery and evasive quality to those strong in this sign – which can be a strength or failing, depending on the circumstances.

In the affairs of the world Pisces (and its modern ruler Neptune) stands for the fictionalisation of life, such as is generated by television, film, public relations, propaganda and the tabloid press. There are things that are positive about television but it also has an insidious narcotic quality which cocoons millions in a pleasant, illusory little world where there is no need for independent thought or action. Soap operas are a refuge from reality for millions. Not only do they dominate the ratings but the fictitious characters in these programmes receive thousands of letters from viewers and sometimes even feature in news broadcasts as if they were part of the everyday flow of world events. Once more, the boundary between fantasy and reality blurs.

Advertising, at least much of it, is a bizarre combination of reality and fantasy in which an attempt is made to ennoble mundane objects such as soap (essentially fat and caustic soda) by coupling them with glamorous or romantic images. Coca-Cola is basically carbon dioxide, sugar and water, but you wouldn't think so to see it ludicrously inflated on the television or cinema screen. For centuries people have bought, sold and exchanged goods without recourse to images and without pretending the goods were anything other than what they were. It is called commerce and is symbolised in astrology by Mercury. Today we have commercialism, which is symbolised by Pisces and its ruling planets, and which like any -ism involves the exercise of non-rational faculties.

Pisces is the twelfth and final sign of the zodiac so, in the symbolic scheme of things, it ends a cycle but at the same time prepares for a new beginning. It is a forward-looking sign in that it seeks to temper a harsh today with the vision of a better tomorrow, but it also looks back, sometimes nostalgically, sometimes with bitterness, ruing lost opportunity. But symbolically Pisces has to come to terms with the past, draw a line under it.

The sign can be understood in terms of a seed process (to use a botanical analogy). A seed is the end product of a growth process, alone escaping decay and transmitting life into a new cycle. In Pisces the individual might be likened to the seed; the rest of the plant, which sooner or later perishes, to those forces, cultural and circumstantial, that helped create it. So Pisces becomes a sort of battleground between the decaying processes of the old cycle, and the individual attempting to extract some harvest from the past – a meaning, an understanding – to metamorphose into the germ of a future cycle. It is a duality suggested in part by the sign's glyph: fishes knotted together and swimming in different directions.

Much of Dane Rudhyar's writing about this sign comes back to the theme of endings or (more accurately) transitions. He suggests the task in Pisces is to overcome the pull of the past. The great need of the Piscean temperament, he states, is 'to endure. Endurance is the ability to remain one's self under the impact of the cyclic dissolution of all things.'[20]

Capricorn, the tenth sign, represents the culmination of the socialising process, manifesting symbolically as empire and state. Aquarius, the eleventh sign, equates to a blossoming of the collectivising force in things such as education and culture. Finally, with Pisces, we pass to the decadent phase of a civilisation, a time of disintegration, where, as Rudhyar puts it, 'society [is] breaking down under the weight of its crystallisations'.[21] Collective man must look once more to his own resources, for there is no social stability to cling to. Pisces stands for the general degeneration of life quality – the suffering, degradation, exploitation and marginalisation – that often results from the processes of urbanisation and industrialisation. Similarly it stands for the sense of impotence and confusion experienced by the individual caught up in forces over which he has no control. In Pisces, symbolically, man has to claim back the identity that has been eroded or conditioned by social forces. He must 'learn to stand alone and rely only upon his own inner voice'.[22]

In Virgo, the polar complement of Pisces, the need is for an individual to relinquish some of the will to control circumstances, so we find characters who have to submit to some kind of external fate, or must in some way open themselves to chance, mystery or disorder. But in Pisces the balance point is obtained by moving in the opposite direction. Pisces has to learn to resist oppressive circumstances, both fateful and those that are generated by the processes of collective living. The individual's will must be asserted against larger forces, gross and subtle, and often in Piscean writing this takes the form of some small act of defiance, or some purely personal moral assertion. Piscean characters often struggle to find a still centre in a complex world of events, or a sense of permanence within the flow of time. In another guise, they struggle to regain an identity that has been blurred by the weight of others' expectation.[23]

More Pisces writing

Many of **Edward Albee**'s plays clearly embody Piscean symbolism. In some there is a focus on religion – on sacrifice and salvation more specifically – but more apparent are themes relating to falsity, social fictions and disillusionment. The ambience of *The Death of Bessie Smith* has been described as 'a universe of illusion, frustration and lies'.[24] Another critic has said *Box* and *The Thoughts of Chairman Mao Tse Tung* 'attempt to bring together the whole meta-structure of illusions which together create the fabric of the private and public world'.[25]

Albee's best known play is *Who's Afraid of Virginia Woolf?* A brief synopsis – after hours with an inebriated, bickering foursome – is unpromising, yet the play deserves its reputation as a humorous, intelligent and entertaining work. The action occurs in the residence of George, a college lecturer, and his wife Martha in the early hours of the morning following a campus party. They entertain Nick, also a lecturer, and his wife. The time passes in a haze of alcohol and an atmosphere of shifting sand where the boundary between truth and fiction is blurred. Thus:

Martha: That is not true! That is such a lie!
George: You must not call everything a lie, Martha. (To Nick)Must she?
Nick: Hell, I don't know when you people are lying or what.[26]

We are never quite sure if George and Martha are serious about the abuse they hurl at one another. We do not know if the stories about George's past are true or not, nor for most of the play if the son they speak about is fantasy or reality.

The crux of the play is escapism, or the illusions people cling to to avoid facing an unpalatable existence. 'The refuge we take when the unreality of the world weighs too heavy,'[27] as Martha remarks in a moment of rare lucidity. The title of the play, as Albee has explained, also relates to escapism. 'Who's afraid of Virginia Woolf?' is a little ditty that surfaces periodically in the course of the play, an echo of a joke from the party. It relates to 'who's afraid of the big bad wolf?' That is, who's afraid of facing reality?

In one respect the play is an analysis of a marriage, for it is the author's contention that illusion often stands in the way of genuine relationship. Certainly George and Martha are out of touch with reality. Martha has difficulty relating to real men because she idealises her father and has unrealistic expectations of both George and Nick. George, for his part, has retreated into a world of arid intellectualism, partly to avoid the challenge of ambition and partly, we suspect, to escape the Kali-like Martha. The fictitious son symbolises the sterility of the marriage in an obvious way: it has not born fruit. But it is a means by which the couple avoid facing up to their problems, instead projecting them on to the figment. George insists the boy was unhappy at home because of Martha's rampant maternalism; Martha has it that the boy was unhappy because of George's failure to excel in the academic world.

In the end the play is about dis-illusionment. The son is killed off, and it is then that we get the only moment of human tenderness in the whole play. The final lines see George consoling Martha, who admits she is indeed 'afraid of Virginia Woolf', that is, living life without comforting illusions.

Henrik Ibsen, *Ghosts*

Ibsen's *Ghosts* has nothing to do with the supernatural but is a play about disillusion and coming to terms with the past, the ghosts of the past. At one point one of the central characters, Mrs Alving, says:

I'm timid and frightened because I can never really be free of the ghosts that haunt me ... But I'm inclined to think that we're all ghosts, Pastor

> Manders; it's not only the things from our fathers and mothers that live on in us, but all sorts of dead ideas, and old dead beliefs, and things of that sort. They're not actually alive in us, but they're rooted there all the same and we can't rid ourselves of them.[28]

The play centres about deceit and demystification, and the dead Captain Alving is a pivot. A legend has built up around Alving which in the course of the play is revealed to be false. He is not, as we are first led to understand, a philanthropic benefactor whose bequest will fund a new orphanage. On the contrary, it turns out Alving was a dissolute wastrel. The estate's wealth was generated largely through the efforts of his long- suffering wife, who hid the truth of the situation. The flesh and blood Alving has been dead for years and does not appear in the play. What we do have is an exalted, yet false, image of the man. It is this ghost, this lie, which is finally exorcised.

But beyond this, we find in *Ghosts* themes that appear often in Piscean works:

1. Pastor Manders is one of Alving's greatest admirers but in the course of the play he is disenchanted. His belief that the Captain is a great human being is finally shattered, though only finally. For much of the play he continues to fool himself, rationalising facts which contradict his rosy view. Evidence that the Captain was a lecher, for example, is dismissed as being the healthy folly of a young and spirited man.
2. Mrs Alving is a martyr. She suffered and, in that puzzling Piscean way, needs to suffer.
3. Scandal is uncovered. Regina, the servant girl, is not Engstrand's daughter but Alving's bastard.
4. Oswald, Alving's son, is a victim. He has inherited syphilis, and wants to marry Regina so she can nurse him. The ghost lives on: like alcoholic father, like son.
5. Regina too is disenchanted. She yearns for escape from her small world. Oswald is a poet and scholar, and before she learns of his ailment she dreams of marrying him and leading a fashionable life in Paris. The disclosure of his illness shatters this illusion. What remains is the prospect of marriage to a man who will need to be selflessly nursed.

John Steinbeck, *The Grapes of Wrath,* and *Of Mice and Men*

The Grapes of Wrath is a novel about suffering, blameless oppression, escape and social breakdown. It is set at a time and place in history, in America in the Great Depression, when a world was breaking down. The sharecropping system whereby for generations the Joads, and tens of thousands of others, eked out an existence on the land is no longer viable. One man and a tractor can do the work of a dozen families and so it makes economic sense for the banks that own the land to drive off the families.

The Joads have not brought about their downfall, but rather are victims of circumstances beyond their control, of an economic system turned bad. It is banks and finance houses who repossess their farms. These are driven by profit, which in turn is determined by remote and unpredictable factors, such as bank rates and commodity prices, which in turn can be controlled by the weather, natural disasters or political events in foreign parts. The forces that oppress are remote and amorphous, and all the sharecroppers can do is bend before them. In a mass migration, they flee the past and their homeland for the promise of a better life. The forces are far too powerful for them even to contemplate opposing – at least as a single unit. One of Steinbeck's abiding beliefs is that in order to counter this overwhelming pressure you have to create something equally as large, something much greater than the individual. As Tom Joad says at one point: a person is just 'a little piece of a great big soul ... his little piece of soul wasn't no good 'less it was with the rest, an' was whole.'[29]

Elsewhere in this novel Steinbeck writes of 'the screaming fact that sounds through all history: repression works only to strengthen and knit the oppressed.'[30] In *The Grapes of Wrath* the migrating families are united in their misfortune, and they help each other the best they can. And yet the critical point has not been reached. There are the beginnings of organised resistance, but by and large the migrants just suffer, and bend, and flee. It is in Steinbeck's later novels, such as *In Dubious Battle*, that we see people unite and through strike action push back against repression.

The Joads must bear much, yet they survive. They take what little luck comes their way, are sustained at times by the kindness of others, and, when the pressure becomes too great, they simply move on. Steinbeck has coined a phrase – a strong survival quotient – to describe people like the Joads' capacity to resist destruction. The final pages of the work seem to summarise their situation. When it appears things couldn't be any worse the rains come, the river bursts its banks, and the floodwaters rise towards the abandoned railroad box-car that has become their home. Quite literally a hostile tide threatens to engulf the family. Their attempts to resist are futile. A dam is built, but then easily swept away. Part of the box-car is demolished and likewise the platform they construct to keep their possessions from the rising waters. But in the end they are forced to flee to higher land.

The Grapes of Wrath is also a novel about disillusion. The past has effectively disappeared for these people, yet the future is still uncertain. California is the goal, and indeed to start with it promises much, and the migrants let themselves dream of a life that will be better. But once they arrive they are confronted by the hostility of the law and local people, by shortage of work, by starvation wages and farmers who exploit them. In the end all they can do is survive, and then barely.

Disillusion, delusion and the futility of escape are recurring Steinbeck themes and are evident, for example, in *Of Mice and Men*. The main characters, Lennie and George, are once more individuals firmly fixed at the lower end of socio-economic life. They are itinerant labourers, but dream that one day they might have a farm of their own to work. The novel ends in tragedy just as it seems their hopes may be realised. Lennie is a powerful giant, but a simpleton, and in one sense a destroyer. He has an affection for small and helpless animals – such as mice – but in his enthusiasm to coddle he ends up killing, just as individuals like George and Lennie are crushed by life as it rolls impersonally and clumsily by.

Of Mice and Men is also a story of compassion and self-denial. George has sympathy for his simple friend, but without his cumbrance he could fare better in the world and have a greater chance of realising his dream. One part of George would like to abandon Lennie, yet another side of him is a martyr and needs a burden. Self-denial such as this is peculiarly Piscean and occurs often in life as well as literature.[31]

Alan Sillitoe, *The Loneliness of the Long Distance Runner*

This is a story of a youth who resists external pressures, in the form of others' expectations, and which also illustrates the Piscean paradox of winning by losing. Smith, the central character, is convicted of theft and sent to borstal, where he impresses the governor with his running. High hopes are placed on him to win the annual cross-country race against a local public school. Indeed, he looks set to win but stops just short of the winning tape to let the opposition's runners pass him. This is a deliberate sacrifice on Smith's part. To win would bring freedom of sorts – more privileges, the right to continue training outside the borstal confines. But it would be a spurious freedom, for he would still be a prisoner, and false also because it would be gained by doing what the prison authorities want him to do. The authentic freedom is the one that has his assent, the one he chooses. By choosing to lose, he writes himself out of the governor's – and society's – script. He proves in the only way open to him that he is not powerless, but an individual capable of willing his own destiny. He loses his external freedoms but gains an inner liberation in recompense.

Anthony Burgess, *A Clockwork Orange*

This is another novel that pivots on the idea of choice under duress. Written in the late 1950s, and set in the 'not too distant future', the work proved uncomfortably prophetic, with its vision of tower blocks, violent crime, corrupt police, over-crowded prisons and an apathetic populace pacified by drugs and trivial entertainments. It is a society in its decadent phase, one that has lost its vigour. It is teenage gangs who resist the tides of social decay. They assert themselves through anti-social behaviour – particularly violence – and there is at least the implication in the book that evil action is preferable to apathy. Alex, the novel's narrator, is at least his own person (even if he suffers one of the more less-attractive traits of Pisces: he can be a self-pitying whiner at times).

Alex's life of crime comes to an end when he is betrayed by his gang and imprisoned for murder. However, while in prison he volunteers to take part in a government experiment designed to cut crime and take the strain off the over-burdened jails. He is subjected to a form of aversion therapy so that he experiences extreme discomfort even at the thought of committing violence. As Brodsky the head therapist says: 'He [Alex] will be your true Christian ready to turn the other cheek, ready to be crucified rather than crucify.'[32]

Alex is released and does indeed, because of fear of the pain, eschew violence. However, he has in a sense been emasculated and in a kind of enforced penitence he suffers vengeance at the hands of some of his former victims. Once his self-assertion – his violent nature – is chemically excised, he becomes the victim. He becomes caught up in a scheme to topple the government, and for reasons of political expediency his brainwashing is undone. In the final chapter Alex is part of a new gang but in time loses his enthusiasm for ultra-violence and concludes it might just be a better thing to settle down and get married. In short, he decides to reform himself.

What is central to the story is the question of free will. The aversion therapy takes away Alex's power to act, and for moral choice substitutes fear of pain – a point made by the prison chaplain to a government minister more concerned with expediency than religious nuance. Alex is not turning the other cheek, he is simply coerced by fear of pain. But the message of Pisces, and the theme of *A Clockwork*

Orange, is one of integrity of the will, of needing to act of one's own volition and not from outside pressure.

Mike Leigh, *Vera Drake, Meantime*

Vera Drake is the story of a back-street abortionist, set in London in the early 1950s. Vera is full of kindness and sympathy and with a charitable attitude to her work. She doesn't take payment, but performs abortions, as she puts it, to help put girls in trouble back on their feet. In this she shows characteristic Piscean self-delusion, for it allows her to evade the reality of what it is she does. Also typical of this sign is the idea of things not being as they appear to be – Vera keeps her work secret from her family and they only find out about it when the law intervenes. There is moral ambiguity too. The revelation of the secret stuns her adoring family, but it is only her son who is troubled by the bigger picture, by the fact that a kind, caring, lovable woman can also be a destroyer.

Meantime, written for television, is set in the 1980s amongst the tower blocks, poverty, defeated lives and unemployment of London's East End, and focuses on the Pollock family, particularly its two sons. One, Colin, is dull-witted and seems to gain social acceptance through the role of village idiot thrust upon him. His brother, Mark, is far sharper than Colin, although provocative and anti-social. He is more like the youth in *A Clockwork Orange*, a focus of vigour in his immediate world. His rebellion is formless however, simply an assertion that he refuses to be sucked down by his circumstances. He verbally bullies Colin and appears at first to be the villain of the piece.

At a critical point in the play fortune seems to smile on Colin through an affluent aunt who offers him work. Partly this is altruism, partly, we suspect, the surfacing of a repressed maternal instinct from the childless woman. Mark, however, does all he can to sabotage the arrangement, and it is not immediately plain why, although his family put it down to jealousy and bloody-mindedness. But there is more at work than this. What the brother really objects to is the fact that Colin is put upon, is tossed around like a rag-doll and is a receptacle for everyone else's needs and feelings. Indeed Mark's wounding nickname for his sibling is 'Muppet'.

Colin loses the way and never arrives at his aunt's home, and so the opportunity of a respite from his dreary existence is lost. The play ends with the small act of defiance that seems to characterise Pisces. Colin shaves his head, and the significance of this lies in the fact that it was his own choice, a willed act, an indication that he has begun to swim against the tide. His brother, who has perhaps consciously been working to this end, is pleased by the turn of events. His attitude towards Colin changes, with a new-found respect symbolised by a change in nickname to the more flattering 'Kojak'.

Ralph Ellison, *Invisible Man*
This novel, published in 1952, centres on loss of individual identity in a hostile world. It is the story of a black man in the United States of America who concludes he is 'invisible'. People don't see *him* but simply 'a coloured man'. In one scene he is repeatedly mistaken for someone else, each mistake being a different facet of the man's personality. The world forces its version of reality upon the nameless narrator, until he finally rebels and retires to the seclusion of a New York basement in order to understand himself. He reviews his life and concludes he was simply living up to others' expectations. At a college for black students, for example, he essentially functioned as a pawn in a guilt-shedding exercise for rich benefactors. And when he works for the 'Brotherhood', an organisation fighting for black liberation, he concludes, he is still only functioning as a mouthpiece for something much bigger than himself.

Henrik Ibsen, *The Lady from the Sea*
The action is set one summer in rural Norway at the home of the Wangel family, the doctor, his two daughters and their stepmother, Ellida, a woman out of her element and the lady of the title. The play centres on a crisis in a marriage in which secrets emerge, and on the exorcising of a ghost from Ellida's past. She is haunted by a seaman who exerts a strange influence over her. In the early part of the play she confesses that she had a relationship with this man and went through a ceremony that bound them together in a ritualistic way. He took a key-chain, slipped two rings on to it, one of his, one of Ellida's, and then threw it into the sea.

The stranger represents the sea for Ellida, and beyond that an unknown, a fearful, yet fascinating and compelling unknown. In Act 3 she talks of the sea as being some kind of natural element:

> if only men had chosen from the very beginning to live on the sea – or even in the sea – we should have reached a perfection quite different from our present state – both better and happier.[33]

And in reply to the point that it is too late to put it right now she replies: 'Yes that's true, unfortunately, and I believe that mankind knows it too, and it haunts us like a secret sorrow.' This 'secret sorrow', this yearning for spiritual wholeness and freedom beyond the mundane world, is symbolised in astrology (in part) by Pisces.

Ellida lives in two places. One part of her takes its place in the domestic life of the Wangels, yet the better part of her consciousness is focused in mystery and the 'infinite'. She tells her family this. At one point in the play the children are bedecking the house in flowers and decorations for 'mother's birthday', which turns out to be their real mother's (who has died), and not Ellida's, their stepmother. And when she learns that her husband and stepchildren are 'cherishing memories' she had no part in, she does not seem perturbed, because, as she remarks, 'I have a life myself, in which they have no part'.[34]

At the critical point in the play the two worlds converge. A steamer docks in the fjord on which the Wangels live. The stranger is on board, and comes to claim his 'wife', for he looks upon the ritual with the rings as a legitimate marriage ceremony. He presents Ellida with an ultimatum: come with him when the steamer leaves the next day, or forget him forever. The arrival of the seaman changes Ellida. Before his arrival, in the company of her family, she is distant and vague, as if perpetually beguiled by the mysterious freedom the absent stranger represents. But in his presence she grows fearful and demands protection from her husband. She is not yet ready to surrender to the infinite.

It is at this point in the play that the couple are forced to face up to the lie upon which the marriage had been built. They married shortly after the death of the doctor's first wife, not out of love, but because of the need he had for a housekeeper, a companion and a mother for his children. Ellida agreed to the proposal because at the time she was 'bewildered and alone', although later realises the decision to marry was flawed, because it was made under duress, forced by circumstances. The bond with the seaman, on the other hand, was authentic, because it was a promise freely given.

What resolves the twin-fished split between the mysterious unknown symbolised by the seaman and the down-to-earth domesticity of the Wangels is free will. The doctor agrees to absolve her of her marriage vows so the choice she makes is truly her own, and not one dictated by bonds of duty and obligation. Once she is free to choose, the seaman looses his fascination. A small act of individual freedom dispels the lure of an infinite freedom.

Ben Okri, *The Famished Road*

One of the main ideas in *The Lady from the Sea* is to be found in a novel set in a very different place and time. The central character of Okri's work, Azaro, is a spirit child, one for whom the boundary between the world of flesh and the world of spirit is porous. We are told:

> There are many reasons why babies cry when they are born and one of them is the sudden separation from pure dreams, where all things are made of enchantment and there is no suffering.[35]

Spirit children make a pact with their friends in the spirit world to return soon after birth but Azaro, because of a love for his parents, resists the call of the spirits and remains in the world of space-time. Consequently, he is haunted by hallucinations and remains bound to that other world by 'spirit tokens'. He will continue to feel the pull of that world 'for as long as my cord to the other world remained intact, for as long as my objects were not found'.[36] Other Piscean themes are present in this work. It is set in the urban squalor of post-colonial Nigeria where Azaro's parents work hard but still struggle to exist in dire poverty. His father is a dreamer, but also has the physical and spiritual strength to rebel. He berates the city's underclass for their apathy, for accepting suffering and believing the lies of the politicians.

Notes

1. W H Auden, *Forewords and Afterwords*, Random House, 1973, pp69-70.
2. *Twentieth Century Writing*, ed K Richardson, Newnes Books, 1969, p583
3. *Contemporary Novelists*, ed James Vinson, St James Press, 1976, p495
4. *Contemporary Authors* (Permanent Series), Vol 2, ed Christine Nasso, Gale Research, 1978, p521
5. *Encyclopaedia of World Literature in the Twentieth Century*, Vol 1, St James Press, 1999, p552
6. *Contemporary Dramatists*, ed James Vinson, St James Press, 1977, p321
7. *Encyclopaedia of World Literature in the Twentieth Century*, Vol 2, St James Press, 1999, p552
8. Alrik Gustafson, *A History of Swedish Literature*, University of Minnesota Press, 1961, p148
9. *Contemporary Dramatists*, ed James Vinson, St James Press, 1977, p92
10. *Contemporary Poets*, ed James Vinson, Macmillan, 1980, p446
11. *Encyclopaedia of World Literature in the Twentieth Century*, Vol 1, St James Press, 1999, p326
12. *Contemporary Novelists*, ed James Vinson, St James Press, 1976, 782
13. ibid, 631
14. *Dictionary of Scandinavian Literature*, ed Virpi Zuck, St James Press, 1996, p393
15. *World Authors 1950-70*, ed J Wakeman, H W Wilson Co, 1975, p1116
16. *Dictionary of Scandinavian Literature*, ed Virpi Zuck, St James Press, 1996, p347
17. *Contemporary Novelists*, 7th edition, St James Press, 2001, p776
18. Charles Baudelaire, *La Revue Fantaisiste* 1861, cited in *Nineteenth Century Literary Criticism*, 3, Gale Research

19. *Twentieth Century Writing*, ed K Richardson, Newnes Books, 1969, p382

20. Dane Rudhyar, *An Astrological Triptych*, ASI, 1978, p85

21. Dane Rudhyar, *Astrological Signs, the Pulse of Life*, Shambhala, 1978, p124

22. ibid, p125

23. This issue of identity concerns other of the sign's writers. We note the following observation of the work of Stanislaw Witkiewicz (born 24 February 1885):

> The way in which the problem of disintegrating personal identity becomes extended into the social realm is a fundamental issue in [his] later plays and novels. (*European Writers*, vol 10, Charles Scribner's Sons, 1985, p1209)

Dramatist Mike Leigh observes:

> Many people are frustrated ... the greatest frustration comes from being unable to be yourself, from being forced to play the roles that society imposes on us. (Quoted in *The Films of Mike Leigh*, Ray Carney and Leonard Quart, Cambridge University Press, 2000, p82)

24. Gilbert Debusscher, 'The Death of Bessie Smith', in *Edward Albee: A Collection of Critical Essays*, Prentice Hall, 1975, p54

25. C W Bigsby, 'Box and Quotations from Chairman Mao Tse-Tung: Albee's Diptych', in *Edward Albee: a Collection of Critical Essays*, Prentice Hall, 1975, p152

26. Edward Albee, *Who's Afraid of Virginia Woolf?* Penguin Plays, 1973, p 118

27. ibid, p111

28. Henrik Ibsen, *Ghosts*, Penguin Classics, 1981, p61

29. John Steinbeck, *The Grapes of Wrath*, Minerva, 1995, p278

30. ibid, p492

31. In Kobo Abe's *The Woman in the Dunes* an insect collector on an expedition is held prisoner – along with a mysterious woman – by villagers in a vast sandpit and made to work for them, endlessly filling buckets with sand. He tries to escape, but is recaptured. When, finally, they do give him an opportunity for freedom he elects to stay with the woman, whom he has come to love and pity. The man decides he has more real freedom here than in his mundane existence as a teacher. The sandpit forms a metaphor for a world both hostile and unstable, and like other Abe writing, the novel deals with the difficulty of establishing identity in just such a world.

32 Anthony Burgess, *A Clockwork Orange*, Penguin, 2000, p98

33. Henrik Ibsen, *The Lady from the Sea*, Penguin Classics, 1982, p280

34. ibid, p256

35. Ben Okri, *The Famished Road*, Jonathan Cape, 1993, p4

36. ibid, p9

Appendices

1: Example of a birth chart

Figure 1 shows the birth chart (or horoscope) of the celebrated writer H G Wells. It is essentially a representation of the heavens (from a geocentric perspective) at the time and place he was born, which was 4.30pm (GMT), 21 September 1866, Bromley. The time of birth is generally not recorded on English birth certificates, but in this case his mother noted it in her diary:[1]

> Friday passed a restless night, got worse after breakfast, very ill all day, got dinner over, cleared away, sent Fred with a note to Mrs Harvey before he went to school. 3 Mrs H came and Mr Morgan quarter to 4. Baby half four. Grateful humble thanks, may I never forget to give thanks.

The circle shows the signs of the zodiac, indicated here by their glyphs. Constellated about the circle are the ten planets (including the Sun and Moon), once more indicated as glyphs. The horizontal line bisecting the circle is the ascendant axis; the second bisecting line is the midheaven axis. The nature of planets situated close to either axis will generally play a significant part in the life of the individual, as will the sign of the ascendant, the one rising over the eastern horizon at the time and place of birth (note that horoscopes are drawn with north at the bottom). In Wells' case the sign is Aquarius and it signifies, among other things, his broad readership, his immense popularity, his urge to be a teacher to mankind, his great social vision and, on the more immediate level, his sociability and need for independence. Aquarius is doubly emphasised in the chart, because the Moon is also situated in this sign. Moreover, it is close to the ascendant, which in itself lends a distinct colour to his character. In a positive sense, it contributed to his writing skills. A strongly placed Moon suggests imagination and the tendency to absorb and store impressions from his environment. It suggests a close bond with his mother and a liking for female company in general. It also accounted for his irritability and a tendency to petulant outbursts. But it would contribute some human warmth to what is otherwise a rather cold, objective, detached chart.

The angular relationships between planets are also emphasised in traditional astrology, particularly the conjunctions (where planets lie within 10 degrees of each other on the circle of zodiacal longitude). In Wells' case, there are three conjunctions: Sun/Mercury, Venus/ Saturn and Mars/Uranus. The psychological schools of astrology might see the latter two as an indicator of Wells' singular sexual nature, which seemed to be compounded of obsession, fantasy and a predatory urge for excitement, which he satisfied outside of his marriage with a string of mistresses. He had a great need for freedom in his relationships, something that was embodied in his utopian New World Order, where there would be no place for possessiveness and jealousy, or any of the other messy aspects of relationships. As he noted in his autobiography:

> I developed my adolescent fantasy of free, ambitious, self-reliant women who would mate with me and go their way as I desired to go my own way. I had never in fact seen or heard of any such women; I had evolved

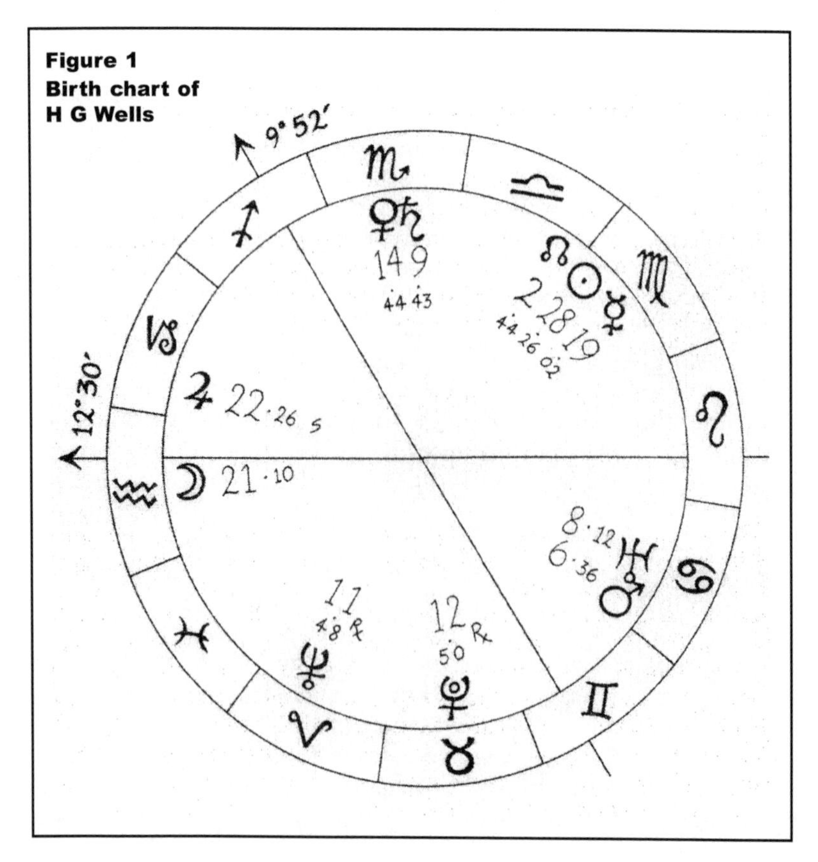

Figure 1
Birth chart of
H G Wells

> them from my inner consciousness. This was my preliminary fantasy of love ... it exerted a ruling influence upon my conduct for many years.[2]

There are other facets of Wells' character that could be explored from an astrological perspective, but it is perhaps important to state here some of the things that are not shown. We can not say from simply looking at the chart that it represents a writer, or a man who achieved great international fame and respect, to the point that without too much difficulty he could gain an audience with both President F D Roosevelt and Joseph Stalin. A chart speaks in its own way and can tell us much, but this sort of information doesn't seem to be given.

Appendix 2: Signs and constellations

Constellations are groupings of stars as they appear to the terrestrial observer that generally bear only a superficial resemblance to what they are supposed to represent, have ill-defined boundaries and are of unequal size. For example, the constellation of Virgo occupies 46 degrees of zodiacal longitude, while Libra occupies only 18 degrees. The signs, on the other hand, are an idealised version of the constellations, occupying equal 30-degree segments of the circle. The so-called tropical zodiac, the one used by the great majority of western astrologers, is not in effect determined by physical star patterns but is founded upon an essentially unchanging relationship between the sun and the Earth, in which there are four critical points, the solstices and the equinoxes. Because of the earth's tilt and movement the sun's position can be measured by latitude – declination – as well as by longitude. Moreover, this changes from day to day. On 21 March, the first day of spring, the solar axis and the earth's equator are aligned. Declination is zero at this point, but progressively changes as the sun appears to move north, until the summer solstice, the first point of Cancer, when the sun culminates directly overhead at 23 degrees north, the Tropic of Cancer. At the autumn equinox, corresponding to the first point of Libra, the sun, as it were, moves south once more, and continues to until it has a declination of 23 degrees south, at the first point of Capricorn, the winter solstice in the northern hemisphere. The tropical zodiac, then, utilises the vernal equinox as its starting point, irrespective of the particular star pattern that appears behind the sun at this point. The first 30 degrees of the ecliptic are then allotted to Aries, the next 30 to Taurus, and so on for the full circle.

The sidereal zodiac, which is utilised in Indian astrology, uses the backdrop of star patterns rather than the seasonal cycle as its reference. It is in effect a moving zodiac, as the constellation that lies behind the sun at the spring equinox changes over the centuries because of a phenomenon related to the earth's axis called precession. Around 2000 years ago – it is not known exactly – this so-called vernal point coincided with the first degree of Aries. However, this point moves backwards through the zodiac at the rate of about one degree every 72 years, so that it now lies in the early part of Pisces.

It is this confusion between the *signs* of the zodiac as a working model, and an approximate circle of star patterns, that underlies a lot of ignorant criticism of astrology.

Appendix 3: The work of the Gauquelins

The work of Michel Gauquelin (1928-1991) was touched on in the introduction. He was a French psychologist who as a young man had an interest in astrology, but later grew sceptical. He decided he would prove once and for all that astrology did not work and to do this he turned to the major research tool of his profession, statistics.

Figure 2: The Gauquelin effect for writers

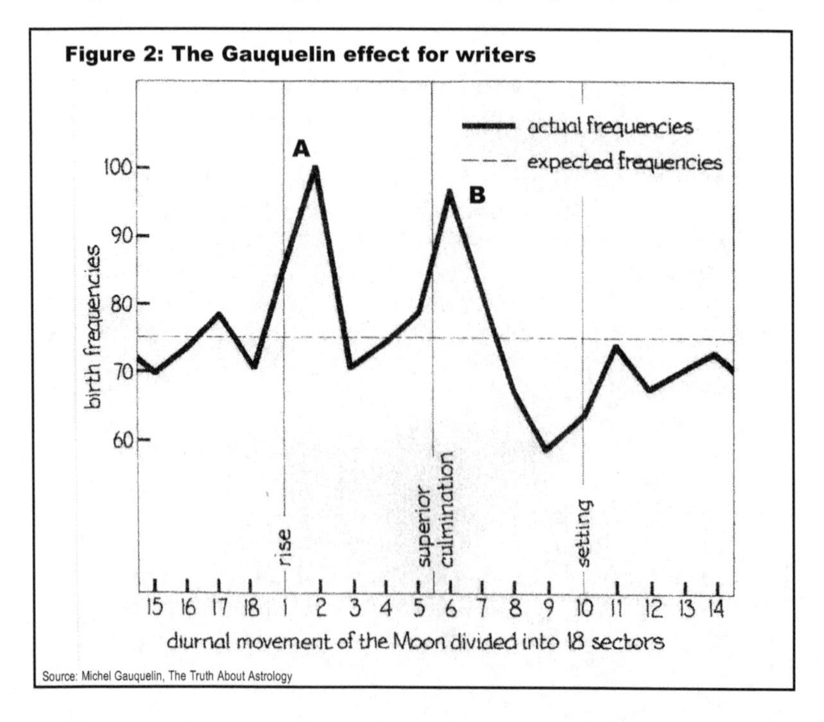

Source: Michel Gauquelin, The Truth About Astrology

Working with his wife, Françoise, he set about collecting the raw birth data of individuals classified by vocation – scientists, politicians, athletes, actors and writers. It was a mammoth task that involved searching public records for tens of thousands of individuals. To his surprise he discovered strong statistical patterns emerged for each of the vocational groups. These patterns related not to the zodiac, but to the diurnal circle also used in astrology, the one based on the ascendant and midheaven axes and which comes about because of the 24-hour rotation of the Earth about its own axis. We know the sun rises, culminates and sets, but so also do the moon and the other planets.

What Gauquelin discovered was that certain planets tended to be rising and culminating in the cases of those who excelled in certain professions. Figure 2 shows this for the Moon and 1,352 European writers. The sample includes some distinguished names, such as Anouilh, Artaud, Baudelaire, Rimbaud, Camus, Sartre and Malraux, and some lesser known ones. He divided the diurnal circle into 18 sectors and calculated the frequency for each planet in each sector over the total sample.

The highest frequencies are observed at points A and B, which in physical terms represent the Moon just rising at that place on the earth, and just past its highest point in the sky, its culmination. If there was no connection between writers and the moon position we would not, over a large number of cases, get peaks and troughs, but a straight line distribution of equal numbers in each sector. In statistical terms the distributions were highly significant and very unlikely to have occurred by chance. Similar results were found for the other vocations – sports champions, politicians, scientists, doctors, actors – although it was planets other than the Moon which were prominent.[3]

Gauquelin's methodology doesn't quite accord with traditional astrology, which uses 12 houses rather than 18 sectors. He also takes into account a planet's latitude as well as its longitude in determining a placement on the diurnal wheel, which once more differs from traditional astrological practice. Thomas Shanks (of Astro Computing Services) has analysed the data in terms more familiar to astrologers. He discovered, amongst other things, that there was a statistically significant tendency for the Moon to fall in Sagittarius and Gemini, two signs that tradition has linked more than any other with writing and publishing.

The Gauquelins' work has been criticised and the results questioned, although much of this has come from disciples of scientism, for whom nothing could validate astrology. But the more open-minded among the scientific community have been quietly impressed with his work.

Some critics have questioned the quality of the basic data, the times recorded in European birth records, mostly from the 19th and early 20th centuries. Gauquelin has published these and if we analyse them we discover that the times as originally recorded by the civil authorities have in many cases been rounded. For example, in birth records for French artists, in around 85 per cent of cases the time is given only to the hour. There is no reason why babies should be born on the hour. We would expect a random distribution of times about the hour, and indeed this is more the case with other samples of recorded birth times (in post-war Scotland, for example).[4] Astrology generally requires times more accurate than the nearest hour, as a birth chart can change significantly over even a 10- or 15-minute period (particularly as we move to latitudes away from the equator). However, this quirk in the data does not in my view invalidate Gauquelin's conclusions, as he is dealing with large sample sizes and it is reasonable to assume rounding errors in the times will tend to balance out.

It can be argued that the work of the Gauquelins represents a landmark in human thought because, as far as I am aware, it is the first time that something 'occult' has been expressed in the precise language of mathematics (albeit to a limited degree). However, from a *practical* point of view the results remain marginal. Quite what is proved by a statistically significant result is open to debate, but is perhaps not the point anyway. What Gauquelin established is a statement about a *group* of writers, a sort of summary of the individuals that make up that group. We can not then take that summary, that generality, and apply it to individual cases. Rather, it is a statement that applies everywhere at once but nowhere in particular (the familiar case of the average family having 2.4 children). The majority of prominent writers still do *not* have the Moon rising or culminating, just as many people with the Moon in these positions have *not* become famous writers.

Appendix 4: Systems of knowledge congruous with astrology

The Cabbala is the esoteric teaching of Judaism. Fundamental to it is the Tree of Life which can be understood as a model of the universe. Halevi[5] describes it as 'an objective diagram of the principles working throughout the universe. Cast in the form of an analogic tree it demonstrates the flow of forces down from the Divine to the lowest world and back again.' Eleven sephiroth (or spheres) mark the successive phases of this involution. They are linked by 22 pathways, which are regarded as successive stages of unfoldment of cosmic realisation in human consciousness. Kether is the first sphere on the Tree but beyond it, according to cabbalistic teachings, lie realms of unmanifest or negative existence. Such states as these symbolise are beyond human comprehension, as are the magnitude of stellar distances, but they do at least provide some kind of far-flung reference point from which we can take a bearing and begin to appreciate the topography of human totality.

The planets can be equated directly to the sephira and the signs

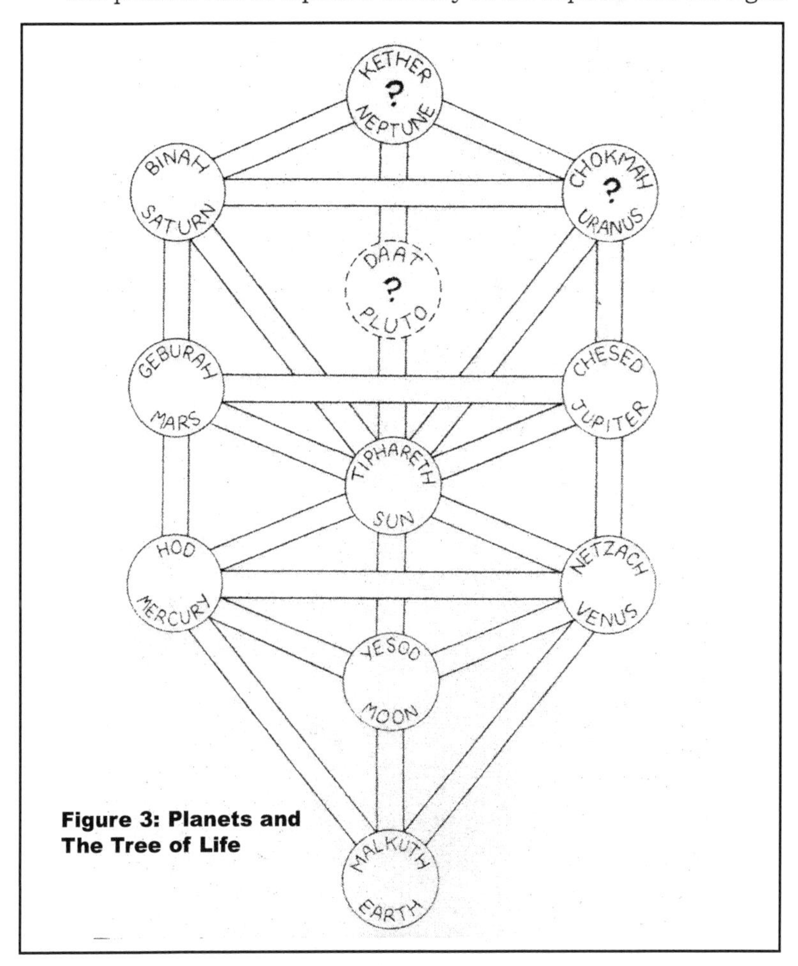

Figure 3: Planets and The Tree of Life

to the pathways, although there are a number of correspondences in the latter case and no agreement upon which is best. The discovery of the planets Uranus, Neptune and Pluto in modern times precludes their inclusion in the original schema of the Tree, although they have since been allocated spheres conveniently left vacant in the original formulation. Just as planets symbolise dimensions of human experience, so too do sephiroth, and much can be learned by comparing the two.

For 3000 years or more the **I Ching** (or Book of Changes) has had a considerable influence on Chinese thought and culture. It stands as a system of knowledge that reduces the world to 64 inter-related hexagrams, combinations of yin and yang lines. This reflects the concept of a manifest world built upon the interplay of two alternating primal states of being, themselves the expression of a unity. These dual strands are held to pattern any fundamental pair of opposites – night/day, winter/summer, creative/receptive and so on. In the initial formulation a body of imagery drawn from the worlds of nature and man came to be associated with the various groupings of lines, or trigrams. These were then doubled to form 64 hexagrams which form a kind of model of the transitory manifest world. The *Book of Changes* can be read as a book of knowledge, but over the centuries it has primarily functioned as an oracle. A hexagram is cast using coins or yarrow stalks for the moment of asking a question. The cast hexagram is then a representation of the quality of that moment – much like a horoscope – and also how that moment is likely to change and develop. It offers the inquirer advice on how to act in the particular situation.

The history and rationale of the I Ching are given in detail in what has become the definitive English language version, the Richard Wilhelm translation.[6] Wilhelm describes how certain of the hexagrams have come to be associated with 'months', or phases of the year. For example, he tells us hexagram 1 is related to May-June, which corresponds to the sign Gemini, which runs from about 21 May to 21 June. It is the cyclic arrangement of these 12 monthly, or seasonal, hexagrams that provides a basis for comparison with the zodiac, and thus a source of insight into the signs.

Figure 4 shows the relationship between the signs of the zodiac and the so-called seasonal cycle of I Ching hexagrams. The rhythmic change of yin to yang (and vice versa) is plain to see.

The philosopher and composer **Dane Rudhyar** (1895-1985) has written copiously and in great depth about astrology, and in terms of ideas and understanding was well in advance of his contemporaries. There is a website (www.khaldea.com/rudhyar) that details information about the man and the extent of his writings and I often quote him in the text of *The Literary Zodiac*. What I find particularly valuable is his application of Taoist thought to the zodiac. He does not directly equate hexagrams and signs but more broadly uses the idea of the zodiac as a cyclic interplay of polar opposites as a framework for understanding the signs. This is the Day/Night force cycle he describes in *Astrological Signs, The Pulse of Life*. He views each sign as representative of a state of human experience in which more or less of two basic forces are active. These he calls Night force

Figure 4: Zodiac signs and their equivalent I Ching hexagrams

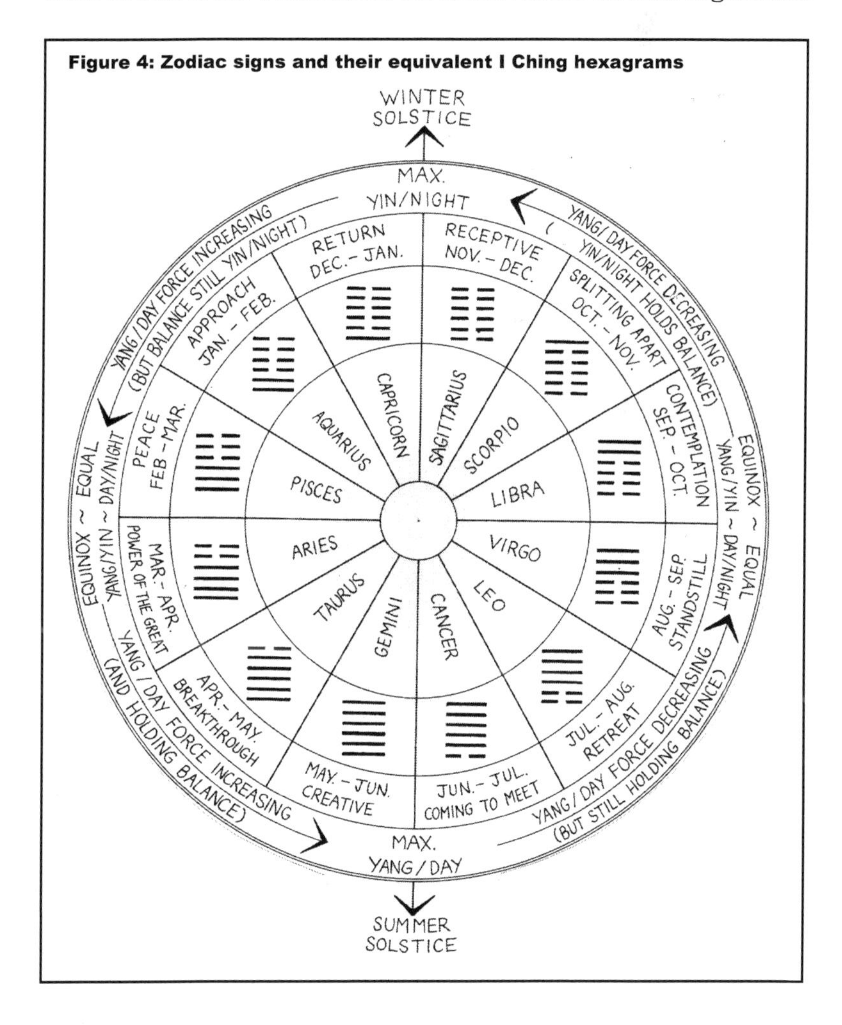

and Day force, and they correspond broadly to yin and yang. (See Figure 4)

The Day (yang) force is a personalising energy, one that 'forces ideas, spiritual entities, abstractions, into concrete and particular activity'.[7] It stresses the primacy of the individual and is to the fore in the early part of the zodiac, maximising in Gemini/Cancer. The Night (yin) force, on the other hand, is a collectivising or in-gathering energy. It emphasises values relating to society. It waxes at the expense of the Day force from the summer solstice onward, maximising in Sagittarius/Capricorn. By examining the balance of the Day and Night force at any stage of the zodiac we can get an immediate bearing on the nature of a sign. It is a simple idea, yet powerful in its capacity to elicit understanding. Each sign can be understood quite simply in terms of the balance of the two primary forces and by the tendency in change of this balance.

Notes

1. Information provided by the H G Wells Society of Great Britain.
2. H G Wells, *Experiment in Autobiography*, Gollancz, 1934, p185
3. Michel Gauquelin, *The Truth About Astrology*, Hutchinson, 1984, pp32-36
4. See Paul Wright, *A Multitude of Lives*, Parlando, 2009, pp 8-10
5. Z'ev ben Shimon Halevi, *Tree of Life*, Rider, 1972, p13
6. *I Ching*, Routledge & Kegan Paul, 1975
7. Dane Rudhyar, *Astrological Signs, The Pulse of Life*, Shambhala, 1978, p22

Appendix 5: Change of Sun sign by date

The approximately one monthly divisions of the zodiac are as follows:

Aries: 20 March to 20 April
Taurus: 20 April to 21 May
Gemini: 21 May to 21 June
Cancer: 21 June to 21 July
Leo: 22 July to 23 August
Virgo: 23 August to 22 September
Libra: 23 September to 23 October
Scorpio: 23 October to 22 November
Sagittarius: 22 November to 21 December
Capricorn: 21 December to 20 January
Aquarius: 20 January to 19 February
Pisces: 19 February to 20 March

Some individuals are born on the cusp, that is, the divide between two signs. However, there is no evidence in astrology that the Sun can share the nature of two signs. It works in quantum fashion rather than as a continuum. For example, there are at least two writers whose sun is positioned very close to the end of Scorpio. André Gide was, according to birth records, born at 3am on 22 November 1869, in Paris. If we calculate the position of planets for that time we find the Sun was situated at 29deg 53min of Scorpio, about 7min of arc (or three hours of clock time) before entering Sagittarius. His creative themes put him firmly in Scorpio. George Eliot was, according to her father's diary, born at 5am on 22 November 1819 with the Sun also in the last degree of Scorpio. Her writing, with a focus on characters that need to shed narrow egotism and, as it were, sink into a level of caring communion with their fellow human beings, is characteristic of the sign.

For those born on a day when the sun changes sign it's necessary to know a time of birth to fix its position more accurately. The table following shows the time (GMT) and date the Sun entered a particular sign for the years 1940-1993. The times were calculated using the Win*Star (version2) software package. If the time you are checking fell when British Summer Time was operative (one hour ahead of GMT), allowance must be made for this. In recent years Summer Time has run from the last weekend in March to the last weekend in October, although it varied before that.

1940
Aquarius, 21 Jan 4.44am
Pisces, 19 Feb 7.04pm
Aries, 20 March 6.24pm
Taurus, 20 April 5.51am
Gemini, 21 May 5.23am
Cancer, 21 June 1.36pm
Leo, 23 July 00.34am
Virgo, 23 August 7.29am
Libra, 23 Sept 4.46am
Scorpio, 23 Oct 1.39pm
Sagittarius, 22 Nov 10.49am
Capricorn, 21 Dec 11.55pm

1941
Aquarius, 20 Jan 10.34am
Pisces, 19 Feb 0.56am
Aries, 21 March 0.20am
Taurus, 20 April 11.50am
Gemini, 21 May 11.23am
Cancer, 21 June 7.33pm
Leo, 23 July 6.26am
Virgo, 23 August 12.17pm
Libra, 23 Sept 10.33am
Scorpio, 23 Oct 7.27pm
Sagittarius, 22 Nov 4.38pm
Capricorn, 22 Dec 5.44am

1942
Aquarius, 20 Jan 4.24pm
Pisces, 19 Feb 6.47am
Aries, 21 March 6.11am
Taurus, 20 April 5.39pm
Gemini, 21 May 5.09pm
Cancer, 22 June 1.16am
Leo, 23 July 12.08pm
Virgo, 23 August 6.58pm
Libra, 23 Sept 4.16pm
Scorpio, 24 Oct 1.15am
Sagittarius, 22 Nov 10.30pm
Capricorn, 22 Dec 11.40am

1943
Aquarius, 20 Jan 10.19pm
Pisces, 19 Feb 12.40pm
Aries, 21 March 12.03pm
Taurus, 20 April 11.32pm
Gemini, 21 May 11.03pm
Cancer, 22 June 7.12am
Leo, 23 July 6.05pm
Virgo, 24 August 0.55am
Libra, 23 Sept 10.12pm
Scorpio, 24 Oct 7.08am
Sagittarius, 23 Nov 4.22am
Capricorn, 22 Dec 5.29pm

1944
Aquarius, 21 Jan 4.07am
Pisces, 19 Feb 6.27pm
Aries, 20 March 5.49pm
Taurus, 20 April 5.18am
Gemini, 21 May 4.51am
Cancer, 21 June 1.02pm
Leo, 22 July 11.56pm
Virgo, 23 August 6.47am
Libra, 23 Sept 4.02am
Scorpio, 23 Oct 12.56pm
Sagittarius, 22 Nov 10.08am
Capricorn, 21 Dec 11.15pm

1945
Aquarius, 20 Jan 9.54am
Pisces, 19 Feb 12.15pm
Aries, 20 March 11.37pm
Taurus, 20 April 11.07am
Gemini, 21 May 10.40am
Cancer, 21 June 6.52pm
Leo, 23 July 5.45am
Virgo, 23 August 12.35pm
Libra, 23 Sept 9.50am
Scorpio, 23 Oct 6.44pm
Sagittarius, 22 Nov 3.55pm
Capricorn, 22 Dec 5.04am

1946
Aquarius, 20 Jan 3.45pm
Pisces, 19 Feb 6.09am
Aries, 21 March 5.33am
Taurus, 20 April 5.02pm
Gemini, 21 May 4.34pm
Cancer, 22 June 0.44am
Leo, 23 July 11.37am
Virgo, 23 August 6.26pm
Libra, 23 Sept 3.41pm
Scorpio, 24 Oct 0.35am
Sagittarius, 22 Nov 9.46pm
Capricorn, 22 Dec 10.53am

1947
Aquarius, 20 Jan 9.32pm
Pisces, 19 Feb 11.52am
Aries, 21 March 11.13am
Taurus, 20 April 10.39pm
Gemini, 21 May 10.09pm
Cancer, 22 June 6.19am
Leo, 23 July 5.14pm
Virgo, 24 August 0.09am
Libra, 23 Sept 9.29pm
Scorpio, 24 Oct 6.26am
Sagittarius, 23 Nov 3.38am
Capricorn, 22 Dec 4.43pm

1948
Aquarius, 21 Jan 3.18am
Pisces, 19 Feb 5.37pm
Aries, 20 March 4.57pm
Taurus, 20 April 4.25am
Gemini, 21 May 3.58am
Cancer, 21 June 12.11pm
Leo, 22 July 11.08pm
Virgo, 23 August 6.03am
Libra, 23 Sept 3.22am
Scorpio, 23 Oct 12.18pm
Sagittarius, 22 Nov 9.29am
Capricorn, 21 Dec 10.33pm

1949
Aquarius, 20 Jan 9.09am
Pisces, 18 Feb 11.27pm
Aries, 20 March 10.48pm
Taurus, 20 April 10.17am
Gemini, 21 May 9.51am
Cancer, 21 June 6.03pm
Leo, 23 July 4.47am
Virgo, 23 August 11.48am
Libra, 23 Sept 9.06am
Scorpio, 23 Oct 6.03pm
Sagittarius, 22 Nov 3.16pm
Capricorn, 22 Dec 4.23am

1950
Aquarius, 20 Jan 3.00pm
Pisces, 19 Feb 5.15am
Aries, 21 March 4.35am
Taurus, 20 April 5.59pm
Gemini, 21 May 3.27pm
Cancer, 21 June 11.36pm
Leo, 23 July 10.30am
Virgo, 23 August 5.23pm
Libra, 23 Sept 2.44pm
Scorpio, 23 Oct 11.45pm
Sagittarius, 22 Nov 9.02pm
Capricorn, 22 Dec 10.13am

1951
Aquarius, 20 Jan 8.52pm
Pisces, 19 Feb 11.10am
Aries, 21 March 10.26am
Taurus, 20 April 9.48pm
Gemini, 21 May 9.15pm
Cancer, 22 June 5.25am
Leo, 23 July 4.21pm
Virgo, 23 August 11.16pm
Libra, 23 Sept 8.37pm
Scorpio, 24 Oct 5.36am
Sagittarius, 23 Nov 2.51am
Capricorn, 22 Dec 4.00pm

1952
Aquarius, 21 Jan 2.38am
Pisces, 19 Feb 4.57pm
Aries, 20 March 4.14pm
Taurus, 20 April 3.37am
Gemini, 21 May 3.04am
Cancer, 21 June 11.13am
Leo, 22 July 10.08pm
Virgo, 23 August 5.03am
Libra, 23 Sept 2.24am
Scorpio, 23 Oct 11.22am
Sagittarius, 22 Nov 8.36am
Capricorn, 21 Dec 9.43

1953
Aquarius, 20 Jan 8.21am
Pisces, 18 Feb 10.41pm
Aries, 20 March 10.01pm
Taurus, 20 April 9.25am
Gemini, 21 May 8.53am
Cancer, 21 June 5.00pm

Leo, 23 July 3.52am
Virgo, 23 August 10.45am
Libra, 23 Sept 8.06am
Scorpio, 23 Oct 5.06pm
Sagittarius, 22 Nov 2.22pm
Capricorn, 22 Dec 3.31am

1954
Aquarius, 20 Jan 2.11pm
Pisces, 19 Feb 4.32am
Aries, 21 March 3.53am
Taurus, 20 April 3.20pm
Gemini, 21 May 2.27pm
Cancer, 21 June 10.54pm
Leo, 23 July 9.45am
Virgo, 23 August 4.36pm
Libra, 23 Sept 1.55pm
Scorpio, 23 Oct 10.56pm
Sagittarius, 22 Nov 8.14pm
Capricorn, 22 Dec 9.24am

1955
Aquarius, 20 Jan 8.02pm
Pisces, 19 Feb 10.19am
Aries, 21 March 9.35am
Taurus, 20 April 8.58pm
Gemini, 21 May 8.24pm
Cancer, 22 June 4.31am
Leo, 23 July 3.25pm
Virgo, 23 August 10.19pm
Libra, 23 Sept 7.41pm
Scorpio, 24 Oct 4.43am
Sagittarius, 23 Nov 2.01am
Capricorn, 22 Dec 3.11pm

1956
Aquarius, 21 Jan 1.48am
Pisces, 19 Feb 4.05pm
Aries, 20 March 3.20pm
Taurus, 20 April 2.43am
Gemini, 21 May 2.13am
Cancer, 21 June 10.24am
Leo, 22 July 9.20pm
Virgo, 23 August 4.15am
Libra, 23 Sept 1.35am
Scorpio, 23 Oct 10.34am
Sagittarius, 22 Nov 7.50am
Capricorn, 21 Dec 8.59pm

1957
Aquarius, 20 Jan 7.39am
Pisces, 18 Feb 9.58pm
Aries, 20 March 9.16pm
Taurus, 20 April 8.41am
Gemini, 21 May 8.10am
Cancer, 21 June 4.21pm
Leo, 23 July 3.15am
Virgo, 23 August 10.08am
Libra, 23 Sept 7.26am
Scorpio, 23 Oct 3.24pm
Sagittarius, 22 Nov 1.39pm
Capricorn, 22 Dec 2.49pm

1958
Aquarius, 20 Jan 1.29pm
Pisces, 19 Feb 3.49am
Aries, 21 March 3.06am
Taurus, 20 April 2.27pm
Gemini, 21 May 1.51pm
Cancer, 21 June 9.57pm
Leo, 23 July 8.51am
Virgo, 23 August 3.46pm
Libra, 23 Sept 1.09pm
Scorpio, 23 Oct 10.11pm
Sagittarius, 22 Nov 7.29pm
Capricorn, 22 Dec 8.40am

1959
Aquarius, 20 Jan 7.19pm
Pisces, 19 Feb 9.38am
Aries, 21 March 8.55am
Taurus, 20 April 8.17pm
Gemini, 21 May 7.42pm
Cancer, 22 June 3.50am
Leo, 23 July 2.45pm
Virgo, 23 August 9.44pm
Libra, 23 Sept 7.08pm
Scorpio, 24 Oct 4.11am
Sagittarius, 23 Nov 1.27am
Capricorn, 22 Dec 2.34pm

1960
Aquarius, 21 Jan 1.10am
Pisces, 19 Feb 3.26pm
Aries, 20 March 2.43pm
Taurus, 20 April 2.06am
Gemini, 21 May 1.34am
Cancer, 21 June 9.42am
Leo, 22 July 8.37pm
Virgo, 23 August 3.34am
Libra, 23 Sept 0.59am
Scorpio, 23 Oct 10.02am
Sagittarius, 22 Nov 7.18am
Capricorn, 21 Dec 8.26pm

1961
Aquarius, 20 Jan 7.01am
Pisces, 18 Feb 9.17pm
Aries, 20 March 8.32pm
Taurus, 20 April 7.55am
Gemini, 21 May 7.22am
Cancer, 21 June 3.30pm
Leo, 23 July 2.24am
Virgo, 23 August 9.19am
Libra, 23 Sept 6.42am
Scorpio, 23 Oct 3.47pm
Sagittarius, 22 Nov 1.08pm
Capricorn, 22 Dec 2.19am

1962
Aquarius, 20 Jan 12.58pm
Pisces, 19 Feb 3.15am
Aries, 21 March 2.30am
Taurus, 20 April 1.51pm
Gemini, 21 May 1.17pm
Cancer, 21 June 9.24pm
Leo, 23 July 8.18am
Virgo, 23 August 3.13pm
Libra, 23 Sept 12.35pm
Scorpio, 23 Oct 9.40pm
Sagittarius, 22 Nov 7.02pm
Capricorn, 22 Dec 8.15am

1963
Aquarius, 20 Jan 6.54pm
Pisces, 19 Feb 9.09am
Aries, 21 March 8.20am
Taurus, 20 April 7.36pm
Gemini, 21 May 6.58pm
Cancer, 22 June 3.04am
Leo, 23 July 1.59pm
Virgo, 23 August 8.58pm
Libra, 23 Sept 6.24pm
Scorpio, 24 Oct 3.29am
Sagittarius, 23 Nov 0.49am
Capricorn, 22 Dec 2.02pm

1964
Aquarius, 21 Jan 0.41pm
Pisces, 19 Feb 2.57pm
Aries, 20 March 2.10pm
Taurus, 20 April 1.27am
Gemini, 21 May 0.50am
Cancer, 21 June 8.57am
Leo, 22 July 7.53pm
Virgo, 23 August 2.51am
Libra, 23 Sept 0.17am
Scorpio, 23 Oct 9.21am
Sagittarius, 22 Nov 6.39am
Capricorn, 21 Dec 7.50pm

1965
Aquarius, 20 Jan 6.29am
Pisces, 18 Feb 8.48pm
Aries, 20 March 8.05pm
Taurus, 20 April 7.26am
Gemini, 21 May 6.50am
Cancer, 21 June 2.56pm
Leo, 23 July 1.48am
Virgo, 23 August 8.43am
Libra, 23 Sept 6.06am
Scorpio, 23 Oct 3.10pm
Sagittarius, 22 Nov 0.29pm
Capricorn, 22 Dec 1.40am

1966
Aquarius, 20 Jan 1.20pm
Pisces, 19 Feb 2.38am
Aries, 21 March 1.53am
Taurus, 20 April 1.12pm
Gemini, 21 May 1.32pm
Cancer, 21 June 8.33pm
Leo, 23 July 7.23am
Virgo, 23 August 2.18pm
Libra, 23 Sept 11.43am
Scorpio, 23 Oct 8.51pm
Sagittarius, 22 Nov 6.14pm
Capricorn, 22 Dec 7.28am

1967
Aquarius, 20 Jan 6.08pm
Pisces, 19 Feb 8.24am
Aries, 21 March 7.37am
Taurus, 20 April 6.55pm
Gemini, 21 May 6.18pm
Cancer, 22 June 2.23am
Leo, 23 July 1.16pm
Virgo, 23 August 8.12pm
Libra, 23 Sept 5.38pm
Scorpio, 24 Oct 2.44am
Sagittarius, 23 Nov 0.05am
Capricorn, 22 Dec 1.16pm

1968
Aquarius, 20 Jan 11.54pm
Pisces, 19 Feb 2.09pm
Aries, 20 March 1.22pm
Taurus, 20 April 0.41pm
Gemini, 21 May 0.06pm
Cancer, 21 June 8.13am
Leo, 22 July 7.08pm
Virgo, 23 August 2.03am
Libra, 22 Sept 11.26pm
Scorpio, 23 Oct 8.30am
Sagittarius, 22 Nov 5.49am
Capricorn, 21 Dec 7pm

1969
Aquarius, 20 Jan 5.38am
Pisces, 18 Feb 7.55pm
Aries, 20 March 7.09pm
Taurus, 20 April 6.27am
Gemini, 21 May 5.50am
Cancer, 21 June 1.55pm
Leo, 23 July 0.48am
Virgo, 23 August 7.43am
Libra, 23 Sept 5.07am
Scorpio, 23 Oct 2.11pm
Sagittarius, 22 Nov 11.31am
Capricorn, 22 Dec 0.44am

1970
Aquarius, 20 Jan 11.24am
Pisces, 19 Feb 1.42am
Aries, 21 March 0.56am
Taurus, 20 April 0.15pm
Gemini, 21 May 11.37am
Cancer, 21 June 7.43pm
Leo, 23 July 6.37am
Virgo, 23 August 1.34pm
Libra, 23 Sept 10.59am
Scorpio, 23 Oct 8.04pm
Sagittarius, 22 Nov 5.25pm
Capricorn, 22 Dec 6.36am

1971
Aquarius, 20 Jan 5.13pm
Pisces, 19 Feb 7.27am
Aries, 21 March 6.38am
Taurus, 20 April 5.54pm
Gemini, 21 May 5.15pm
Cancer, 22 June 1.20am
Leo, 23 July 0.15pm
Virgo, 23 August 7.15pm
Libra, 23 Sept 4.45pm
Scorpio, 24 Oct 1.53am
Sagittarius, 22 Nov 11.14pm
Capricorn, 22 Dec 0.24pm

1972
Aquarius, 20 Jan 10.59pm
Pisces, 19 Feb 1.11pm
Aries, 20 March 0.21pm
Taurus, 19 April 11.38pm
Gemini, 20 May 11pm
Cancer, 21 June 7.06am
Leo, 22 July 6.03pm
Virgo, 23 August 1.03am
Libra, 22 Sept 10.33pm
Scorpio, 23 Oct 7.41am
Sagittarius, 22 Nov 5.03am
Capricorn, 21 Dec 6.13pm

1973
Aquarius, 20 Jan 4.48am
Pisces, 18 Feb 7.01pm
Aries, 20 March. 6.12pm
Taurus, 20 April 5.30am
Gemini, 21 May 4.54am
Cancer, 21 June 1.01pm
Leo, 22 July 11.56pm
Virgo, 23 August 6.54am
Libra, 23 Sept 4.21am
Scorpio, 23 Oct 1.30pm
Sagittarius, 22 Nov 10.54am
Capricorn, 22 Dec 0.08am

1974
Aquarius, 20 Jan 10.46am
Pisces, 19 Feb 0.59am
Aries, 21 March 0.07am
Taurus, 20 April 11.19am
Gemini, 21 May 10.36am
Cancer, 21 June 6.38pm
Leo, 23 July 5.30am
Virgo, 23 August 0.29pm
Libra, 23 Sept 9.59am
Scorpio, 23 Oct 7.11pm
Sagittarius, 22 Nov 4.39pm
Capricorn, 22 Dec 5.56am

1975
Aquarius, 20 Jan 4.36pm
Pisces, 19 Feb 6.50am
Aries, 21 March 5.57am
Taurus, 20 April 5.07pm
Gemini, 21 May 4.24pm
Cancer, 22 June 0.26am
Leo, 23 July 11.22am
Virgo, 23 August 6.24pm
Libra, 23 Sept 3.55pm
Scorpio, 24 Oct 1.06am
Sagittarius, 22 Nov 10.31pm
Capricorn, 22 Dec 11.46am

1976
Aquarius, 20 Jan 10.25pm
Pisces, 19 Feb 0.40pm
Aries, 20 March 11.50am
Taurus, 19 April 11.03pm
Gemini, 20 May 10.21pm
Cancer, 21 June 6.24am
Leo, 22 July 5.18pm
Virgo, 23 August 0.18am
Libra, 22 Sept 9.48pm
Scorpio, 23 Oct 6.58am
Sagittarius, 22 Nov 4.22am
Capricorn, 21 Dec 5.35pm

1977
Aquarius, 20 Jan 4.15am
Pisces, 18 Feb 6.31pm
Aries, 20 March 5.42pm
Taurus, 20 April 4.57am
Gemini, 21 May 4.14am
Cancer, 21 June 0.14pm
Leo, 22 July 11.04pm
Virgo, 23 August 6.00am
Libra, 23 Sept 3.29am
Scorpio, 23 Oct 0.41pm
Sagittarius, 22 Nov 10.07am
Capricorn, 21 Dec 11.23pm

1978
Aquarius, 20 Jan 10.04am
Pisces, 19 Feb 0.21am
Aries, 20 March 11.34pm
Taurus, 20 April 10.50am
Gemini, 21 May 10.09am
Cancer, 21 June 6.10pm
Leo, 23 July 5.00am
Virgo, 23 August 11.57am
Libra, 23 Sept 9.26am
Scorpio, 23 Oct 6.37pm
Sagittarius, 22 Nov 4.05pm
Capricorn, 22 Dec 5.21am

1979
Aquarius, 20 Jan 4.00pm
Pisces, 19 Feb 6.13am
Aries, 21 March 5.22am
Taurus, 20 April 4.35pm
Gemini, 21 May 3.54pm
Cancer, 21 June 11.56pm
Leo, 23 July 10.49am
Virgo, 23 August 5.47pm
Libra, 23 Sept 3.17pm
Scorpio, 24 Oct 0.28am
Sagittarius, 22 Nov 9.54pm
Capricorn, 22 Dec 11.10am

1980
Aquarius, 20 Jan 9.49pm
Pisces, 19 Feb 0.02pm
Aries, 20 March 11.10am
Taurus, 19 April 10.23pm
Gemini, 20 May 9.42pm
Cancer, 21 June 5.47am

Leo, 22 July 4.42pm
Virgo, 22 August 11.41pm
Libra, 22 Sept 9.09pm
Scorpio, 23 Oct 6.18am
Sagittarius, 22 Nov 3.41am
Capricorn, 21 Dec 4.56pm

1981
Aquarius, 20 Jan 3.36am
Pisces, 18 Feb 5.52pm
Aries, 20 March 5.03pm
Taurus, 20 April 4.19am
Gemini, 21 May 3.39am
Cancer, 21 June 11.45am
Leo, 22 July 10.40pm
Virgo, 23 August 5.38am
Libra, 23 Sept 3.05am
Scorpio, 23 Oct 0.13pm
Sagittarius, 22 Nov 9.36am
Capricorn, 21 Dec 10.51pm

1982
Aquarius, 20 Jan 9.31am
Pisces, 18 Feb 11.47pm
Aries, 20 March 10.56pm
Taurus, 20 April 10.08am
Gemini, 21 May 9.23am
Cancer, 21 June 5.23pm
Leo, 23 July 4.16am
Virgo, 23 August 11.15am
Libra, 23 Sept 8.46am
Scorpio, 23 Oct 5.58pm
Sagittarius, 22 Nov 3.23pm
Capricorn, 22 Dec 4.38am

1983
Aquarius, 20 Jan 3.17pm
Pisces, 19 Feb 5.31am
Aries, 21 March 4.39am
Taurus, 20 April 3.50pm
Gemini, 21 May 3.07pm
Cancer, 21 June 11.09pm
Leo, 23 July 10.04am
Virgo, 23 August 5.08pm
Libra, 23 Sept 2.42pm
Scorpio, 23 Oct 11.54pm
Sagittarius, 22 Nov 9.18pm
Capricorn, 22 Dec 10.30am

1984
Aquarius, 20 Jan 9.05pm
Pisces, 19 Feb 11.16am
Aries, 20 March 10.24am
Taurus, 19 April 9.38pm
Gemini, 20 May 8.58pm
Cancer, 21 June 5.02am
Leo, 22 July 3.58pm
Virgo, 22 August 11.00pm
Libra, 22 Sept 8.33pm
Scorpio, 23 Oct 5.46am
Sagittarius, 22 Nov 3.11am
Capricorn, 21 Dec 4.23pm

1985
Aquarius, 20 Jan 2.58am
Pisces, 18 Feb 5.07pm
Aries, 20 March 4.14pm
Taurus, 20 April 3.26am
Gemini, 21 May 2.43am
Cancer, 21 June 10.44am
Leo, 22 July 9.37pm
Virgo, 23August 4.36am
Libra, 23 Sept 2.08am
Scorpio, 23 Oct 11.22am
Sagittarius, 22 Nov 8.51am
Capricorn, 22 Dec 10.08pm

1986
Aquarius, 20 Jan 8.46am
Pisces, 18 Feb 10.58pm
Aries, 20 March 10.03pm
Taurus, 20 April 9.12am
Gemini, 21 May 8.28am
Cancer, 21 June 4.30pm
Leo, 23 July 3.24am
Virgo, 23 August 11.26am
Libra, 23 Sept 7.59am
Scorpio, 23 Oct 5.14pm
Sagittarius, 22 Nov 2.44pm
Capricorn, 22 Dec 4.02am

1987
Aquarius, 20 Jan 2.40pm
Pisces, 19 Feb 4.50am
Aries, 21 March 3.52am
Taurus, 20 April 2.58pm
Gemini, 21 May 2.10am
Cancer, 21 June 10.11pm
Leo, 23 July 9.06am
Virgo, 23 August 4.10pm
Libra, 23 Sept 1.45pm
Scorpio, 23 Oct 11.01pm
Sagittarius, 22 Nov 8.29pm
Capricorn, 22 Dec 9.46am

1988
Aquarius, 20 Jan 8.24pm
Pisces, 19 Feb 10.35am
Aries, 20 March 9.39am
Taurus, 19 April 8.45pm
Gemini, 20 May 7.57pm
Cancer, 21 June 3.57am
Leo, 22 July 2.51pm
Virgo, 22 August 9.54pm
Libra, 22 Sept 7.29pm
Scorpio, 23 Oct 4.44am
Sagittarius, 22 Nov 2.12am
Capricorn, 21 Dec 3.28pm

1989
Aquarius, 20 Jan 2.07am
Pisces, 18 Feb 4.21pm
Aries, 20 March 3.28pm
Taurus, 20 April 2.39am
Gemini, 21 May 1.54am
Cancer, 21 June 9.53am
Leo, 22 July 8.46pm
Virgo, 23August 3.46am
Libra, 23 Sept 1.20am
Scorpio, 23 Oct 10.35am
Sagittarius, 22 Nov 8.05am
Capricorn, 21 Dec 9.22pm

1990
Aquarius, 20 Jan 8.01am
Pisces, 18 Feb 10.14pm
Aries, 20 March 9.19pm
Taurus, 20 April 8.26am
Gemini, 21 May 7.37am
Cancer, 21 June 3.33pm
Leo, 23 July 2.21am
Virgo, 23 August 9.21am
Libra, 23 Sept 6.55am
Scorpio, 23 Oct 4.14pm
Sagittarius, 22 Nov 1.47pm
Capricorn, 22 Dec 3.07am

1991
Aquarius, 20 Jan 1.47pm
Pisces, 19 Feb 3.58am
Aries, 21 March 3.02am
Taurus, 20 April 2.08pm
Gemini, 21 May 1.20pm
Cancer, 21 June 9.19pm
Leo, 23 July 8.11am
Virgo, 23 August 3.13pm
Libra, 23 Sept 0.48pm
Scorpio, 23 Oct 10.05pm
Sagittarius, 22 Nov 7.36pm
Capricorn, 22 Dec 8.54am

1992
Aquarius, 20 Jan 7.32pm
Pisces, 19 February 9.43am
Aries, 20 March 8.48am
Taurus, 19 April 7.57pm
Gemini, 20 May 7.12pm
Cancer, 21 June 3.14am
Leo, 22 July 2.09pm
Virgo, 22 August 9.10pm
Libra, 22 Sept 6.43pm
Scorpio, 23 Oct 3.57am
Sagittarius, 22 Nov 1.26am
Capricorn, 21 Dec 2.43 pm

1993
Aquarius, 20 Jan 1.23am
Pisces, 18 Feb 3.35pm
Aries, 20 March 2.41pm
Taurus, 20 April 1.49am
Gemini, 21 May 1.02am
Cancer, 21 June 9.00am
Leo, 22 July 7.51pm
Virgo, 23 August 2.50am
Libra, 23 Sept 0.22am
Scorpio, 23 Oct 9.37am
Sagittarius, 22 Nov 7.07am
Capricorn, 21 Dec 8.26pm